Also by Anne Wolrige Gordon

PETER HOWARD, LIFE AND LETTERS

Dame Flora

the biography of
Dame Flora MacLeod of MacLeod

by

ANNE WOLRIGE GORDON

HODDER AND STOUGHTON
LONDON SYDNEY AUCKLAND TORONTO

Contents

		page
1	The MacLeods	9
2	The Northcotes	14
3	Early Childhood	18
4	Childhood in Edinburgh	23
5	The Last Walk	29
6	Granton House	34
7	Flora Comes Out	41
8	India, 1900	47
9	Marriage	61
10	Brussels and Berlin	70
11	The First World War	78
12	Chelsea Politics, 1919	87
13	The End of an Era	94
14	Early Years in Skye	101
15	Fire at Dunvegan	111
16	The Second World War	118
17	Canada—the First Clan Tours	127
18	America	139
19	Australia and New Zealand	151
20	The First Clan Parliament	161
21	Politics	173
22	Peter Howard	184
23	Old Age	198
	APPENDIX I: The Fairy Flag	206
	APPENDIX II: A Short Clan History	208
	APPENDIX III: The MacLeods—Genealogy of a Clan	212
	APPENDIX IV: Dame Flora and her Family	214
	INDEX	217

Illustrations

Dame Flora MacLeod of MacLeod[1]   *frontispiece*

                                                      facing page
Sir Reginald MacLeod of MacLeod   48
Agnes Northcote   48
Sir Reginald, Flora and Olive   48
Flora MacLeod of MacLeod, 1911   49
Olive, 1910   49
Hubert Walter   49
Beneath Sir Reginald's portrait, Dunvegan   64
Dame Flora with her grandsons, John and Patrick Wolrige Gordon[2]   64
The Clan Parliament at Dunvegan[3]   65
John downing the horn[3]   65
Welcoming HM the Queen, HRH the Duke of Edinburgh and HRH
    Princess Margaret[3]   96
The Royal Party meeting the MacLeod national groups[3]   96
The Royal Party leaving for the landing stage[4]   112
A royal farewell to Skye[3]   113
In New York and Dallas, 1962   144
In Wellington and Auckland, 1955   145
Australian MacLeod week, 1957[5]   145
With the author in Japan, 1963   176
In India[1]   177
Ninety-third birthday celebration[6]   192
At a London Ceilidh, 1971   192
With the author at Dunvegan   192
Dunvegan hospitality[7]   193

Acknowledgments

1 David Channer
2 Press Association Reuters
3 Scottish Tourist Board
4 George Outram & Co Ltd
5 Sydney Morning Herald
6 Scottish Daily Express
7 Life Magazine

Acknowledgments

THERE ARE MANY PEOPLE WITHOUT WHOM IT WOULD HAVE been impossible to write this book, and I would like to thank the following for the loan of their letters, their recollections, or for their invaluable assistance over the past three years: Miss Gallagher; Mr. R. Gandhi; Mrs. Gordon; Mrs. M. Henderson; Mr. Charles Heron; Miss M. J. Holme; the librarians at the House of Commons; Mrs. P. Howard; Mr. Heyward Isham; Miss Hopeton Kneeland; Mrs. Alison MacGibbon; Mr. Bruce MacLeod; Mr. Don MacLeod; Mr. J. MacLeod Nicol; Mr. Norman MacLeod of Suardal; members of the Clan MacLeod Societies; Miss J. Nicolls; Miss Mary Northcote; Mrs. Smith; and Mrs. W. Lang for many months of untiring work in preparing the manuscript.

I am particularly grateful for information obtained from Dr. I. F. Grant's book, *The MacLeods: The History of a Clan*; Mrs. Alice Macnab of Macnab and Mrs. Joan Wolrige Gordon, Dame Flora's daughters, who most generously allowed me to use and quote from many of their personal letters and who were of great assistance in correcting the manuscript and Joan Wolrige Gordon for providing the short histories of the clan and the Fairy Flag which appear in the Appendices; my husband, Patrick, for his patience and encouragement during three years when I have had too little time to spare; most especially, Dame Flora herself (my dear Baloo), without whom I could have written nothing. I am particularly grateful to her for the long hours spent in tape-recording memories of her childhood and early life about which there was no written record; for the letters, notes and articles, which she has allowed me to read and, in many cases, from which I have quoted. Throughout these months she has been a constant source of inspiration. She has allowed me to write a balanced book, revealing not only her great successes and achievements, but also some of those universal mistakes and frailties common to us all. That she has permitted this in her lifetime, shows an unusual largeness of heart for which I admire her. I hope both friends and strangers, and her clansmen in all parts of the world, will discover, as I did, that through knowing the truth about her they love her more.

A.W.G.

The MacLeods

IN 1847 AND 1848 THE GREAT POTATO FAMINE STRUCK THE highlands of Scotland nearly as severely as it did Ireland. Potatoes were the staple food in those stricken countries where families proliferated and there was almost no agriculture, no industry to provide food, and no money to pay for it. During those two dreadful years there was virtually no harvest.

Seventy years earlier the clearances had forced thousands of Highlanders to leave their homes and seek a living in distant parts of the world. One of the few estates in Scotland where no tenant or crofter left against his will was the MacLeod estate in the island of Skye. When the island was hit by the potato famine, this tradition was carried on by the thirty-five-year-old 25th Chief, Norman MacLeod of MacLeod. This romantic Highlander, with his kind, well-set eyes, fine features and wiry shock of hair, was an extrovert, endowed with great charm and a delightful sense of humour. He had married the Hon. Louisa St. John of Bletso, daughter of the 13th Lord St. John of Bletso, and one of the oldest titled families in Britain. Together they had come to Dunvegan Castle, the traditional home of the MacLeods for over 600 years.

The young English bride was a beautiful woman with dark chestnut hair swept back over her ears, an oval face and a slender, graceful figure. She was a complete aristocrat, and believed that people born of good blood should automatically inherit certain privileges. Although she had married into a great Scottish family, it cannot have been easy for her to adjust to the rigours of living in an isolated Highland castle. In those days the castle had very few comforts, and even its nine-foot-thick walls cannot have kept out the cold when the gale-force winds blew off the Atlantic in winter. It was dark inside the castle, and there was little shelter outside it.

With great energy the young MacLeods made many valuable improvements to the castle. At that time the main rooms were all passage rooms, and the offices on the ground floor opened directly on to the guncourt. Here, they built a passage, reducing the size of the guncourt by a few feet. The dining-room above was accordingly extended, which made possible a passage on the other side. They raised the top of the tower and added to the outside walls the little turrets which became a delightful feature of the architecture. Close by the castle, they made a round garden, surrounded by a beech hedge enclosing green lawns and symmetrical flower beds. It is embedded in trees, and from it there are glimpses of the sea and the rock upon which the castle stands. In the background thunders the music of the waterfall. It became a magical oasis in the wild and sometimes savage beauty of the Fairy Island.

On February 1st, 1847, the MacLeods' fourth child and third son, Reginald, was born. He was the only one of their five children to be born at Dunvegan, and a fairy lullaby was chanted over his cradle. It was said to be the same haunting melody as had been sung by the fairy wife of a former chief. This fair and blue-eyed baby boy was apparently born into a world bathed in history and magic, but he was not long to enjoy its enchantments.

Reginald's birth coincided with the acute distress of the potato famine. Without hesitation, the young chief sold his private fortune with all his possessions, including pictures, plate and furniture, and with the money paid for road-making, bridge-building and drainage. The entailed estate and land he could not sell. Some help came from outside, but very little. Norman MacLeod spent from £225 to £300 a week, and in 1847 he wrote in a letter that he was feeding between six and seven thousand people. His personal resources could not long stand up to this burden, but he wrote, 'Ruin must be faced rather than let the people die.' Never once did he question where his duty lay, nor what a landlord and chief must do for his people. They owed him their lives, but when the famine ended he was totally ruined.

Dunvegan Castle was leased. Norman MacLeod and his twenty-nine-year-old wife left the home they loved and went to London, where he obtained a job first as a junior clerk in the Civil Service at a modest salary of £105 per annum, and later he became the head of the Science and Arts Department of the South Kensington Museum.

The shock suffered by his protected and beautiful wife is not difficult to imagine. Her world was shattered. The home she had created was gone. Her five pregnancies were all some years apart, and it may be conjectured that she suffered several miscarriages which undermined her health. Her husband's sacrifice had been noble and heroic, but she may not have seen it that way. She was not brought up in the Highland tradition, and she now found herself in entirely different circumstances from those she had expected by right. Whatever the reasons, her health broke down completely and for the rest of her life she was constantly referred to as a *malade imaginaire*. Her failing health gradually became her principal interest.

Reginald MacLeod's childhood was not particularly happy. He saw his mother suffer and his tender heart went out to her. Louisa MacLeod's ordeal was not yet over, for when he was only twelve and away at school, her second son, Torquil, died of tuberculosis. Reginald was himself a frail boy and suffered from poor health. He was first educated at a day-school in Blackheath. When he was sent to Harrow, instead of living in a normal house with other boys, he had to live in a tutor's house where he was fed on a special diet and forbidden to play games. Perhaps because Reginald had been born in the castle she loved and remembered, or because of his delicate health, Louisa felt instinctively drawn towards him. He had inherited his father's charm and good looks. He possessed such compassion for his poor invalid mother that from his earliest days he was the member of the family who assumed the duty of caring for her, and he was her favourite child.

Norman MacLeod probably never understood his wife's attitude, and he found her ill-health tiresome. It is quite possible that the hardships entailed upon himself and his family embittered him. In any case, the marriage never regained its original happiness. He did not mention his misfortunes, and hardly ever referred to his childhood or early married life again. With courage and optimism he put the past behind him. When his circumstances improved he resumed his social Scottish life, at which he excelled and in which his wife could not share. In later years he was often abroad and had many foreign friends. He held a fatal attraction for women, enhanced by an absent wife. In her despair Louisa turned to Reginald, and he gradually took his father's place in his mother's affections.

In 1860, when Reginald was thirteen, he returned to Skye with his father for the first time. They lived together in a little house near Sligachan in the Cuillins. Lord Hill was the tenant at Dunvegan, and it was as his guest that Reginald first saw the house where he was born. These summer visits to Skye continued over the years and, when her health allowed it, Louisa came too. The link with Skye and the love of the castle was not lost, although it could never be quite the same again. As the years passed and the family fortunes were partially restored, Norman MacLeod lived at the castle for the summer months and invited his friends there. Although he founded the Wine Society in London, he used to order a perfectly ordinary case of wines from the Army and Navy Stores for the entertainment of his guests. One visitor was convinced that in such an ancient castle there must be a marvellous cellar. At dinner he complimented his host on the quality of the claret and added that it was a treat to have wine in such perfect condition. This was too good a chance for Norman MacLeod to miss, and, turning to his son, he said, 'Well, if he likes this wine, I think we had better give him a bottle from our special bin.' Reginald knew there was not one. He finally decided the only thing he could do was to take two spoonfuls of port and mix it with the claret. When the evening came, the unsuspecting guest was 'transported'. 'I have never tasted anything to compare with it,' he said, and added that it was the most memorable and marvellous wine he had ever met. Father and son shared this merry sense of humour, and were united in their love of Skye and her people. It must often have been hard for them to realise what their life might have been had fortune smiled on them.

Reginald MacLeod left Harrow and went up to Trinity College, Cambridge. He was a popular student and made many friendships, including one with Arthur Balfour which lasted all his life. During one summer vacation the two of them, with Lord Kinnaird, made a daring voyage round the south end of Skye in Rob Roy canoes. They paddled from

Dunvegan to Rhum and on to Eigg, where Reginald MacLeod spent the night in a cave with the unburied bones of the unfortunate MacDonalds, suffocated by his ancestor, Alasdair Crotach, the 8th Chief, in the sixteenth century. The following day they passed through the Sound of Sleat to Kyleakin, and those who know the violent seas which guard the Hebrides may feel they were fortunate to return alive.

Louisa MacLeod did not make life easy for Reginald. Her eldest son, Norman, had been given a commission by the Duke of York in the 73rd. Her daughter was now married and she did not feel as close to her youngest son, Roderick. All her demands and sorrows were poured out upon Reginald, and she clung to him tenaciously. Whenever he left home she would say miserably, 'I shall never see you again.' Many young men might have fled from such control, but Reginald did not. He treated his mother with infinite patience, although he differed from her in one significant respect. His father's experience had convinced him that nobody was born to privilege, and that it had to be fought for and won. Accordingly, in 1872 he took a modest job in the Civil Service as Inspector of Factories in England. The salary was so meagre that in his view it did not permit him to marry the girl with whom he had fallen in love. She could not wait for him and decided to marry somebody else. It was a wound to his tender heart. It was difficult enough for this devoted mother's son to break away from home, without the added burden of a broken romance. It was not until 1876, when Reginald MacLeod was twenty-nine, that he finally became engaged to Agnes Mary Cecilia Northcote.

The Northcotes

AGNES NORTHCOTE, THE ELDER DAUGHTER OF SIR STAFFORD Northcote, was born in 1848. In 1876 Sir Stafford was the Chancellor of the Exchequer in Lord Beaconsfield's government, and reaching the climax of a distinguished political career. He was a Balliol scholar, an intellectual with a great love of literature, and a particular passion for the works of Sir Walter Scott. At Oxford he had supported Mr. Gladstone, but had gradually changed his political views and was now a convinced Tory. Although he was not an ambitious man, his family life was inevitably largely sacrificed to his political career.

Lady Northcote had ten children, two of whom died in childhood, and she spent most of her time at the family home of Pynes, near Exeter in Devon, while her husband was in London. No doubt economies in the country were highly necessary, with six sons to educate at Eton and Oxford. Sir Stafford loved children and there is a charming story of how he returned from the House of Commons late one evening to find his daughter ill. A night-nurse had been called to Downing Street. She brought with her a fractious baby who kept the household awake. Sir Stafford took the baby in his arms, calmed it and spent the night pacing the corridors with the child so that the nurse should not be worried.

Lady Northcote was brilliant and socially gifted in her own right, so it is no surprise that this was a home where intellectual achievement took precedence. The children were encouraged to excel at their studies and they had inherited their parents' love of books. Lady Northcote's fragile appearance was deceptive, for she had a will of iron and a determination to match it, both of which were inherited by her daughter, Agnes. It made the relationship between mother and daughter far from easy.

14

Agnes was highly intelligent and rather unusual. She spoke French and German. She played the organ each Sunday in the parish church of Upton Pyne. Like the rest of her family she was widely read, and books were her abiding passion. She was interested in social work, and, no doubt inspired by Florence Nightingale in the Crimea, had wanted to become a nurse—an idea which caused infinite distress to her family. She was twenty-eight years old and it was now time for Margaret, her only sister and eight years her junior, to come out. In those days the only correct way for a girl to leave home was to get married. Agnes had lived through one unhappy romance and by now found the increasing conflict with her mother an added reason for going. Her engagement to Reginald MacLeod was an obvious solution. There was no romance about this marriage, and none of the magic which had heralded Reginald's birth twenty-nine years earlier in the wintry mists of Skye. This was an age when love was not a prerequisite for marriage and this one had the necessary Victorian label of being 'perfectly honourable'. During the engagement Agnes told her future husband that her health was poor and that the doctors were concerned about her eyesight. She offered to release him. Reginald MacLeod was far too chivalrous to accept the suggestion. He had lived for so long under his mother's dominating influence that he inevitably looked for a strong personality in the woman he was to marry. In Agnes Northcote he had found it.

Norman MacLeod rejoiced in his son's good fortune, and that summer he gave a family party at Dunvegan Castle. Sir Stafford Northcote was persuaded to come when he was assured that even in that remote part of the Highlands there was a daily post. The Northcotes arrived late in the evening at Portree and travelled to Dunvegan by night. Reginald was awakened by the ringing of bells in the early hours of the morning and raced downstairs to welcome his guests. We can only imagine how the days passed, with Reginald enthusiastic in his love of the castle, and no doubt eager to share its history with Agnes and her family. There were picnics and walks and perhaps boating expeditions. A photograph was taken at the foot of the castle rock to record the visit for posterity. Sir Stafford and Lady Northcote stand on one side of the engaged couple, and the MacLeods on the other, surrounded by numbers of relations and friends. The ladies are dressed in long dresses and most unsuitable shoes and bonnets, while the gentlemen wear the kilt or sport tweed trousers, jackets and matching shooting-hats. No smile appears to pass any lip as they gaze fixedly out across the waters of Loch Dunvegan, but it must have been more enjoyable than it looked, for Sir Stafford wrote in a letter that he saw 'familiar sights', including 'Flora MacDonald's stays, the sword of Rory Mor and the mysterious Fairy Flag which brings victory to the MacLeods.' It inspired him to record the occasion in poetry.

Reginald and Agnes MacLeod were married in the Henry VII Chapel of Westminster Abbey in April 1877. It was a wedding studded with political brilliance. Arthur Balfour was the best man, the wedding breakfast was held at 10 Downing Street, and Lord Beaconsfield proposed the bridal toast. Although it appeared to be a marriage of great splendour, this was not entirely the case. Sir Stafford had too large a family to be able to give his daughter much money. Reginald MacLeod was not wealthy and had to start his married life on a narrow budget, so the young couple rented a furnished house in Hobart Place. Their poverty was only comparative, for they had a small staff and were able to entertain their friends to dinner. The flowers on the table at their first dinner-party were threepenny cypress pot-plants, and Reginald took them to Skye and transplanted them into the round garden, where they thrive today as healthy bushes. The young MacLeods had a wide range of friends and were entertained in political and social circles in London, but their early married life was far from lavish.

In late January 1878, Agnes MacLeod left Hobart Place and returned to her parents' home for the birth of her first child. 10 Downing Street is the official residence of every British Prime Minister, but Lord Beaconsfield was now a widower with no children. Sir Stafford Northcote, his Chancellor, friend and neighbour at No. 11, was a man with a very large family living in much too small a house. The two men had, therefore, agreed to exchange houses. So it was that three days after Reginald MacLeod's thirty-first birthday, on Sunday, February 3rd, 1878, Agnes MacLeod gave birth to a daughter at 10 Downing Street. As she lay peacefully in her cot in the glorious ambience of Downing Street, the proud father and mother could not see the strands of their lives which were so deeply woven into the spirit and soul of this tiny but perfect little girl. Her fair skin and blue eyes were certainly inherited from her father and were entirely Scottish, but the way those eyes absorbed the world around them with a clear appraisal was English and Northcote. The romantic charm of the MacLeods and the strength of Highland moor and mountain combined in her with the intellectual brilliance, social gifts and steely determination of the Northcotes. Like two great rivers they merged and yet were to remain strangely separate and distinct.

Many years later Agnes MacLeod told her granddaughter how the doctors had first informed her that she had given birth to a son. When asked whether she was disappointed to learn of their strange mistake, she replied that she 'was too exhausted to care', but it was perhaps prophetic, for this baby was to grow up wishing to be a boy and thinking men better than women.

In accordance with Sir Stafford Northcote's taste in literature, this granddaughter was called Flora after the heroine of Sir Walter Scott's novel *Waverley*, and Louisa Cecilia after her two grandmothers. This decisive Northcote influence was thus established from the moment of Flora's birth.

Early Childhood

FLORA BEGAN HER LIFE IN LONDON IN THE SIMPLE surroundings of the house in Hobart Place. She had a nurse and, like most Victorians, her parents played only a small part in her infant life. For one hour each afternoon she was brought to the drawing-room to enjoy their company, and subsequently removed upstairs to bed. However, Reginald and Agnes MacLeod led an interesting social life and this was a home frequented by some of the great political figures and important personalities of the day. The unseen wall which divided the nursery from the rest of the house was occasionally infiltrated with the colour and excitement of these visits.

Early one morning, no doubt held up to the window by her nurse, the little girl upstairs saw an officer on horseback, wearing full-dress uniform, canter to the door of her house. He had come to tell her father that Sir Garnet Wolseley wished to see him at the Foreign Office. The Government was sending troops to quell the Glendale uprising in Skye,* and wanted Reginald MacLeod's advice on the best place to land. The rush of hasty footsteps on the stairs, and the brilliant

---

* The Glendale uprising was a local revolt by crofters against the payment of rents. Reginald MacLeod was consulted because he could give information about logistics and topography, and the War Office sent a small platoon to enforce payment.

The people welcomed the soldiers and a most cordial relationship was established. The Crofters Commission held a court in the parish church of Dunvegan, and Norman MacLeod heard himself denounced and abused. On the way out he said to one of the crofters, 'I never thought to hear you speak like that of me. I thought we were good friends.' The man flung his arms around him. 'Indeed, MacLeod,' he said, 'we all love you but I had to say what I did.'

The two ringleaders served a very short sentence in prison, and many years later a monument was erected to the two 'Glendale martyrs'. The Court gave the crofters ownership of their own crofts, but it was something of a pyrrhic victory since they now had to pay their entire rates, whereas previously these had been shared between landlord and tenant. The rates naturally became increasingly heavy, and it was a relief to all concerned when crofts were eventually derated.

figure on horseback galloping away were to remain Flora's earliest memory.

Flora's next encounter with high politics was as a bridesmaid for one of her parents' friends, and Mr. Gladstone was among the guests at the wedding. When he walked solemnly up the aisle past Flora's footstool, she pushed it under his feet in a moment of childish determination and very nearly toppled her grandfather's main political opponent.

On February 18th, 1880, when Flora was two years old, she was taken into her mother's bedroom at Hobart Place to see her new-born baby sister, Olive. This was very different from the glories of 10 Downing Street which had surrounded her own birth, but the baby was not unlike her. She had the same fair hair and penetrating blue eyes with their formidable gaze.

That autumn, in another bedroom in London, an old lady lay dying. She had been dying for so many years now that it seemed impossible to believe her time had really come. Louisa MacLeod's mind searched intermittently among the memories of long ago. There was a round garden with roses in it; a castle on a rock which she had loved; a handsome Highlander whom she had married but who for some reason was not now with her; there were people struggling in poor crofts with no food; and now there was a little granddaughter who sometimes crawled on her bed and laughed and whose fat little fingers clutched hers. The memories came and went like the hushed voices in the room around her. More vivid than all these was the picture of a boy with golden hair who had now grown into a man. He had laughter and warmth in his eyes, a laughter and warmth she had desperately needed and clung to. Even now, she could hardly let him go. Her hand clutched his for a moment and she was at peace. It was over. Reginald MacLeod had sat by his mother's bedside like this in all the years he could remember. He had comforted and sustained her and wiped away her tears. Now his task was over. His mother's beautiful oval face, marked by the years of sorrow and ill-health, was to him still lovely. This death which would mean release was still infinitely painful to his warm heart. Without his two little babies at Hobart Place and the strong personality of his devoted wife, upon whom he now leant for support but whom he never crossed because he hated conflict and admired her brilliant mind and forceful

will, he would scarcely have been able to face the end of this
chapter in his life.

Downstairs, Reginald MacLeod could hear Flora's
pattering footsteps, and in a few moments the door would
open and the nurse would bring her in—a ray of sunshine
into a room darkened by death. 'My nurse carried me in her
arms to see my grandmother dead in bed,' wrote Flora long
afterwards. 'I thought she was asleep and I was not at all
frightened. I am sure the nurse peeled some grapes for me,
as I remember toddling after her while she was holding the
bunch in her hand.'

Reginald MacLeod had the greatest difficulty in reaching
his father with the news of his mother's death, for he was
abroad on one of his many visits. For Norman MacLeod the
death of his wife came as no shock, for they had been long
since estranged. The following summer there was a house-
party at Dunvegan, and among the guests was a fascinating
and psychic Austrian baroness, Hanna von Etingshausen.
Her father had been given his title because he had a very good
collection of fossils which interested Emperor Franz Joseph.
Agnes MacLeod acted as hostess for her father-in-law, and
with her husband's help entertained his colourful
cosmopolitan guests. One day, walking near the waterfall,
Agnes lost a ring. Murmuring in German, 'Holy St. Anthony,
help me', Hanna removed some leaves and uncovered the
jewel. One of the young guests was captivated by her youth
and mystery, but Reginald MacLeod protested so strongly
that the guest desisted. Bitterly did Reginald regret his
altruism, for in 1882, within two years of his wife's death,
Norman MacLeod had himself married Hanna von
Etingshausen. It was a knife through his son's heart, and
proved to be a marriage which virtually estranged Norman
MacLeod from his family and friends. 'Aunt Hanna', as she
was called by the family, made him a devoted wife for
thirteen years until he died in 1895. They lived together in the
dower house at Uiginish, over the water from the castle which
had been his home.

Norman MacLeod's remarriage, the death of his wife,
Louisa, and the natural tendency for a mother's family to
play the largest part in the family life meant that the
Northcotes were the major influence in the young lives of
Flora and Olive. Sir Stafford Northcote was a master at

story-telling. Flora used to sit on his lap and listen with rapture to the Fairy tales of Comtesse d'Aulnois. One was called *The Bee and the Orange Tree*. Once on a stormy, wet day at the end of a story, the sun suddenly burst forth from behind a cloud and Flora turned to her grandfather and said, 'Oh, Grandpapa, the clouds have stopped to hear you.' Lady Northcote glittered like a brilliant diamond in the eyes of her small granddaughters. 'She was ravishing, amusing, original and entirely delightful,' wrote Flora. Uncle Olly, their mother's younger brother, was an undying favourite and sent his nieces five pounds every Christmas. It was a gift they remembered, for Agnes MacLeod lived in a world which was dominated by intellect and not by affection. In all their young lives Flora and Olive could not remember receiving one birthday present or Christmas gift from her. She did not wrap her children lovingly in her arms, but trained them from the earliest age that self-discipline and devotion to duty were the most important virtues. It was left to her tender-hearted husband to lavish affection on these two small girls, and because he felt his wife was hard on them and not very well, he probably spoiled them.

Flora wore her straight hair shoulder-length with a deep fringe over her forehead. It gave her already compact figure a decidedly square appearance. Her family named her 'Poohooh', a name she herself gave to all small girls she met. Olive had an abundance of curls and was prettier than her sister, but because they were so close in age, sharing the same daily routine and enjoying the same surroundings, they became inseparably fond of each other. The steely Northcote will ran strongly through them both, but Flora submitted more readily to discipline, while Olive flouted authority with fierce obstinacy. When Flora was four, it was decided that Olive, being two years her junior, should go up to bed first. Olive refused. Clearly, the nursery staff at Hobart Place disgraced their contemporary Victorians, for the terrible scene which followed only ended when Flora took Olive by the hand and went upstairs with her. The matter was not raised again. It established an unbroken principle that the two sisters shared everything and did everything together. Even Agnes MacLeod could not resist their powerful domination. She soon reached the conclusion that it was useless to punish Olive. If she was told to go to bed, she would go to bed, but then she would never get up. If she was deprived of some favourite treat, she decided she no longer liked it. Flora was amazed at Olive's courage, and regarded her as superior in every way, but this was not entirely justified. Flora herself excelled as a story-teller, and with Olive as a captive audience she would hold her spellbound with tales of magic and suspense. Sometimes it was too much for Olive, who would call to her nurse, 'Flora says there is a wolf behind the door and I half believe it.'

The enjoyment of the nursery must have meant everything to Reginald MacLeod, for he had to face, very early in his married life, the fact that his wife's health was an increasing anxiety. It was a real tragedy for them both, for she was able, and ambitious for her husband's success. The friends among whom they mixed enjoyed far greater affluence than they, and in an effort to improve their situation, Reginald MacLeod invested in some shares. By nature he was a generous over-optimist and not altogether practical. The venture turned out badly, and he soon discovered that he had lost a considerable amount of their small capital. It was a mistake they could ill afford. Sir Arthur Hobhouse (later Lord Hobhouse) had recently retired from being Chief Justice of India and a member of the Viceroy's Council. His wife was Mary Farrar, Agnes MacLeod's aunt, and she lent her neice money. She would probably willingly have made it a gift to a dearly-loved relation, but the young MacLeods were proud and felt they could not grant themselves anything until they had paid it all back.

This financial crisis dislodged the family from their rented house in Hobart Place. Flora and Olive were removed from the warmth of their Northcote relations and from the nursery they enjoyed. To escape from the pity of his friends and shame at his own plight, Reginald MacLeod accepted the post of Conservative Agent for Scotland, and took his family far from the bright lights of London to the simple austerity of a lodging at 7 Manor Place, Edinburgh.

Childhood in Edinburgh

As REGINALD MACLEOD MADE THE LONG JOURNEY NORTH TO Scotland with his family, his thoughts must occasionally have turned to another young MacLeod, forty years before, who had travelled from Skye in the wake of financial ruin. History, with its strange twists and turns, now repeated itself. Agnes MacLeod had lived all her life in England and left behind her not only the home she loved, but also the warmth and interest of family and friends, for a country strange to her and a climate admitted to be harsh even by those who love it most.

In the years during which the MacLeods lived in Edinburgh, and as their financial position slowly improved, they moved house three times, first to a place called Woodlands and then, a year later, to Wood Hall in the village of Juniper Green. Their original home at Manor Place was dreary and cold. Comforts and amenities had to be foregone until the fatal debt was paid off, and for the first time in her life Agnes MacLeod suffered real hardship. Her husband had many Scottish friends and loved Scotland. From his earliest years he had accepted a life of unselfishness and severe self-discipline. His wife was given a warm welcome, but she found Scottish society cold and intellectually far less congenial than that of London. The anxieties and deprivations through which she passed must have closed still further a heart which was rather frigid at the best of times, and the Scots in turn were shy of this English lady with whom they had so little in common. The eyesight which had caused concern continued to deteriorate, and the Edinburgh winters, followed by the traditionally cold springs, did not improve Agnes MacLeod's health.

In their bare little nursery at Manor Place, Flora and Olive were unaware of the trauma through which their parents were passing. They now had a German nurse called Pussy to whom they were devoted. She no doubt pitied their arid existence and showed them more affection than her Germanic reticence would otherwise have allowed. The nursery revolved round Agnes MacLeod's health. Pussy was not particularly strict, but she kept to a rigid routine and punctuality was observed at all times. The children were trained to be unselfish and to put their mother's interests first. They were expected to do as they were told without complaint. 'Do not make a fuss saying you do not want to or you cannot,' they were told. 'Nothing is so boring or so tiresome.' This was reinforced by the story of the little bird who used to sing whenever the child was going to be naughty, 'If you wish to be happy—be good, be good.' Olive's formidable will must have resisted this doctrine, but even she submitted to Pussy's benevolent discipline. The afternoon hour in the drawing-room and the monotony of daily walks remained unbroken. Only at rare intervals was the regime interrupted, for there were apparently no other children with whom Flora and Olive could play. Instead, Agnes MacLeod encouraged a love of books in her daughters in much the same way as her parents had done with her. She read them poetry or the stories of Greek mythology and Roman history long before most children of their age had even looked at a picture-book. No doubt she thought Edinburgh a most uncultured place, but the parched and regimented life she made for Flora and Olive was unusual even in those days.

When the family moved from Manor Place to Wood Hall, the two sisters chased each other round the scattered trees on the small patch of lawn like calves enjoying their first taste of freedom in the spring sunshine. On birthdays, Flora and Olive were allowed to choose their favourite pudding, and, no doubt because of the austerity of their lives, they invariably chose rice pudding and stewed pears.

The long months in Edinburgh were interrupted only for a few weeks each summer, when Reginald MacLeod rented an almost endless stream of small country lodgings in which to give his family a holiday. There was a little garden plagued with snails which Flora and Olive gathered and put into pails of salt water. Once a visitor came, whose heart no doubt went out to the two small girls with so few toys and almost no luxuries, and he brought with him a parcel. 'Olive and I were given a superb doll,' wrote Flora, 'with eyes which opened and shut and golden ringlets and a pink satin dress. This was the crowning outrage to the shabby old doll we loved. So we took her straight out into the garden and stamped on her silly wax face.' The tread of those childish feet as they trampled on that painted face betrayed a strangely sad story of loyalty and loneliness, shared only between two sisters. The steel of the Northcote will was there, strong and immovable, ready to sacrifice the greatest treasure for the sake of pride. It was a determined pride, and Flora and Olive hated being wrong. Once when they were taken for a summer holiday to Dunvegan, Flora walked with her nurse by the gate of the walled garden, past a cherry-tree laden with fruit. 'You may eat one cherry,' the nurse told her. Flora ate two. The nurse then asked, 'Did you eat more than one cherry?' 'No,' replied Flora. 'I saw the second stone drop,' said the nurse. The shame and bitter resentment which burned in Flora's heart was never forgotten. Truthfulness had been a virtue always stressed by Pussy, but Flora could not bring herself to admit that she had told a lie. 'It was the nurse's fault,' she said. 'If she had declared she had seen the second cherry being eaten, I would not have denied it.' When a plate belonging to the dolls' tea-service was broken, Flora hid it for fear of the nurse. Ever afterwards she remained convinced that children only told lies out of fear and never from wilfulness.

Caroline, Countess of Seafield, was broken-hearted by the death of her husband and only son, and the two great houses at Castle Grant and Cullen were now hers. Reginald and Agnes MacLeod were her devoted friends and she found much comfort in their visits and was exceptionally good to their children. Flora and Olive were given their own garden plots in the castle grounds, complete with gooseberry-bushes and flowers. Bowls of bilberries and milk were eaten for elevenses under the trees in the forest and for a few golden days they enjoyed a magic world. It was a different story on Sunday, which was celebrated with spartan discipline. No books or knitting were allowed, and there was a visit of a guest to Flora and Olive's bedroom, where they were told to kneel down while she prayed for and with them.

One autumn a group of important gentlemen arrived at Castle Grant amidst great excitement. Flora and Olive had to practice their curtsies and later that day they were presented to the future King Edward VII, after he had shot over one of the famous grouse moors. On another occasion five brace of grouse were delivered to Manor Place and in their parents' absence Flora and Olive ate half a grouse each for lunch, ten days in succession.

In his work as Conservative Agent for Scotland, Reginald MacLeod had a wealth of interesting political stories to bring home, which enlivened the otherwise lonely life of his wife. In 1880 Donald Cameron of Lochiel, 24th Chief of Clan Cameron, stood as Conservative candidate in Inverness-shire, a constituency he had represented in Parliament since 1868. In those days the property qualification was high, and out of a population of 86,369 only 1,994 had the right to vote. The franchise was limited to owners of land of £10 annual value; long leaseholders and lifeholders with £10 yearly interest; and a number of more wealthy tenants. Because of this restriction every vote counted and it was not untrue to say that every vote had its price. Reginald MacLeod worked hard for Lochiel, especially in Skye. There was only one Conservative elector in Stornoway and the Conservatives sent a boat to bring him over to vote in Portree. The large body of Liberal voters waited at the quayside but was not allowed to embark and was left behind. Nevertheless, as Reginald MacLeod accompanied the ballot-boxes to Inverness he saw Sir Kenneth Mackenzie, the Liberal candidate, board the train at Stromeferry amidst jubilant crowds flaunting yellow ribbons and a forest of pipers, and his heart sank. When he arrived in Inverness he told the local agent that he could not face the count, and would return to his Edinburgh office. the agent replied, 'Mr. MacLeod, I wouldn't be so sure.' 'What reason have you for saying that?' asked MacLeod. 'Well,' answered the agent, 'two days before the election I heard that the Liberal candidate had sent second-class tickets to all the voters within reach. When I heard that, I hired every horse and cart and carriage I could get and sent every voter first-class tickets with Lochiel's compliments, and I think that's done it.' Reginald MacLeod stayed for the count. He heard the returning officer announce that Lochiel had received 808 votes to his Liberal opponent's 779, and had thus retained his seat with a majority of 29.

Flora must often have heard her father talk of his political work, for over eighty years later she could still remember the exact voting-figures of Lochiel's victory, and it was always politics which appeared to excite her interest. Reginald MacLeod himself stood twice unsuccessfully for Parliament, in 1885 and again in 1911. On both occasions he fought in Inverness-shire and although he had invitations to represent safe Conservative seats elsewhere in Scotland, he always refused. It had to be his own county or nothing. It was during these campaigns that he experienced a dramatic and permanent improvement in his health. He had to walk many miles across moorland, for with such a limited franchise it was imperative to visit each voter in his home. Everywhere he was received with traditional Highland hospitality. In place of the dram of whisky he asked for milk. He consumed gallons of it and was thereafter never again troubled by poor health.

On November 3rd, 1883, Sir Stafford Northcote was installed as Rector of Edinburgh University. Flora and Olive, aged five and three, were dressed as little rectors and sold programmes at the ceremony. It was the last time they were to share a great occasion with their illustrious grandfather. On July 6th, 1885, Sir Stafford took his seat in the House of Lords as Earl of Iddesleigh, the name derived from his family estate in Devon. Although he subsequently became First Lord of the Treasury and later, in 1886, Foreign Secretary, it was a move he deeply regretted. He wrote, 'This has apparently been my last night in the House of Commons. I have sat in it rather more than thirty years and it has become part of my life.' In the final weeks of 1886, Lord Randolph Churchill made his now famous unexpected resignation as Chancellor of the Exchequer in Lord Salisbury's Government. Although Lord Iddesleigh disapproved of Lord Randolph Churchill's action, he automatically placed his seat in the Cabinet at the Prime Minister's disposal.

On a bleak afternoon in Edinburgh in January 1887, Flora and Olive sat with their mother in the sitting-room at Manor Place when the door opened and their father came in and asked them to go upstairs. The past week had been one of anguish. Lord Salisbury had accepted Lord Iddesleigh's resignation, but for some unknown reason the letter telling him so had not arrived. It was from the announcement in the newspapers of January 4th that he first read the news. Lord Iddesleigh was an honourable man who had given long

service to his country, and it was the greatest possible shock.
He was old, his health was now failing, and he should
probably have resigned before, but this was a sad way to go.
On January 12th he had completed his affairs at the Foreign
Office and said goodbye to old friends. It was naturally a
moment of great emotion, and afterwards he walked to 10
Downing Street to see the Prime Minister. 'On reaching the
ante-room,' wrote his biographer,* 'he sank into a chair
where Mr. Henry Manners and Lord Walter Gordon-Lennox
found him very ill and breathing with difficulty. He never
spoke again and died at five minutes past three in the
presence of Lord Salisbury, Mr. Henry Manners, and two
doctors.'

10 Downing Street, the house which had played a
distinctive role in the lives of the Northcote family for a
decade, where Flora had been born and where her mother
had lived, now played its final part in the last moments of
Lord Iddesleigh's life. Gently Reginald MacLeod broke the
news to his grief-stricken wife. It was a sad farewell for her, so
far from the comfort of her family. She had an infinitely
loving husband to sustain her and together that night they
took the train to Devonshire.

Lord Iddesleigh was beloved in Scotland. The following
day *The Scotsman* carried a black band round the full page
which recounted his life and death. It described him in
Chaucer's lovely line as 'a varray parfit gentil knight'. Flora
and Olive had new black dresses and were the principal
mourners at the memorial service in St. Giles' Cathedral. As
their small black figures walked erect up the cathedral aisle,
all eyes were upon them. It was with a sense of tragedy and
sorrow that the crowded congregation watched these golden-
haired little girls in mourning for their beloved and famous
grandpapa. Flora and Olive did not allow a tear to fall or lip
to quiver, and no doubt their grandfather would have been
proud of their courage and their flair for a great occasion.
'Olive and I enjoyed—I am very much afraid we did
enjoy—our days of fame,' wrote Flora.

---

* Andrew Lang, *Life of the First Earl of Iddesleigh*

The Last Walk

THE GREY LIGHT OF THE EDINBURGH SKY SHONE THROUGH THE windows of Wood Hall on to the figure who now lay motionless upon the bed. Agnes MacLeod often had reason to remember her recent visit to the English oculists and their harsh diagnosis that within a few years she would be totally blind. It was a death-sentence for a woman whose greatest pleasure was reading books and music.

Together she and her husband had hurriedly planned the journey to Dr. Pagenstecher's world famous eye-klinik in Wiesbaden. She remembered that endless train journey to Germany with Flora and Olive, and the parting from her husband, who must return to his work in Edinburgh at a time when she most needed his support. She and the children had lived in the *klinik* and shared their meals with the other patients at the great *standtisch* under the notice on the wall which read, 'Patients are requested not to talk of the subject of their afflictions'. How hard she tried to carry out those instructions, making pleasant conversation to her neighbours at mealtimes! Once she had translated a thunderstorm as a *donnersturm* instead of using the correct *gewitter*. The gales of raucous laughter with which this had been greeted had made Flora and Olive blush with mortification.

Dr. Pagenstecher had slowed down the deterioration of Agnes's eyes to a considerable extent, but he could not repair the detached retina which was the cause of her failing sight. The outcome was inevitable and by degrees during those days her last hopes of recovery faded. Dr. Pagenstecher looked at the children's eyes and prescribed reading-glasses for Flora, and forbade both her and Olive to do needlework.

Agnes MacLeod could hear again the music of those lovely afternoon concerts in the Kurgarten, music which had been a balm to the fears and anxieties which forced their way into her mind. How much the children had enjoyed those concerts! The journey home through Lucerne in Switzerland was made in a brave effort to alleviate the pain of facing the future. Reginald MacLeod had taken Flora and Olive up the Rigi Mountain in a cable-car and these two unspoiled little girls had found it 'altogether wonderful'. When the moment came to leave the hotel, their kind, unpractical father discovered he had not enough money to pay the bill. He left his daughters 'in pawn' with Pussy and on arrival in England sent a cheque to release them.

Within months of the return to Scotland, Agnes MacLeod developed a creeping paralysis. Slowly but steadily the joints in her limbs stiffened until walking became almost impossible. She had walked out with her daughters for the last time. It was 1889. She was only forty-one, and Flora was just eleven. The iron will which had dominated Agnes's life now became her greatest resource. Slowly she forced herself out of the despair and self-pity which threatened her and replaced them with a determination to live. If she could not go out, Flora and Olive must stay in. If she could not accompany her husband on social occasions, he must forego them, for otherwise people would think ill of him for neglecting his wife. This world in which Agnes MacLeod was imprisoned must be shared by those she loved, whether they wished it or not.

Flora and Olive now had to live their lives to a disciplined routine which suited their mother, who commanded the household from her invalid bed. The daily governess bicycled from Edinburgh each morning and gave the children lessons for two hours. 'The lessons were primitive,' wrote Flora; 'exercises in French and German corrected with a key. Our arithmetic, now called mathematics, was of the standard

Multiplication is a vexation
    Division is as bad.
The rule of three doth puzzle me (it does still)
    And practice drives me mad.

After lunch for two hours each day, with unbreakable monotony, Flora and Olive had to read aloud to their mother the books she could no longer enjoy for herself. It was a ritual which was observed even when the children were ill.

They read biographies, literature, history and poetry. They read in French and German as well as in English. Their clear childish voices floated across the room afternoon after endless afternoon. They read beautifully and absorbed most of the great literary works. When other children were playing in the park with their nanny, or enjoying a day at the seaside, Flora and Olive were at home reading to their mother and acquiring the intellectual excellence she so much admired. They did not complain for they very much enjoyed reading aloud and liked the unchanging rhythm of their lives. It was merely the terrible restriction of never being able to break the routine which oppressed them. Flora did her best to disguise her feelings, but she could not hide the boiling cauldron of resentment which welled up inside her from time to time. In those moments she vowed she would never be ill, nor would she ever impose upon anybody the life which Agnes MacLeod had imposed upon her. She and Olive were passionately sorry for their father, for they felt he was being deprived of all the gaiety and enjoyment which he deserved.

After tea each afternoon a neighbour and friend came in to read to Agnes MacLeod while she lay in her room. This was the golden hour to which Flora and Olive looked forward, when they could escape from their sedentary life for the one playtime of their day. They rushed out into the garden and romped on the grass, for at heart they were still children, albeit rather old for their age. Although in almost every other respect they were virtually uneducated, they soon became aware that they were much more widely-read than their contemporaries. 'We were boastful of our "shop window",' wrote Flora, 'which we liked to believe deluded even intelligent people into thinking we were educated in depth.'

Once a year in the winter the MacLeods took their daughters to London to visit Lord and Lady Hobhouse in their large house in Bruton Street. Flora and Olive had their meals in the housekeeper's room with Mr. and Mrs. Whitchurch and Miss Smith, the lady's maid. As they grew older they were increasingly allowed in the dining-room for lunch. Apart from the summer holidays, these were the only weeks of the year when they did not have to think of their mother, and they enjoyed their freedom with undiluted enthusiasm. There was always a visit to the pantomime which they did not much enjoy, and later a Gilbert and Sullivan opera. This was an immediate favourite and they described their first visit to *HMS Pinafore* as 'epoch making'.

It was a sad reflection on Agnes MacLeod's life that the only treats her children remember having were when their mother was not there. It was not altogether her fault. 'My mother had to do all the disciplining,' wrote Flora, 'and my father did all the giving, so of course we adored my father. We respected my mother. Even if we begged and begged and begged she would not give way unless, which rarely happened, we convinced her. With my father very little coaxing had the desired effect.' Agnes MacLeod was a good disciplinarian, but she could sometimes be very hard. Flora once developed a serious throat infection during a holiday in London. It was not diphtheria, but Agnes MacLeod refused to call the doctor until Flora's fever was very high. When he eventually came the doctor said he had seen far less dangerous diphtheric throats. This strange ruthlessness was repeated when Flora caught scarlet fever. She was gravely ill, but Agnes MacLeod insisted that she must be made to get up. It was only the pleading of Reginald MacLeod for his loved daughter that finally persuaded Agnes MacLeod to leave her in bed where she lay.

In 1890, Reginald MacLeod was appointed Queen's and Lord Treasurer's Remembrancer, and represented the Treasury in Scotland. For many years he had written articles on financial affairs for *The Scotsman*. By slow degrees and with careful stewardship he had at last paid off the Hobhouse debt. In 1891, when Flora was thirteen, he could afford to give her an allowance of £1 a month with which she was expected to buy her own stockings, shoes, boots and gloves. It was one of the absolute rules of the family that nobody ever bought anything they had not got the money to pay for, and Flora kept it religiously.

The increase in salary which no doubt accompanied Reginald MacLeod's new appointment made it possible in 1893 for him to rent Granton House, four miles from Edinburgh. Flora was fifteen, and after the strange succession of houses in which she had lived, this was the first she ever regarded as home. 'It was a charming place belonging to the Duke of Buccleuch,' she wrote, 'and stood on a bank which sloped down to the estuary of the Firth of Forth. It had a good garden and a fine flat meadow which was kept mown so that Olive and I could indulge our passion for cricket.' The MacLeods could now afford to employ three maids, a gardener and a coachman who drove an open landau drawn by one horse. Flora and Olive, who had grown accustomed to their life of austerity, felt they had arrived in paradise.

Granton House

THE MACLEODS LIVED AT GRANTON HOUSE FOR SIX YEARS FROM 1893-1899. It was a place which lent itself to a life which Flora and Olive had not yet been able to enjoy. There was a woodland path at the bottom of the garden, with a gate which opened on to the shore. Agnes MacLeod allowed her daughters to bathe in the estuary when the thermometer registered 60° or more, but otherwise the rigid pattern of life continued and was accepted without question. 'There was tea for breakfast on weekdays and coffee as a special treat on Sunday—the day we drove in our open landau to St. Mary's Cathedral, Edinburgh, for morning service,' wrote Flora. 'Every weekday my father bicycled to his office in the city and our governess bicycled the four miles out to Granton House and back.' The lessons were followed by the daily two hours of reading aloud, alleviated only by occasional games of chess played with a set made for the blind.

Once a week Flora and Olive were taken to the Bessire School in Edinburgh for drill and deportment classes, at which they did not excel. They worshipped the girls at the French school, in particular Mary Hunter and Mamie Bailey. 'They were goddesses,' said Flora, 'and we were rabbits.' One of the features of the school was an excellent cricket team and it was from there that Flora and Olive developed their love of the game. The bi-annual cricket matches on the meadow at Granton House were the high spot of the summer season. 'The home side was composed of neighbours and friends,' wrote Flora, 'and was always shamefully defeated. Men players were invited to swell the ranks of the scratch team and had to play left-handed. The bowling was extremely slow.' A distinguished Edinburgh K.C. remembered playing as a small boy on Flora's side at Granton House in the position of long stop. To his shame he let a ball pass and was wishing the earth would cover him up when Flora, as captain and wicket-keeper, called out, 'Well tried!' and completely restored his self-respect.

Uncle Olly's annual Christmas gift of £5 had been put in the savings bank at the rate of £2.10s. a year. 'When women's bicycles burst upon Edinburgh, Olive and I were greatly relieved to find we could each afford one at a cost of £14,' wrote Flora. 'We learnt to ride at "the shop"—a long oblong building provided for tuition. Unfortunately our instructor always allowed us to complete the circuit in the same direction, so we consistently made right-hand turns. When we first took our bicycles out at Granton House, we were unable to turn left, hit a tree, and ignominiously fell off.'

Uncle Olly's health had broken down after the sudden death in 1885 of his beloved American wife, Edith Hamilton Fish. He was working in America at the time and brought his two small children to England and made a home with his newly widowed mother. From there he made frequent visits to Granton House, to which Flora and Olive greatly looked forward. Perhaps he understood the strange world which his invalid sister had created for his two nieces, for he devoted himself to them. 'He was an inspiration to read to and with,' wrote Flora, 'and a marvellous playfellow.' At croquet he played two balls against Flora and Olive who had one each. 'Our balls were named after Scottish heroes,' wrote Flora. 'Uncle Olly was Marmion, after Sir Walter Scott's famous narrative poem, with two Squires, Blunt and FitzEustace, who were successively promoted, or degraded if their strokes miscarried. We thought this inconceivably brilliant.'

For six weeks in the year Uncle Olly took his sister abroad and gave Flora and Olive a holiday which they loved. It was in the summer of 1893 that Flora, at the age of fifteen, first consciously remembered being taken to Dunvegan Castle. The family arrived by boat, so it was from the sea that she first grasped the beauty and magic of the castle which was to play such a big part in her life. Her grandfather was standing on Dunvegan pier with Aunt Hanna to greet them. It was one of the last times she ever saw him, for in 1895 he died. He was entitled to think he had secured the estate, as he had three sons, but they had only two daughters each. Under an entail made in 1866 the estates, failing a male heir, were to go to the eldest daughter of the last chief. Until two brothers were dead, nobody knew who the last chief would be. When Norman MacLeod succeeded his father, he was already an old man and sometimes called the oldest eldest son in Britain. He was living in England with his English wife, and although he was greatly loved in Skye, devoted to Dunvegan—upon which he spent much of his money—and would willingly have made it his permanent home, his wife said the climate did not suit her. As the years passed they lived increasingly in England and built their home in Sussex. Some years after the birth of his daughters Canon Roderick C. MacLeod, the youngest of the three brothers, had a son, Ian Breac, and Dunvegan had a male heir at last. The question of the future ownership of the castle was naturally of no interest to Flora in her childhood and now the chances of her becoming Chief at Dunvegan seemed extremely remote.

The governess at Granton House was an excellent music teacher and an enthusiast. She taught both girls to play the piano, and later Flora played the viola and Olive the flute in the Edinburgh Ladies' Orchestral Society. They were good enough to play duets on two pianos at small charity concerts. Their father loved to hear them and he used to take them to play at the annual *ceilidh* of the first and newly-formed Clan MacLeod Society in Edinburgh. Music now became the one passion and enjoyment of their lives. The Carl Rosa Opera company came to Edinburgh for a short season every year and Flora and Olive were taken to see *Carmen* and some of the light operas.

In 1895, Reginald MacLeod and his elder brother were each left £15,000 by their great-aunt Perceval. She was Anne Eliza MacLeod of MacLeod, daughter of the 23rd Chief, sister of John Norman, the 24th Chief, and very proud of her MacLeod connection. She was also the daughter-in-law of Spencer Perceval, the Prime Minister assassinated in the House of Commons in 1812, and it was assumed by the MacLeods that the inheritance was part of the money paid in compensation to the Perceval family at the time of the assassination. She left each of her four great-nephews a quarter of her estate. Reginald MacLeod had long wished to give Flora and Olive a few of the pleasures he had been unable to afford in the past, and this surprising bonus enabled him to tell them that he would take them for a fortnight to the Wagner Festival at Bayreuth. When Wagner had died in 1883, his famous theatre had been bankrupt and everything had been sold. Now the *Ring der Nibelungen* was to be played in its entirety for the first time in twenty years and Richter, who had been trained by Wagner as his special conductor, was to conduct the first cycle. The theatre had been re-equipped and this was its first opening.

Flora and Olive were in a state of euphoria. 'Olive and I devoted many months beforehand to studying *The Ring* profoundly,' wrote Flora. 'I played the male singer's part on my viola and Olive played the girl singer's part on her flute. We worked night and day. It was a tremendous moment when we got to Bayreuth, because the whole world was waiting for *The Ring* after twenty years. The theatre was marvellously built in a sort of oval. It was plunged into darkness and there was dead silence. Suddenly the long E-flat of the horns stole on the air—the birth of the universe. Slowly other harmonies crept in and became the smooth-flowing water of the Rhine. It was a revelation, a shattering experience. I think it changed my life.'

At the end of the performance Flora and Olive were in such a frenzy of excitement that they begged their father to let them stay for the second cycle. Naturally, the seats were all sold, but the theatre management was so moved by the emotion of the two young girls that they found them seats. There was a young man called Burghstaller, who sang the part of Siegfried. Flora and Olive thought he was 'inspired' and wrote him a letter in German expressing their 'highest reverence' for his 'genius'. To their sorrow he did not reply, but they both returned to Edinburgh transformed by the depth of *The Ring*

Jessie Low, the daughter of a Scottish judge, and one of Flora's and Olive's Edinburgh friends, was invited to Granton House. She spoke no German, but they now had an unlimited passion for Wagner, and their friends were expected to share it. Jessie was made to assist Flora and Olive in their disastrous attempts to act out the Wagner plots.

It was a paradox that Flora and Olive, whose lives had been harshly disciplined and deprived of almost every enjoyment, emerged from their childhood with spirits uncrushed and, indeed, with dominating personalities and wills of their own. Living four miles from Edinburgh with no public transport and a one-horse landau limited social

contacts to an infinitely small circle, outside very close
neighbours. Flora and Olive did not easily make friends with
their contemporaries in Edinburgh and it was not surprising,
for their lives had been totally devoid of normal human
relationships. They had never experienced the give and take
of playing with other children. 'Intellectually,' wrote Flora,
'we did not belong to the Edinburgh set and found their
company dull.' The Edinburgh set no doubt regarded Flora
and Olive as colossal intellectual snobs. This was possibly
what Agnes MacLeod had intended, but if her daughters
were mentally superior to other girls, they were tragically
immature in almost every other respect. She refused to tell
them the facts of life. When Olive once commented that the
gardener's wife was getting very fat Agnes MacLeod
reprimanded her so severely that she crept away and hid for
hours under a dresser. On another occasion she was made to
kneel down on the floor in front of her mother and apologise
for having asked a simple question.

Flora's small, compact figure with its active little hands
and tiny narrow feet was not unattractive, but the strong blue
eyes and determined features were not altogether feminine.
She had a man's mind, polished and sharpened by a mother
who was interested in little else. She loved her father and
Uncle Olly and already preferred men's company to
women's. Indeed, she always thought being a man far better
than being a woman. She played cricket, chess and croquet,
and indulged in ice-cold bathing—all generally regarded as
masculine pursuits. She had never once held a needle or a
paint-brush, and in an age when it was accepted that girls of
good breeding did no work, she had naturally never cooked
or cleaned anything in her life. In spite of the efforts of the
Bessire School, her deportment left much to be desired. Her
clothes were only remarkable because they had probably
been unironed, and at a time when an eighteen-inch waist was
the vogue, Flora's was never less than twenty-three. A mutual
friend was horrified by the lack of grooming and described
Olive in a photograph as looking like 'an out-of-work hop
picker'.

Flora's and Olive's appearances were easily excused on the
grounds of their mother's partial blindness. She had enclosed
them in a world bereft of beautiful things. They had never
seen women in lovely clothes, so they had poor taste. They

had never arranged flowers or chosen wools for tapestry, so they had no sense of colour. Above all, they had never experienced the love of a mother, and so they did not really know how to love other people.

This lack of mother love was not necessarily unusual in those days, but it had an unfortunate and permanent effect upon Flora, for it largely destroyed her ability to make reciprocal friendships. She had several infatuations and she was to become the subject of much hero-worship herself, but true friendship was to be a rare occurrence in her life. It was a plight which incurred pity rather than dislike. Fortunately, she had inherited her father's warm heart and sparkling disposition. She had an infectious enthusiasm described rather unkindly by a friend as 'a gust of fresh air—overpowering, like a gale-force wind'. She had the natural exuberance of a child and referred to this period in her life as, 'when I was a little girl'. In fact, she was nearly eighteen and about to come out. Life must now inevitably separate the two inseparable sisters. There were three great balls in the Edinburgh winter season. One was given by the Benedicks (married men), another by the bachelors, and the third by the members of the New Club with an elected membership from the whole of Scotland. Reginald MacLeod was delighted to have a partner at his side after so many years of social starvation, and noticed few of Flora's imperfections. He took her with him to the banquets at Holyrood Palace and the breakfast-parties given in those days by the Moderator of the General Assembly.

Olive was naturally annoyed that Flora was doing things without her for the first time. She offered Flora criticism and advice, and laid down a stringent code of behaviour. 'In no way was I to make myself conspicuous,' wrote Flora. 'To dance more than three times with one partner was to make oneself conspicuous, and this a well-brought-up girl would be ashamed to be. I did my best to live up to Olive's instructions, sometimes under difficulties, as when my father, who was thoroughly enjoying himself, would fail to collect me after the third dance. I confessed these lapses to Olive and they were criticised but ultimately excused. The standard was markedly relaxed when Olive herself came out.'

Once at an important ball-party in the Borders, the ladies had withdrawn after dinner and were discussing the absence

of a particular friend who was 'expecting'. 'Expecting what?'
asked Flora. The initial silence which ensued was broken by a
chorus of embarrassed titters. Later, to the partner who
asked her what she used her fan for—she was twirling it
about for the first time in her life—Flora answered truthfully,
'To yawn behind.' It was apparent that Flora was sadly
unprepared for her emergence from childhood, but she was
not long to remain so.

Flora Comes Out

IN 1896, LORD IDDELSLEIGH, AGNES MACLEOD'S ELDEST BROTHER, invited her to bring Flora to Pynes for the Exeter ball and the small neighbour's dance which followed it. Flora's parents accompanied her to Devonshire, although obviously her mother did not go to the dance. We shall never know what the Iddesleighs thought of their Scottish niece but they were probably unimpressed, for Flora herself said afterwards, 'I had none of the thrill and rapture and intoxication which I ought to have felt. I was just shy and clumsy, totally deficient in appropriate small talk, and a real country bumpkin.'

From Pynes, Flora went without her parents to Brocket, the famous home of the Melbournes, now owned by Lord and Lady Mount Stephen. Lord Mount Stephen was proud to tell the story of his early years as the barefoot son of a crofter father in the Scottish Highlands. At the age of seventeen, with two friends, he had made his way first to London and then to Canada, where he became renowned for his part in the construction of the Canadian Pacific Railway. Like so many men of humble origin, when he subsequently became a millionaire and was given a peerage, he gloried in his success and enjoyed the membership of a titled world and the hospitality he could offer—to Royal guests among others. His adopted daughter, Alice, had married Sir Henry Stafford Northcote (later Lord Northcote), Agnes MacLeod's younger brother. Aunt Alice, as Flora called her, had a charming and powerful personality. She dressed beautifully, was a great social success and a perfect hostess. The parties she gave were often memorable. She had no children of her own and at once regarded Flora as a daughter in need of rigorous training. She saw beyond the immediate impression which Flora made with her gauche behaviour and dowdy clothes, to the highly intelligent mind, the desire to shine, and the appreciation of success which lay behind them. 'She showed uncanny flair when she enclosed me in her world and gave me her affection,' wrote Flora, who was deeply impressed by her Aunt's poise. It was not long before she loved her and eventually worshipped her shamelessly. Not everyone shared Flora's enthusiasm, for some people regarded Alice Northcote as an extremely wordly and ambitious woman. This opinion was probably valid, but, as Flora admired both these qualities, it did not matter to her.

Flora arrived at Brocket on the occasion of two important society balls. One of these was at Hatfield House, the historic home of the Cecils, and at that time the residence of the Prime Minister, the Marquess of Salisbury. As the glittering house-party arrived, Flora was made increasingly aware of her deficiencies. 'I felt less and less qualified to be part of their dazzling, beautiful and unreal world,' she wrote. That evening at dinner, Lord Mount Stephen suddenly banged the table till the wine-glasses rang and, looking at Flora, called out. 'Excuse me, Ma'am—(Royalty, was present)—it's that little girl slouching.' Flora was horrified, but Lord Mount Stephen repeated this ritual until she held herself straight. Small wonder that she learned the lesson quickly and for life!

There was once a large party when their Highnesses the Duke and Duchess of Teck were present. 'He was an anxious guest because he had a violent and at times uncontrolled temper, so every care had to be taken to avoid provoking it,' wrote Flora. 'It was bad enough that he should storm at the footmen waiting at table, but I was really terrified when told to be Uncle Harry's partner at whist, with instructions that the Duke of Teck *must* win. What can one do when the wrong side holds all the cards and the right side none?' Flora and Uncle Harry survived. Another guest at Brocket was the Duchess of Albany, the widow of Prince Leopold, Queen Victoria's youngest son. 'She was very stout,' wrote Flora, 'for besides eating heartily at meals she had a cold pheasant in her bedroom at night. I found her charming and kind.' She brought with her her daughter Princess Alice who later became the Countess of Athlone. She was only a few years younger than Flora and they enjoyed each other's company on the few occasions when they did things together.

Occasionally the Mount Stephens went up to London for the day by rail. 'Smoke made the trains very dirty and there were many tunnels,' wrote Flora. 'It was my duty to open and close the windows. Aunt Alice always instructed me to take a clean pair of gloves to wear when I arrived. I once suffered a great humiliation and a severe scolding from her because Lord Mount Stephen had to stand still in Piccadilly when my shoelace, "disgracefully and most carelessly tied", had come undone.' Aunt Alice took a particular interest in Flora's clothes and she was fitted with a bright blue cloth dress and short, tight-fitting coat with steel embroidery, made by a famous dressmaker in Dover Street called Kate Reilly. 'It cost the fabulous sum of £30,' wrote Flora, 'but I do not think I ever loved it.'

In 1896 Flora was presented at Buckingham Palace. Aunt Alice and Lady Mount Stephen both had the entrée—the entrance reserved for specially qualified people—and therefore escaped the long wait of the less privileged. Courts were then called drawing-rooms and were held at 3 o'clock in the afternoon. 'We had our hair dressed in the morning and in the afternoon we drove to the Palace in our low-cut dresses with a long train and three feathers in our hair,' wrote Flora. 'There was a great queue of carriages, and people jumped on the footboards to stare inside at the smart dresses. The Princess of Wales, afterwards Queen Alexandra, flanked by the whole Royal Family, was present all the time. And there was an old, dumpy, dowdy lady, dressed in black and yet infinitely majestical, seated in a chair.'

It was not many months after Flora's first and only encounter with Queen Victoria that Lady Mount Stephen died. When Flora returned to Brocket late in 1898, a new mourning livery was being made for the men-servants, and her aunt and uncle were living with their bereaved father. Miss Tufnell, a lady-in-waiting to one of the lesser Royalties, chose this moment to visit Brocket, and Flora was instructed to look after her and make sure Lord Mount Stephen was not troubled. 'I very soon realised this was the last thing Miss Tufnell intended, nor was it desired by him,' wrote Flora. 'Shortly after her visit, he announced their engagement. It was a painful shock to my aunt and uncle, who had sacrificed much to care for him, and doubly hurtful coming so soon after his wife's death. Meals became dreadfully gloomy. I felt it was my duty to try to be cheerful and talk naturally. At dinner I embarked on one of my father's Skye stories, told in the lovely soft Highland tongue. It concerned a crofter who lived on a great cliff called Biedermore. His cow had fallen over the cliff and his wife had died. A visitor condoled with him but the crofter replied, "The ways of Providence are inscrutable. The coo I hae gotten the noo is a better coo, and the wife a bonnier wife, too." Once I had started it was impossible to stop. I sat there and wished the earth would swallow me up.'

In 1897 Reginald MacLeod took his daughters to Vienna. His father's widow, Aunt Hanna, had now remarried a wealthy and distinguished Austrian, Count Vincent de Latour. So great was her devotion to Skye that she made her husband promise to live six months of the year in Uiginish, and it was only when he agreed that she consented to spend the other six in Vienna. Aunt Hanna and her husband gave the MacLeods a warm welcome and generous hospitality in Vienna. 'They gave us a splendid luncheon in excessively hot weather,' wrote Flora. 'It began with iced beer. Olive and I thought it horrid. At the same time, we were terribly thirsty. My mother had enjoined us under no circumstances ever to drink water. With the first course some claret came round. We thought that was very much nicer than beer. So we deflected from our tankards of beer on to the claret. With the next course there came champagne. At the end of luncheon they produced some wonderful liqueur—a special recipe—which we could not refuse. Afterwards they lent us their carriage, and we drove to the great palace and gardens of Schönbrunn. Olive said she was feeling unwell, so I agreed to stay with her, sitting on a seat, while my father went to look at the gardens. Suddenly, Olive, became extraordinarily queer. She said she felt giddy and remarked that a little girl's hoop was going 'round and round and round.' Then she began weeping and said how terribly miserable she would be if I died. I was sick with fear. I could not think what had happened. When at last my father came in sight, I rushed to him. He took one look at Olive and said we must go straight home. We managed to get her into the carriage.'

Flora had a strong head which was always unaffected by drink, and Olive soon recovered from her hangover. Their father now gave them a dress allowance of £80 a year, which they were careful never to overspend. 'We were taught whenever we went out with other people, no matter how much older or wealthier they might be, to offer to pay our share of the cost,' said Flora.

In 1899, Reginald MacLeod was appointed Registrar-General to take the 1901 census. He was naturally pleased with his appointment. It was twenty years since he and his wife had left their house in Hobart Place in difficulty and distress. Now, with his fortunes restored, he moved his family back to London to prepare for his work. He bought a house in Draycott Place. A wing consisting of two bedrooms, a bathroom and a small sitting-room was added to it and made a perfect London home for Flora and Olive. They revelled in their good fortune, which included the new attractions of electric light and a motor-car, but their happiness was clouded by the news that Uncle Olly was now desperately and fatally ill. In the winter of 1899 he invited Flora to accompany him to the French Riviera and Italy to see some of the great works of art before he died. Flora had been surrounded by illness all her young life and knew how difficult the journey would be, but for Uncle Olly there was nothing she would not do. Accompanied by the Scottish table-maid from Granton House she left with Uncle Olly and his valet for the Continent. 'Each morning I was sent to visit the picture galleries and places of interest and mark out anything especially fine,' she wrote. 'In the afternoons we went together—Uncle Olly in his wheelchair—to visit the chosen works of art. It was a great strain on a very sick man, and in the evening he would return exhausted, and virtually collapse. I admired his gallantry. I shared the joy which this final pleasure gave him and equally the pain which was the price he paid for it. We returned through Paris and he took seats for the Opera. It was a courageous effort but he could not last through the performance. He fainted and had to be carried home.'

It is not difficult to imagine the strain under which Flora lived through these days. She was only twenty-one and had never before been abroad without her family, but her courage under duress was a quality she retained for life. Early in 1900, Uncle Olly died and Flora and Olive experienced the first 'burning sorrow' of their lives. Aunt Alice decided with Flora's parents that she was in need of a change. Together they agreed that she should visit her uncle and aunt in India, where Lord Northcote had just accepted the post of

Governor of Bombay. With the blessing of her family, Flora
set sail from Marseilles at the end of April 1900 on board the
P. & O. liner *Caledonia*, bound for India.

India, 1900

FLORA ARRIVED IN INDIA WHEN THE BRITISH RAJ WAS AT ITS
height. Lord Beaconsfield's dream of Queen Victoria as
Empress of India was fulfilled. Lord Curzon was the Viceroy,
soon to become famous for the splendours with which he was
surrounded. The entertainment of the large European
community was a full-time occupation, consisting of polo
matches, picnics, tennis and garden-parties, race meetings,
boating expeditions and above all glittering society balls,
which kept the staff at Government House and the hundreds
of magnificently dressed Indian servants endlessly busy.

Lady Northcote was an ideal Governor's wife and within
weeks of her arrival in Bombay had been acclaimed a great
success. As a travelling companion for Flora she had chosen
Miss Agnes Beresford Hope, who was neither young nor
good-looking but who had a wasp waist, of which she was
tremendously proud, and a lady's maid called Ida, who
tightened her laced stays with a button hook. Flora did not
really approve of this practice, but Miss Hope told her that
'more men marry a good figure than a pretty face'. Flora took
an immediate and permanent dislike to her.

This was Flora's first long absence from home and her only
parting from Olive since their childhood. To begin with she
felt homesick and awkward. In her first-class cabin on board
the *Caledonia,* with no one but Miss Hope for company, the
two-week voyage in intense heat seemed endless. Apart from
the Europeans on board there was a wealthy Indian
gentleman who was deliberately disregarded by the other
passengers. Flora disapproved strongly of their attitude, felt
it her duty to befriend him, and several times engaged him in
conversation. She soon realised that her approaches were
entirely misconstrued, and she had to break off the acquaint-
ance abruptly.

Flora was in many ways unprepared for society life in India, but she was now accustomed to the exacting standards of Aunt Alice and she learned quickly. She wrote daily and at great length to Olive, who had to wade through letters of never less than twenty and sometimes more than fifty pages. Relieved by her first taste of freedom after the restrictions of home, Flora developed from a child into a woman.

When the *Caledonia* sailed into Bombay harbour on Friday, May 4th, 1900, the European community had already left for the cooler climate of Mahableshwar. On Saturday Flora wrote, 'Yesterday we dropped anchor at 5 a.m. and for more than an hour previous the row getting up cargo was deafening. Apparently these big vessels anchor about a mile out and boats of sorts come for the passengers. Captain Greig came in a private launch at 7.30 a.m. to fetch us. This is the most beautiful city in the world. At night the whole outline of the bay from Malabar Point to Colaba Lighthouse is fringed with brilliant lights, and this is called "the Queen's Diamond Necklace". The reflection of this row of lights in the water is simply glorious.

"The appearance of the whole place—I am including in this the country through which we pass in the train—is burnt and caked with drought. It is brown, brown, brown, no grass, no crops, no wild flowers, nothing but great tracts of parched soil. Release is afforded by the vivid green of the trees, sort of emerald colour, quite different from anything we see in England. The people themselves are even more interesting—a huge jumble of Parsees, Hindus and Mohammedans. The former I have learnt to discern, for the men wear curious glazed caps on their heads and the women lovely sort of embroidered mantillas. Many of the Hindus have different coloured chalk marks on their foreheads. One universal custom is that the babies are all carried astride on their mother's hip.'

The train journey from Bombay to Poona was long and arduous. Plague had broken out and strict precautions were in force. 'At the stations along the line doctors come and feel the pulses of all the passengers,' wrote Flora. 'We had lady doctors who came to us and if anyone's pulse is abnormal he is instantly stopped, isolated and placed under supervision.' These constant interruptions delayed the train, which did not reach Poona until 2 a.m. After light refreshments, Flora and

Her mother, Agnes Northcote

Sir Reginald MacLeod of MacLeod,
27th Chief, Dame Flora's father

Sir Reginald with his
daughters, Flora and
Olive

Flora MacLeod of MacLeod, 1911

Olive, 1910

Dame Flora's husband, Hubert Walter, in later life

Miss Hope were escorted to phaetons—'most beautifully
arranged like beds so that we lay down all the way with
pillows and were very comfy,' wrote Flora. 'We changed
horses five times on the road and at Wai, where the hard
climb begins, we had teams of four mules put on. Then came
enormous excitement for our creatures were "bhobbery
wollahs" (cantankerous creatures) and refused to move.
Finally, when the whole native community ran at them with
sticks and stones, the mules retired to the ditch after a perfect
volley of kicks. At last we were off and kept up a hard gallop
most of the way, the mules being stimulated by the two
assistant *sais* (grooms) with shouts and whips and the hurling
of stones and earth gathered at the roadside.'

Lord Northcote, attended by four members of his staff,
received his niece at Government House. 'You may imagine
the joyfulness of the greetings,' wrote Flora. 'All dirty and
travel-stained, we were whisked through porches, along
verandahs and up an outside wooden staircase to the
Governor's quarters. Here such a loving, warm welcome
greeted us, and Aunt Alice looked as radiant and well as
Uncle Harry.'

Flora was at once enchanted with India, and Aunt Alice
now became the greatest feminine influence in her life. The
powerful and superficial world, of which the British
community at Government House was the centre, gave Lady
Northcote the opportunity to exploit her natural gifts. She
ran everything with smooth efficiency, and it was from her
that Flora learnt to give orders to the servants, talk in a
relaxed and interesting fashion with men, and entertain large
numbers of guests without a qualm. None of these things
came naturally to Flora, and her dependence upon Aunt
Alice was deep. She learnt to smoke because Aunt Alice
smoked. She played the piano after dinner because Aunt
Alice asked her to, but she brought her own natural
enthusiasm to all she did. 'We were thirty-six at dinner,' she
wrote a week after her arrival. 'We got through quite nicely,
although I always perish with fear at first. Aunt Alice was
more than kind and introduced me to hundreds of people.
She made me stand behind her during the reception and
introduced me along. At several times in the evening she
beckoned me up, but what pleases me most of all was that
Captain Wood told Aunt Alice that I was a great help to the

staff and very useful, That, I mourn to say, is a very
charitable exaggeration on his part, but it was nice of him and
pleased Aunt Alice. I refused to dance the first three dances
and stood about and talked to the wallflowers. After that I
got myself engaged right through, but even afterwards fits of
compunction would overwhelm me and I occasionally
sacrificed a dance to dull talk.

'Today has been full of the races and most successful they
were. I wore my white serge costume with the white silk and.
insertion lace blouse, a black sash and my black hat. I have
worn white and black all the time here. Aunt Alice has a
perfect passion to see me always in white, which for me is an
expensive hobby. No dress has much chance of her approval
unless it is white.'

It was Flora's duty to accompany her aunt on official visits
and, as Lady Northcote had a reputation for hard work, the
pace was often exacting. She had been known to visit
nineteen people in a single morning, and in one day Flora and
Miss Hope called on Lady Wingate, Major and Mrs. Grant
of Rothiemurchus, Mrs. Metaxa 'who had a dog killed by a
panther only the other day', and Mrs. Carter who had 'shot
four tigers herself'. These were all Europeans and the
meetings with native Indians were rare and, therefore,
exciting. 'Yesterday, I was introduced to some rather
amusing little people,' wrote Flora. 'They were the daughters
of the Rani of Akalkot. The mother herself is a widow and in
purdah (no strange man may see her face), but the three little
daughters go about. The eldest is just marriageable, thirteen
years old, the second ten and the third three. They are very
tiny but extraordinarily old for their ages. I was much
puzzled to know how to address them but was finally
instructed, "My dear". The two eldest girls wore green silk
bodices and pink gauze skirts, and on their heads two black
caps covered all over with embroidery and real pearls! Then
in their black hair they have great diamond stars fastened in,
and in their left nostrils and on their foreheads more
brilliants. Their ear-rings were colossal emeralds, and round
their necks were strings of pearls, emeralds and diamonds.
Even the baby girl had ropes of pearls and precious stones all
over. They say it takes them one-and-a-half hours to dress,
and when they dress in their best it takes four hours.'

Aunt Alice carefully instructed Flora on the class

distinctions of the guests who came to Government House, but it was a lesson Flora was incapable of learning. She continually made mistakes. 'I disgraced myself yesterday at the purdah party,' she wrote. 'In the corner of the dining-room sat a tall, dark lady in elaborate Persian dress. Attributing her solitude to her nationality, I flew up and in my broken Urdu invited her in to tea. The lady rose and preserving the most complete silence followed me into the dining-room. I was just offering her a chair and treating her to the full courtliness of my nature when Aunt Alice rushed up and said, "Good heavens, you have made a muddle. That's the ayah who should never come in here. Leave her now and don't take any more notice of her." There must have been two or three hundred people there and the European ladies were loud in their enjoyment.'

On the tennis court or on picnics, Flora's fresh-air quality came into its own and she made herself popular, but she was not a flirt. Her friendships with men were almost invariably limited to the older and married members of the staff, with whom she felt far more in sympathy than the young army officers who were her dancing-partners. She immersed herself in a Hindustani manual 'for I cannot bear not to be able to ask for what I want,' she wrote. 'It seems to me quite unnecessary to understand anybody else, but to be able to volley forth your own commands is most desirable.'

The small group of people who surrounded the Northcotes at Government House lived with discipline and formality even when they were alone. Each morning before breakfast, escorted by two members of the staff, Flora was expected to ride on horseback or a bicycle. She was afraid of horses and disliked riding, but she forced herself to do it. 'The Queen's health is drunk every night,' she wrote. 'Uncle Harry stands up and says, 'The Queen Empress' and we all say it after him and then drink. On a band night we stand with our glasses in our hand while the band plays *"God Save The Queen"* Outings and expeditions were equally formal. 'Today started with the most heavenly picnic,' Flora wrote, 'among the grandest scenery I ever saw in my life, to a place called Elphinstone Point, eight miles away. We started at about 11.30 so it was pretty hot, but we were well protected against the sun. The gentlemen had started off before breakfast on their beat. However, they received us at a most charming little bungalow commanding a beautiful view, where the most sumptuous luncheon was prepared—pies, cold fowl, cold lamb, mint sauce, *aloyau de boeuf,* hot potatoes and peas, different kinds of tarts, strawberries and cream, bananas, mangoes—everything you could conceive. The delightful feeling of no strangers acted like champagne on the party, and Uncle Harry was in tremendous form and produced pun after pun, which were received with volleys of laughter.'

Later that day Flora was told that the Queen's *phirita* (or letter) had arrived and must be read in state. 'The gentlemen joined us ladies in the drawing-room,' she wrote, 'and we solemnly took our seats. There was an impressive hush. The dining-room door was flung open and a procession entered headed by a *chopdar* (personal bodyguard to the Governor) with a silver mace. We instantly rose to our feet. Captain Wood followed, looking with firm determination on nothing at all. Then the staff in pairs, Captain Greville bearing on a cushion a large envelope from which he never moved his eyes. Uncle Harry followed last looking very dignified. I started by wishing to laugh because it seemed so absurd that these men, with whom we had been joking a few minutes back, should suddenly have to go through such an absurd pantomime. The arrival of the *phirita* was announced to His Excellency and it was presented to him. He touched it and then desired Mr. Hill to read it. The seals were broken. While we all stood up, Mr. Hill began, "Victoria, by the grace of God, etc." I was so absorbed in the nervous anxiety to suppress a giggling fit that the beginning rather escaped me until suddenly there was an awful "tche" from Captain Purves. Mr. Hill, who had been reading with difficulty, stopped suddenly. Captain Wood was seen shaking all over and Captain Greig devoured his handkerchief alive. Colonel Croly, Major Leigh, and Captain Greville looked very grave and Uncle Harry said with an angry voice, "Order, gentlemen." Silence was soon restored and Major Leigh took the document from the impeccable Mr. Hill. He then resumed "that in consideration of the dangers of Mahableshwar it became necessary to appoint two new members of the staff—Agnes Beresford Hope to be Assistant Military Secretary, and Flora MacLeod to be A.D.C." After this, of course, there was no attempt to conceal laughter.' Flora and Miss Hope were given black evening dresses with yellow revers and gold buttons 'in imitation of the staff and which we are always to wear when we are alone,' wrote Flora.

On June 9, the Northcotes and their entourage from Government House moved from Mahableshwar to Poona. Aunt Alice insisted that Flora must be inoculated for enteric fever. 'The deed was performed at 8 p.m.,' wrote Flora. 'The paraphernalia is much more alarming than the deed. Colonel Croly performed the operation and his talented assistant, Mr. MacQueen, arranged the instruments. These were many in number, consisting of countless bottles and rolls of bandages, cotton wool, etc. They rubbed on some antiseptic stuff first and then came the injection—simply a pinprick and then some smarting. Then the arm was bound up with cotton wool and lint. Then he, Colonel Croly, said I ought to keep an hourly bulletin, the following example of which much pleases me:

7.30   I feel perfectly well.
8.30   I am very hungry.
9.30   I am less hungry.
10.30   I feel very ill.
11.30   Captain Greig has arrived.
12.30   I think he is the most disagreeable man I have ever met.
12.45   Captain Greville has come.
1.30   I have sent for Uncle Harry's gun. This is unendurable.
2.30   I remember nothing more.

This inoculation prevented Flora from joining the final shooting party at Mahableshwar. Miss Hope, who had been considered too old to need an injection, left Flora behind and joined the party on her own. Flora was furious. Alone in her room and forbidden all food, she longed for 'beefsteak and plum pudding' and imagined Miss Hope enjoying the company on her own. It was extraordinary that Flora should regard Miss Hope as a rival, for she was superior to her in almost every way. It was even more extraordinary that this small incident should convince Flora of the need to destroy Miss Hope's reputation in the eyes of the staff, but it did. 'She holds up her skirts in a way which scandalises the gentlemen,' she wrote. 'It is quite curious, her utter inability to amuse herself and her acute dislike of being alone. Anything rather than that.' After another disagreement between them, Flora wrote, 'I was so provoked that I exploded to Captain Greville in the course of our first dance and he was very sympathetic, remarking, "I always knew she was entirely selfish and never thought of anybody but herself." She is very tactless and too much fond of hostessing and taking the lead. She annoys everybody very much by the way she will take no care of herself or her health. It isn't pluck. It is downright selfish stupidity. If she has an attack of diarrhoea she will stand on the wet grass, eat plum pudding and ice for dinner, and be amazed that she never thought about it.'Flora always said she felt sorry for jealous people and that she was glad she did not suffer from jealousy but she was not good at understanding herself. When the shooting-party returned she wrote to Olive, 'Miss Hope seems to have enjoyed herself thoroughly, but I can't help fancying, from little remarks I heard dropped, that a single woman on a day's shooting is a little in the way. After luncheon she declined to remain in the *tonga* as suggested and walked into the jungle where eventually the head *shikari* disposed of her somewhere. There wasn't any game in the jungle but if there had been her white dress would have frightened it miles away. However, it was her own choice and wish to go and I was thoroughly pleased because of having a delightful quiet day with Aunt Alice. I simply adore her for the care she takes of me. I can never get over my importance here as Uncle Harry's niece. You would be quite amused at the invitations that overwhelm me and which don't come to Miss Hope.'

It took one hundred bullock-carts laden with household equipment from Government House five days to make the journey from Mahableshwar to Poona. The official party left at 5 a.m. and made the twenty-mile drive to Wai. 'There we breakfasted off porcelain with fine silver and linen napkins which had been unpacked specially for the purpose,' wrote Flora. The seven-course breakfast prepared by servants in full-dress uniform was identical with that served daily at Government House. Thousands of people lined the roads to the station and official dignitaries were presented along the route, so the fifty-mile train journey to Poona took five-and-a-half hours.

Government House in Poona was at Ganesh Khind, a few

miles outside the town, and renowned for its grace and luxury. 'I wish I had words to describe its beauty,' wrote Flora. 'It is really a dream. Figure to yourself a large stone grey building with two big entries along the front, one leading to the ballroom and the other to the main entrance. A tower rises up over the principal door, on the top of which floats the flag. At this door there are always sentries on duty and a mounted member of the bodyguard. He looks so well with his lance and his red uniform.

'The dining room is vast and splendid with windows or doors on both sides of the house. Down the passage you come to the salon which is simply gigantic and I should think quite perfect for dancing. It is very lofty and has a grand white and gold ceiling, beautiful candelabra, and furniture very massive in red velvet and gold. During the whole length of the dining-room on the right of the passage there is no building. This is the joy. It is a huge loggia supported on granite columns on a marble floor, surrounded with shrubs and with a fountain playing in the centre. Through the columns you see bright grass, plentifully watered, studded with rose-beds, most luxuriant tropical plants, splendid palms, brilliant crimson gold mohr trees, purple bougain-villaeas, huge crotons, a fountain with lilies in the distance and peacocks sunning themselves in their brightest colours.'

It is difficult to imagine how the real conditions in India ever penetrated this protected and luxurious world, but they occasionally did. There was a severe famine in Poona in June 1900, and in that district alone 50,000 starving people were recorded. Lady Northcote, together with the British officials, worked hard to relieve the terrible conditions. 'Will you please tell mother that money is very badly wanted for the Bombay Famine Fund which Aunt Alice is collecting for,' wrote Flora. 'She would be very grateful if you could tell any people who wish to contribute to send to that instead of the Lord Mayor's Fund. It is very nice that people at home are so keen and anxious to help, for it is very terrible out here. I saw yesterday, when visiting some of the native schools, where children were cared for whose parents had given them up starving because of being unable to feed them. Poor little mites. Although they looked fat, the sisters said they weren't healthy, only swollen out with food.'

When Lord Northcote gave a celebration tea to mark the capture of Pretoria in the Boer War, 12,000 children turned up instead of the expected 5,000. Some had walked twenty miles in the hope of getting a meal. 'Everybody tells me I see nothing of what India is really like, living as I do here,' Flora wrote, 'and that Rudyard Kipling's descriptions of it, however horrible, are vividly accurate. Today I was taken to a native bazaar for the first time and saw men and women asleep on the street. On the way home we passed a common where there were hundreds of cattle lying about, all to be sold, for the poor people cannot feed them. You can buy a cow for two rupees.'

To Government House came those men of the Indian Civil Service who were in need of a rest. Many worked an eighteen-hour day under exhausting conditions, and deaths from plague, cholera and typhoid were common. 'They literally work themselves to death,' wrote Flora. 'I should call the Indian Civil Service the finest profession in the world. If I were a man it is the one I should try for, for a good man is bound to make a career. He has so many opportunities of distinguishing himself, but of course requires great initiative and decision. The work is very grand and very noble and very splendid, and some of the workers are such silent heroes one would be proud to belong to them.'

Queen Victoria took a personal interest in Lady Northcote's work and corresponded with her about it. 'A letter from the Queen by this mail—a long one—filling a sheet and a half, and everything, including the envelope, in her own hand,' wrote Flora. 'It was all about the famine and the work among the poor women and of how Aunt Alice couldn't say enough to them of the interest she, the Queen, took in them.'

Flora now devoted her mornings to reading Kipling and books on Indian history and religion from her aunt's extensive library. 'The darkness and mystery of the Hindu worship gives me a feeling of something grand and terrible,' she wrote. 'I am quite afraid of Vishnu and wouldn't for worlds profane his shrine. Uncle Harry lent me a fascinating book called, *India in 1983*—a skit on the Bengali self-government when England gives India Home Rule. It is brilliantly amusing and I must read it aloud to mother when I come home. The names of the Ministers are simply delightful—Bladeenath Laiktokil, Minister of War; Rathanath Mounterjee, Inspector of Cavalry; Seegren Muchasik, Minister of Marine; Datsdewah Demunny Ghose, Minister of Finance.'

Indian independence was far from the minds of the British in 1900. The reception given by the Northcotes at Ganesh Khind in early July was the largest of its kind ever held there. 'So great was the crush,' wrote Flora, 'that it took one man an hour to drive the short mile from the entrance gate to the house.' Under a blaze of illuminated chandeliers, with fountains playing in the loggia and flaming torches in the garden, hundreds of officers in full-dress uniform danced with their ladies and for an evening forgot the 50,000 starving Indians outside. 'Aunt Alice looked quite beautiful,' wrote Flora, 'in an embroidered white satin dress, trimmed with pink chiffon and carnations, and a perfect blaze of diamonds—her tiara, collarette and necklace.'

Flora herself became increasingly clothes-conscious under her influence. 'I wore my white satin with pink roses and black velvet ribbons in my hair, and my face rouged, powdered and patched,' she wrote. 'This was the dance of my career. My card was filled from beginning to end. The floor was a dream. It is known as the best in India and my experience can't produce a better one. It is so springy that one can dance on and on without stopping.' Yet, for all her enthusiasm, Flora was never in love with any of her partners. One of them, a Captain Roberts, became so attached to her that he twice got himself invited to Government House in order to see her again. He was an ebullient character and wore a black patch over the eye he had lost in a polo accident. 'My sympathy was increased by hearing there is talk of the other eye breaking down,' wrote Flora, 'and that all this rowdiness and noise is to drown care and to have a good time while it is left to him. He has a most gruesome laugh—two characters, a gentleman in solitude and a bounder in public. So my impressions alternate. Anyhow he is interesting.' Essentially, Flora was far more interested in the annual cricket match between the President's XI and the Parsees' XI. This was held in Bombay, with a return match a month later in Poona. She sat in the Governor's box throughout the two-day event, armed with her own score-card and pencil, and oblivious of the heat. 'The windows and roofs of the houses were thick with gazers,' she wrote, 'and even the trees were alive with them, while round the enormous ground people were packed like sardines. 15,000 are estimated to have been present. One half of the ground is given up to the native and one half to the European spectators, but the former certainly vanquish in the power of making a noise.'

Flora impressed everybody with her knowledge of the game. The President's team was defeated in Bombay and the return match in Poona opened badly for them. 'We were all confident the match would be over by lunch-time,' wrote Flora, 'and that the Parsees would only have about thirty runs to make, but the ten-to-one on our crushing defeat was disappointed. Will you believe it, our men went on after lunch and made a hundred runs before Mr. Drysdale was caught in the deep field; The last wicket put on 115 runs. Wasn't it glorious? The excitement was intense and, as they hit about, the excitement in the pavilion was rapturous. Men stood and shouted. It was thrilling. All round were yells, "Well played, Sir, well played." "One, two, no, no, three. One up. Steady, steady, for goodness sake." We were all frantic. When our score reached 336 there was great applause and, as we felt we had now equalled their score in one innings, defeat would be robbed of its disgrace. I know six of the team which gives me a great glow of pleasure.'

It was with the same energetic enthusiasm that Flora toured India before sailing home to England. Accompanied by Miss Hope and Captain Ferguson, she visited Ahmedabad, Delhi, Agra and Bombay. She rose regularly at 5.30 a.m. and, criticising her companions for being 'a bit late', undertook a day's sight-seeing which would have put a modern package-tour to shame. In one day alone she visited Ferozobad, the Kila Kona Mosque, Hummyun's Library, the Jain Mosque and the native bazaars. Miss Hope sat utterly exhausted and dejected on a boulder while Flora climbed briskly to the top of the monuments. She walked for several hours on the Ridge, the scene of the famous siege of 1857, and explored the topography of the battlefield like a general. 'On the highest point of all stands the Mutiny memorial,' she wrote. 'It is remarkable for anything but beauty. The names of battles, fallen officers, and regiments engaged are engraved on it, and tables showing comparative losses. The 60th Rifles

started the siege with 380 men. By the end 379 had been killed
or wounded. Isn't that a terrible casualty list?'

It was only when the party reached Agra on October 14
and visited the Taj Mahal by moonlight that Flora's feminine
heart was touched. 'The absolute perfect beauty of what we
saw is indescribable,' she wrote. 'The Taj looked quite
ethereal with its outlines so melting into the sky. You could
not clearly have designed it. It seemed like a cloud floating
between earth and heaven and one felt as if it were a dream or
bubble one breath would blow away. We sat there till 12.30.
It really was like a peep of heaven and very, very far removed
from this earth. The quiet river on one side and the glorious
garden on the other completed the most beautiful scene I
shall ever see. It was like the most perfect music realised into
form.'

When Flora left the confines of Government House and
the complete loyalty of her aunt and uncle, she discovered
that the main topic of conversation among the British was
their detestation of the Viceroy. 'They say Lord Curzon treats
all the Europeans so *de haut en bas,*' she wrote, 'and at any
public function never mixes with people but either speaks to
no one or else has one or two of the principal swells brought
up to speak to him. Lady Curzon, they say, is very popular
and tries to mix with her guests but Lord Curzon won't have
it, and at their own state dinner-parties they hardly speak to
anyone and go to bed very early. There was great excitement
a short time ago when an order was issued that Lady Curzon
was never to go out driving, not even for shopping or for
pleasure, without an A.D.C. in uniform. On hearing this the
staff resigned in a body and the order was rescinded.'

On Saturday, October 20th, Flora sailed out of Bombay on
board the *Caledonia* As her small figure with its round face
and sparkling eyes watched the outline of India fade over the
horizon, she knew part of her heart remained behind. Behind
her, too, was the shy, awkward child who had left England six
months before. The glory of the British Empire stirred in
Flora's heart and she was possessed of a deep ambition to
serve her country with as much brilliance and success as Aunt
Alice. Behind those very blue eyes there was unusual power
and physical energy to match it.

'Heavenly though it will be to see you all again,' she wrote,
'you will be able to understand that the parting here has been

a sharp pang, and the last letter from the country where I
have spent such happy months and met with such untold
goodness must be rather sad. The visit began with Aunt Alice
and with her it must end. My love and admiration has been
increased even beyond what it was before. My last words
about my happiness while in India must be that I lived with a
truly great and truly good woman who accepts my love and
returns it.'

Marriage

When Flora returned from India she discovered that her six months' absence had been a decisive period in the life of her family. Reginald MacLeod had now rented, in addition to his London home, first a temporary country house and, later, a fine old house called Vinters Park, near Maidstone in Kent. Olive had come out in glittering London society without any of Flora's inhibitions. She had attended Court balls and surrounded herself with a fashionable and interesting group of friends. During Agnes MacLeod's long absences from home, probably for several weeks at a time, when she stayed with Lady Seafield at Castle Grant or Cullen, Olive became her father's London hostess.

Reginald MacLeod and Olive were devoted to each other. After his years of isolation, Olive introduced into his life a galaxy of lively and intellectual young people, prominent among whom were Violet Asquith, Blanche Dugdale, Venetia Stanley, Archie Gordon and Maurice Bonham-Carter. They were constant visitors to Draycott Place and Vinters, where Olive and her father indulged in a positive orgy of entertaining. 'Our host at Vinters,' wrote Sir Lawrence Johns in his book, *An Edwardian Youth,* 'could hardly sit through dinner in his anxiety to begin the after-dinner games. 'And now let us be merry,' he would exclaim, straddling the hearth-rug and rolling his r's like a Frenchman. We called him *Waxworks* because of his pink and white complexion and white cottonwool side-whiskers, and it was difficult to believe that this jovial, hospitable man was the hereditary, secular enemy of countless MacDonalds. The games themselves were fairly exacting: epigrams were extorted; abstruse and abstract conceits must be guessed; you needed to be bookish as well as wide-awake to hold your own in them. Casual visitors, unexercised in our particular sport and disinclined to

61

stand on mental tiptoes after a good dinner, did not always, I fear, appreciate the fun.' The game of aphorisms was a particular favourite in which Reginald MacLeod was once described as 'a sunny peach on a garden wall', Violet Asquith as 'a blooming cornfield', and a particularly colourless cousin as 'a glass of water for a lady'.

Olive considered the most successful party to be one when nobody ever went away. On one occasion when she and her father gave a big dinner-party at Draycott Place, Mrs. Asquith accepted for herself but refused for the Prime Minister. When the evening came, both the Prime Minister and Mrs. Asquith arrived. An extra place was hastily laid and without a qualm Olive seated Mrs. Asquith on her host's left. When the other guests assembled to find the seating disorientated, Olive explained with regret, 'Oh, I am afraid my father has put Mrs. Asquith on the wrong side.' The incident was thus explained and forgotten.

Flora and Olive had been part of one another's lives for so long that it was a shock for Flora to discover that she did not automatically share in her sister's new friendships. In India she had been swathed in admiration and affection by Aunt Alice. Now she wrote, 'I feel like the fifth wheel on the coach.' Olive was surrounded with admirers and had considerable sex appeal. Flora was once present in the room when a suitor crawled on his knees at Olive's feet to beg for her hand. Flora was horrified but Olive was completely unmoved. 'Her beauty was the embodiment of repose,' wrote a friend.

Agnes MacLeod's health had seriously deteriorated and Flora returned to find that her mother was suffering from frequent haemorrhages. In spite of this, or possibly because of it, she was more determined than ever. In the winter of 1900 she insisted on going to Brighton for the day by car. Her doctors said it was sheer madness but nothing would stop her, and her husband could exert no control over her. It was left to Flora to bear the brunt of the argument. In the event, a black fog descended on London and the car could not leave. The doctors advised an hysterectomy—an operation which at that time was regarded as fatal. With resolute self-will, Agnes MacLeod pulled through. 'She explained that she had to live,' wrote Flora, 'because had she died public opinion would have held my father guilty of her death.'

Flora sat in her room at Draycott Place and looked back

on the carefree months in India as a passing dream. Olive now had her own life. Reginald MacLeod was shortly to become an Under-Secretary of State for Scotland, and had an increasing number of business interests in the City. Flora was once again imprisoned in the tragedy of her mother's illness. The reading aloud each afternoon, the games of chess and the monotony of the sick-room grated on the nerves of a girl who only months before had been dancing the night away in the ballroom of Ganesh Khind. There was no friend with whom Flora could talk, for she had made no friends. She did not want to spoil Olive's enjoyment by loading her problems upon her. Aunt Alice, who would have given wise counsel and advice, was many thousands of miles away. In those days, it was considered degradation for the entire family for a daughter to have a career and earn money, so the idea never crossed Flora's mind. If she had been a man, as she so much wished, a career in public life would no doubt have attracted her, but Agnes MacLeod completely believed what she had so often told her daughters—that they would disgrace themselves if they deserted her for any reason other than marriage. There was nobody with whom Flora was in love, but within three months of her return from Bombay she became engaged to Hubert Walter.

Hubert Walter was born on March 12th, 1870, the tenth son and twelfth child of John Walter III, the last of the trilogy during whose lives *The Times* newspaper became famous all over the world. He had grown up in the enormous house called Bearwood, which his father had built on the inherited family estate at Wokingham. It was known as the second palace of Berkshire, but life inside it was far from happy.

John Walter was a Member of Parliament and each night used to leave the House of Commons and go down to *The Times* office with the latest news before returning to his house in Upper Grosvenor Street. With seven step-children and six of her own, with two large houses to keep and a very active social life in the world of politics and journalism, the second Mrs. Walter was not able to spend much time with her children, nor to integrate the two families. Of necessity there was great disparity in their ages, and the children never belonged in any close sense to each other.

Hubert Walter thought his childhood very unhappy. He was the only intellectual in the family and, although he was allowed to win a scholarship to Winchester, his father refused to let him live as a scholar and paid his fees to an ordinary house. He found life a constant frustration. The whole family of suitable age were expected, when at home, to attend a pompous late dinner in evening dress, but no game was permitted afterwards. They sat with their paper or a book in their hands and went to sleep. At the end of every term John Walter's sons were expected to ask their father for a cheque. It was an ordeal Hubert dreaded. His younger brother, Ralph, was far more aggressive. He always tried for more money than the other brothers and was usually successful.

When Hubert Walter left university his one great ambition was to join *The Times*. John Walter was seventy-five years old and had been chief proprietor of *The Times* for forty-six years. He allowed nobody to work for him who had not served an apprenticeship on a local newspaper, so in 1893 Hubert worked for a year on the *Yorkshire Post* before becoming a sub-editor on *The Times*. Although some people suggested that Hubert Walter would never have got his job without his father's influence, it was equally true that once he had got it he was treated no differently from the other journalists. He worked tirelessly, and often sat up until the early hours of the morning. He submitted to his father's domination in the hope that *The Times,* his one source of pride and interest, would one day be his. He was the only Walter, apart from his father, who worked on it and it seemed obvious to him that he should inherit it.

John Walter III died in 1894 and it was then discovered that he had left two-thirds of the paper to his eldest son, and one-third to the third son of the second family. There followed an intensely bitter family row. The first family thought they were going to inherit everything. The second family was horrified because the third son had been picked. Hubert was desperately disappointed. He had been passed over by a father whom he had never loved and who clearly did not believe in him. The subsequent financial arrangements by which each of the disinherited members of the family were given £300 a year did nothing to relieve his misery. It was not money he wanted. *The Times* offered to send him to America to train under their famous correspondent, Smalley. He declined. At the age of thirty-one, a distinguished-looking man with an occasionally

At Dunvegan, beneath Sir Reginald's portrait, 1946

With her twin grandsons, John and Patrick Wolrige Gordon, in 1948

A meeting of the Clan Parliament at Dunvegan, 1956

John downing the horn, the Fairy Flag in the background

brilliant sense of humour and a gift for conversation, he lived alone with his widowed mother in Mount Street and nursed his bitterness.

Flora had met Hubert Walter on a number of occasions. Bearwood was only six miles from Sandhurst Lodge, a house John Walter had rented to Sir William Farrar and his wife, Agnes MacLeod's aunt. Hubert Walter's mother was Miss Flora Macnabb, whose great-grandmother was one of the Miss MacLeods of Raasay who had danced before Dr. Johnson when he and Boswell visited the island on their famous tour of the Highlands in 1773. These connections, coupled with the fact that they had both reached a crisis in their lives, drew Flora and Hubert instinctively together.

Hubert found in Flora a buoyancy and courage he sometimes lacked. She listened sympathetically to his trail of misfortunes and deeply pitied him. She was a dominant personality, attractive to a man who had lived six years with his mother. Although he was probably genuinely in love with Flora when they married, he would reply later when asked about her, 'All my brothers married fools and I was not going to make the same mistake.'

Reginald and Agnes MacLeod felt Flora's engagement was quite acceptable and it was confidently thought that the Walters would be pleased to have the Northcote connection in the family. Even Olive believed her sister was in love, but Flora realised that she had escaped from one prison only to find herself in another. 'I would gaze at my engagement ring,' she wrote, 'and recognise that it was a chain I had not the courage to break.' For the rest of her life Flora would ask happily engaged couples, 'Are you sure?'—on the grounds that if anyone had done that for her she would have answered, 'No.' When Aunt Alice in India heard of the engagement she neither understood it nor approved of it. She had expected Flora to visit her again and had dreams of a brilliant future for her niece. 'It was really a betrayal,' wrote Flora, 'and fundamentally changed our relationship.' Although Flora loved Aunt Alice to the end of her life, and was the only member of the family with her when she died, the treasured bond between them was forever broken.

Hubert Walter possessed the unforgivable fault in the eyes of Aunt Alice of having no ambition. He much disapproved of what became known in the family as 'the Aunt Alice

convention'. This was when Aunt Alice organised readings
from Jane Austen and expected Flora to drop everything and
go, she invariably did. Flora in turn, felt that Hubert
was by nature anti-social, a trait which revealed itself
early in their life together. Hubert Walter was strangely
hostile towards the family friendship with the Asquiths, on
the grounds that it was snobbish. No doubt his views about
Aunt Alice stemmed from the same source, but she had been
immensely loved by friends and servants alike, both in India
and later in Australia. During the First World War she gave
up her home at Eastwell Park, near Ashford in Kent, for the
nursing of wounded Australian soldiers, and she was perhaps
not so totally worldly as he believed.

On June 5th, 1901, at the age of twenty-three, Flora was
married at St. Mary Abbots Church, Kensington. She did not
remember her wedding dress or much of the reception, which
followed the service, in the lovely garden at Cam House, the
home of her cousins, Lord and Lady Phillimore. The
honeymoon was spent at Sandhurst Lodge, where she had
first met Hubert. On the journey down from London the
bridegroom tried to light his cigarette inside his hat and the
lining caught fire. It was unfortunately the only thing which
did. Following the months in India and at home Flora was
considerably run down. She developed a painful abscess on
her face. Hubert visited old friends in the afternoons without
her, and in the evenings after dinner he followed the
Bearwood custom and slept in an armchair.

Soon after her marriage Flora accompanied her husband
for a week-end to Bearwood. 'It was my first and only visit,'
she wrote. 'I remember the chill which pervaded that huge,
bleak, uncompromising house. Hubert's sister took me to the
great picture gallery, seldom visited, unappreciated and
unenjoyed, and remarked as we passed through the living-
rooms that before she entertained a house-party she put away
the *objets d'art* and small ornaments "because you never
knew what you might miss on Monday morning". I then
heard the story of the large dinner-party during which a lady
took off her ring to show her neighbour. It was greatly
admired and passed from hand to hand round the table.
Before the ladies left the dining-room, the owner asked for
her ring back. Nobody knew where it was. With admirable
expertise my host ordered a plate to be brought, and laid a

napkin upon it. The lights were put out and he said the plate would be passed round the table and, if the ring were not upon it when it reached him, he would call the police. Of course the ring was there.'

Hubert and Flora returned to the small house they had taken in Devonshire Terrace, near Paddington. 'We enjoyed having our own home,' wrote Flora, 'although I was completely untrained in the art of housekeeping. We bought frightful wallpapers. In the dining-room we had dreary red-into-copper unified colours. Then we had a very pretty, though quite inappropriate, paper with irises in the background crawling up the staircase. However, the worst was the appalling cornfield which graced Hubert's dressing-room. The dressing-room was very small and the cornfield with its enormous poppies, barley and cornflowers was indescribably awful. We had a cook, a parlourmaid and a housemaid.'

Although married life without real joy was inevitably deprived, Hubert and Flora made the best of it. 'We read in a newspaper of a holiday home for cranks over Easter,' Flora wrote, 'and decided it would be fun. We thought from the first that it would certainly be vegetarian amongst its other peculiarities, so we equipped ourselves with various tins of solid food which we kept in a drawer in our bedroom. The lady of the house had an aura of mauve and yellow and she had her house decorated in mauve and yellow. We were told that we all had auras. We learnt that jargon very quickly. They were a mixed bunch. There was one man whose profession it was to clear the manholes in pavements in London. When we went out walking we picked the buds from the bushes and ate them as we went along. We talked a great deal about polarisation and how very important it was to lie from north to south. We achieved great eminence in that community and the maid said she had never been privileged to clean the rooms of such "high-level spirituality and other-worldliness". We felt had she opened that drawer containing the meat pies, she would have been shocked. We attended various medium sessions. We went into a dark room and sat in a circle where we were expected to hold hands with our neighbours. That was to prevent us clutching the medium when the spirit-body materialised. We sang hymns all the time, including 'Lead Kindly Light'. In the dark the spirit materialised. Of course it was the medium. In all our sessions there was no question about it. When the spirit-form appeared, one person would cry out, "That's my Aunt Maria." It was fun at the time and I enjoyed it thoroughly.'

In 1902 Hubert Walter left *The Times* and was for five years associated with the publishing business of Mr. Edward Arnold. His lack of ambition was a grave defect in his wife's eyes. 'He is not far-seeing,' she wrote. 'He does not grasp his opportunities.' Flora's burning ambition cannot have been easy to live with, and Hubert Walter suffered from moods and depressions. Occasionally at dinner-parties he talked brilliantly, 'and I listened with absolute rapture,' wrote Flora. 'Then if he didn't feel like it he didn't talk.' Flora gave him dutiful devotion but she seldom believed in him as a man. Often a wave of frustration swept over her as she realised how much better she would be at his job. She was not unaware of the danger of the situation and warned him that she would become like her mother unless he made her do things she did not want to do. Hubert Walter regarded Agnes MacLeod as an extremely dominating woman and was critical of the way his father-in-law had allowed her to control both him and his household, but he had not the strength to master Flora. 'You are so sensible,' he told her. 'You do not want to do anything of which I disapprove.'

On June 24th, 1902, Flora gave birth to a daughter. She was called Alice after the aunt Flora loved. Three years later on April 8th, 1905, a second daughter, Joan, was born. They were brought up as Flora had been, in the nursery under the able care of Nanny Cannon. Flora loved her children and for one hour a day poured her affection on to them with an almost obsessive dedication. However, she knew nothing about babies and had no idea of the practical needs of small children. When Nanny Cannon went on her two weeks' holiday, Flora watched the children for the slightest sign of illness. She had a particular fetish about constipation and was always armed with a bottle of castor-oil.

Flora was an addicted games player and as her children grew up she entered into every game with an enthusiasm for which they loved her. In the mornings she would take her daughters one each side of her in bed and teach them the dates of the kings and queens of England. She also taught them the names of the twelve Apostles, but her Bible lessons were seldom a success. She was deeply ambitious for Alice and Joan and wanted them to excel intellectually from the earliest age. She read them books and, like Agnes MacLeod, encouraged them to read themselves.

Hubert Walter was a delightful father with a repertoire of imaginative stories. One particular favourite was about a small chipmunk and a large gopher. When Alice asked, 'How old is the chipmunk?' her father replied, 'One.' 'And how old is the gopher?' asked Alice. 'About five,' came the reply. 'And which do you like best?' she asked. 'I like the gopher,' replied her father, 'he is nearer my own age.' A keen scientist, Hubert Walter put electric light into his daughters' dolls' house and always enjoyed the thrill of a fast car. In 1907 he rejoined *The Times* and was invited to cover the 'Reprise du Congo' as their correspondent in Brussels. Flora and the children accompanied him to Belgium and there followed the happiest months of Flora's married life.

Brussels and Berlin

IN 1907 THE CONGO BELONGED TO KING LEOPOLD, QUEEN Victoria's uncle, and from it he drew a vast revenue. Terrible atrocities were then discovered and the King offered to present the Congo to the Belgian people. The months of debate which followed—for public opinion was widely divided—provided Flora with her first opportunity to mix in the world of politics into which she had been born. She went to Brussels ahead of her family to prepare the house they had rented in the Avenue Louise. There was no central heating in those days and it was so cold that the water froze in her glass. She engaged a staff of three, only to discover afterwards that people were taxed on the number of servants they kept. 'We were considered very rich,' she wrote, 'and it was a sad blow. I discovered that "aul d'Anglan" provided the answer to every shopping problem and in our language meant "old England" pronounced in French.'

The Times correspondent enjoyed particular prestige and the Walters were invited everywhere. Flora spoke fluent French and was widely read in that language, so her presence was invaluable to a husband who was not a linguist. She was a constant source of information and much of what she discovered appeared later in the columns of *The Times*. 'We enjoyed the most amusing society,' she wrote. 'We were accepted at Court, having been presented at the British Court. The diplomats were not allowed to meet any except the Noblesse or Government Party and they were delighted to have intelligent foreigners join their restricted group. We kept the British Ambassador in touch with what was going on in the Middle and Liberal Parties and he was grateful. The Socialist Party was small but brilliant and the Vanderveldes were our special friends. They were intellectual reformists and desired political change, but it was almost impossible to achieve under those conditions. We associated with them all and felt ourselves privileged in comparison with the embassies.'

Hubert Walter made several visits to London during the months in Brussels and when he did so he left Flora in charge. It was a responsibility she took seriously. On one occasion a public debate took place while Hubert was away. The young Secretary at the British Embassy should have attended the debate but decided instead to play golf. Flora found such indifference incomprehensible. She went herself and afterwards, when it turned out to be of some importance, dictated the dispatch to the Foreign Office.

In the summer of 1908 there was a debate on the Belgian question in the British House of Commons. Hubert Walter went over to London to be present in Parliament. 'I was left,' wrote Flora, 'and told that my Belgian contact would keep in touch with me over what happened. Much to everyone's surprise, the Belgian Government decided on that particular day to accept the Congo. I hurriedly cabled *The Times,* and Hubert, seated in the Press Gallery, was startled to hear the Foreign Secretary announce from the floor of the House that *The Times* correspondent in Brussels had just telegraphed that Belgium had taken over the Congo.' Flora was overjoyed with her success. 'I felt very much involved,' she wrote, 'and I loved it.'

Following the 'Reprise du Congo', Hubert Walter was given a number of temporary assignments for *The Times* in Paris. Flora went with him for weeks at a time, once with Nanny Cannon and the children. Vinters otherwise provided an ideal home and playground for Alice and Joan, and Flora's presence was an active help to both her parents, and gave greater independence to Olive, whose position as the home-based girl became increasingly irksome. Nanny Cannon was a countrywoman with an interest in animal and wild life which she shared with the children. She had a sense of discipline and there was law and order in the kingdom over which she reigned. She was a kind person, for at the age of five Alice asked her mother 'What does punishment mean?'

It was during these months at home that Hubert Walter went on a climbing holiday in Switzerland with a friend. When he returned, Flora noticed a slight drag of his foot and they went together to see a specialist. 'He diagnosed

disseminated schlerosis,' wrote Flora, 'and told me alone
afterwards that the disease would develop very quickly or
very slowly, but that the tragic end was inevitable. I asked
him, "What does that mean?" He replied, "People become
completely helpless." When I heard that I urged him not to
tell Hubert, so he might enjoy life without that hanging over
him.' Although it was a number of years before this condition
affected Hubert Walter's life, the diagnosis was a shattering
blow for Flora, who knew better than anyone the full
implications of a paralysing illness. She kept her lonely secret
and was convinced her husband never guessed.

In 1909, Hubert Walter was appointed to Berlin as *The
Times* correspondent. He replaced George Saunders, whose
well-documented and powerfully worded articles warned of
mounting danger from an aggressive and rapidly re-arming
Germany. This was not popular in Britain, and Saunders's
relations with *The Times* were increasingly strained. He was
recalled. When Hubert Walter arrived in Berlin his first visit
was to the Military Attaché who told him not to buy a house,
and to make every preparation for departure as war was
inevitable. In spite of the uncertainty, Flora was delighted to
go to Berlin. She had acquired some knowledge of German,
both from reading aloud to her mother and from her German
nurses. *The Times* office was one floor above the Walters'
home, on the first floor of a superior lodging-house at In den
Zelten 20. 'It was a corner house,' wrote Flora, 'and
altogether on a very strategic site. One front faced a street
with the War Ministry opposite, and the other the great
square with the Reichstag on our left, the famous
Brandenburger Tor, and the broad Siegesallee or Victory
Avenue lined with the large statues of kings and emperors
flanked with humble little busts of their assistants. It led
through the Park to Charlottenburger Chaussee, great in
German history. In the centre of the square was a large pillar
made from the metal of captured French artillery after the
1870–71 War. It was called Siegessäule or Victory Column.'

The military atmosphere of Berlin pervaded everything,
even the social life. Flora was shocked, shortly after her
arrival, by a German officer at dinner, who told her that
Britain and Germany, united, could rule the world. 'He was
amazed when I asked, what if the world did not want to be
ruled,' she wrote. Hubert Walter had to register the arrival of

his family and was viewed with considerable suspicion because he could not remember the dates of his children's birthdays. 'Life was run on regimental lines,' wrote Flora. 'From certain streets prams were strictly *verboten* and in others permitted only between specified hours. Journalists were not suitable or qualified to be presented at Court and we were excluded from aristocratic circles. Instead, we enjoyed the company of able, successful and unpopular Jews and wealthy bankers and industrialists. The Socialists had no wish to associate with those they looked upon as hostile, so we seldom met them.'

Flora enjoyed the theatre and loved the concerts, but dinners were always formal. 'We sat in our stiff satins and jewels,' she wrote, 'and played the game of tossing the handkerchief or balloon when it came our way.' From time to time she could glean a bit of news from her neighbours or report an event required by *The Times*. She was familiar with the small print of the German script in which many newspapers were then written and was therefore of active use to her husband, who was accustomed to Roman script and whose eyes were causing him anxiety. With excellent German governesses for the children, Flora increasingly found her way upstairs to *The Times* office and it would not be an exaggeration to say that her work there swiftly became the main interest of her life.

Hubert Walter had been in Berlin only a year when he decided that his deteriorating eyesight made necessary a visit to Dr. Pagenstecher's Klinik in Wiesbaden. He was away for several months and in his absence the office was left in charge of his assistant, James Mackenzie. Mackenzie was a self-made man who by sheer industry and ability had achieved his position on the paper. He and Flora worked together in *The Times* office and she could not conceal the fact that she found him a man of much more drive and initiative than her husband. He was exhilarating to work with and the close friendship between them soon became, in Flora's own words, 'une amitiée amoureuse'. Flora remained completely faithful to her husband, and love and duty anchored her to her children.

It was during these months that Flora achieved her greatest, though necessarily anonymous, journalistic scoop. 'The Socialists announced a mammoth demonstration in a suburb called Treptow Park,' she wrote. 'It was a protest against the rating legislation of Prussia. The Government forbade the demonstration. The Socialists persisted. There was talk of mobilising the troops and police to break the protest up, and the Government massed their forces at Treptow Park. It was to be an almighty crunch. I wanted desperately to accompany James Mackenzie to the demonstration, but he said there could be trouble and he refused to take me. Alice was being nursed with scarlet fever, and sadly I lunched alone with Joan. Suddenly we heard a strange noise, and from my strategic window I could see a great crowd of people debouching from the Charlottenburger Chaussee. I seized Joan's hand. We ran out to mount the platform in the square and watch from there, and gradually the crowd thickened. There were a few, very few, mounted police among them. I judged it safer to press forward than to turn back, and we mounted the platform. The crowd began to hurl insults at the police. "Bloody dogs! You don't even know how to ride!" The police charged up the steps. I backed against the column and Joan fell down behind me. The horses swept by and down the steps. The crowd shouted about "bloody deeds" and "women and children". Joan was frightened and cried a little; the Socialist Press crowded round but I maintained our anonymity. We then rushed home to collect my purse in order to pay to climb the stairs inside the column and watch from there, but it was all over. The crowd and the police alike dispersed. When James Mackenzie returned home I asked him what had happened and he replied that it was an utter fiasco. Lots of police but no crowd. I was proud to tell him our great story. He cabled it to London. They endeavoured to confirm it from other sources but without success. Such was their confidence in James Mackenzie that they published his dispatch. The Socialist press spent a lot of paper and ink trying to decide how *The Times* alone knew where to place its correspondent.'

It had never once crossed Flora's mind that to take a child of five into a hostile crowd might prove dangerous. She took Alice and Joan home to Vinters on holiday, elated with the excitement of her exploit. It was while she was there that she received a fateful letter from Hubert, who had since returned to Berlin, informing her that she would not be admitted to *The Times* office again, or people would begin to say he took orders from his wife. A wave of anguish swept through Flora as she read those words and realised that her role as her husband's assistant, and the one part of her married life which now held any meaning for her, was to be taken away. In frustration and despair she fell to the floor and beat her head on the carpet.

For nearly five years Flora had proved of invaluable service to her husband, reading the foreign press for him and using her gift for languages to discover unexpected stories. She did not know how Hubert had reached his decision. She was certain he had received no such instruction from *The Times* and it was her strong suspicion that her husband's younger brother, Ralph, was to blame. She had never liked Ralph. 'I deeply resented his influence over my husband,' she wrote. 'He was jealous of me and any part I might play in Hubert's life. He believed in his own ability and importance and had enough money to be a dilettante with a taste for the arts. Instead of encouraging poor, struggling Hubert, he was critical and disparaging, and ruthlessly undermined his self-confidence.' However likely it is that Ralph Walter played a part in this unhappy episode, there is no evidence to support it. Flora never asked her husband how he had reached his decision, or discussed it with him. She neither saw a letter from Ralph nor heard her husband mention one. Instead she tacitly accepted the restriction as a fact.

It was a paradox that Flora, who had once begged her husband to exert his authority, was deeply and irrevocably hurt on the only occasion when he did. Not once did it cross her mind that a man might resent her continual participation in his work, or that he might guess how little she thought of his ability. It did not occur to her that her feelings for Mackenzie, so well concealed from herself and so transparent to others, might persuade her husband that the time had come to draw a distinct line between his professional and his private life. Although Flora continued to live under the same roof and observe the correct formalities of married life, this was in a sense the spiritual break-up of her marriage. When Flora told her husband of the son she longed for, he replied that he did not want the nuisance of prams and broken nights. Husband and wife now lived as two parallel lines which never crossed, and Flora regarded the care of her husband as 'a life sentence'. In days when divorce meant social ostracism, Flora never considered it. In 1910 she left Berlin with Alice and Joan and never saw James Mackenzie again, nor did they correspond. Mackenzie ultimately succeeded Hubert Walter, and when war broke out he became *The Times* correspondent in London and wrote the famous daily column 'Through German Eyes'. In the winter of 1919, he was a victim of the great 'flu epidemic. Flora heard that he lay desperately ill in lodgings in Ebury Street. She went to the house and the landlady told her that he had been talking of her when he died only a few minutes before she arrived. Joan, aged fourteen, never forgot the scene of intense grief when her mother came home with tears streaming down her face.

Flora's personal sorrow, mostly disguised by her ebullient spirit, was overshadowed in the family circle by a far more public one. Olive had met Boyd Alexander, the explorer, as he was preparing to leave on his last expedition to Africa. He fell in love with her and at once proposed. Olive asked for time to think about it. Boyd Alexander replied that he would give up the expedition if Olive accepted him, but she remained undecided. It is widely believed that she finally accepted the proposal, and the last letter Boyd Alexander wrote before leaving home was to her, but it was too late for him to change the elaborate arrangements for the expedition. He left, and on April 2nd, 1910 was murdered at Lake Chad. 'Olive was completely prostrated,' wrote Flora. 'It became at once accepted that they were engaged and were going to be married when he came home. At that moment Violet Asquith was deeply attached to Archie Gordon, son of the Marquess of Aberdeen. He had a terrible car accident, and, as he lay dying in hospital, Violet flew to him and was at his bedside. When he died Violet wore the deepest mourning and accompanied the family on all the processions from London to Aberdeenshire. When Olive had this blow over Boyd Alexander, Violet was determined to share widowhood with her. We felt that if Violet had not been there, Olive would have taken a long walk and some sandwiches and gone out for the day on the hill and forgotten about it.'

In her own state of depression, it was difficult for Flora to sympathise with her sister's apparently broken heart. Olive and Violet Asquith became bereaved brides and, to the MacLeods' distress, attracted great newspaper publicity.

Olive blamed herself for Boyd Alexander's death and felt deeply enough to accompany the gravestone to Africa with her friends Mr. and Mrs. Talbot, through country where no white women had been before. By the time they arrived at Lake Chad the French were claiming that territory, but their chivalrous hearts were touched at the plight of a fiancée bringing out a tombstone and they surrendered to Olive Boyd Alexander's diaries, which proved that he had got there first. On their way home Olive and the Talbots stopped in Zunguru, where they were received by Charles Lindsay Temple, the Governor of Northern Nigeria, with whom Olive fell in love and whom she eventually married. The wedding was in the village church of Boxley, near Vinters, and Alice and Joan were bridesmaids. Olive's departure for Africa with her husband necessarily made Flora the home-based daughter once again. Her devotion to her father, her sense of duty towards her mother, and the termination of her work in *The Times* office, encouraged her to fulfil the role of a daughter rather than a wife.

The First World War

THE YEARS BEFORE THE FIRST WORLD WAR SAW THE CLIMAX OF the suffragette movement in Britain. Flora had never been a suffragette and heartily disliked the means which they employed to enforce their views. When women chained themselves to the railings of Mr. Asquith's house in Cavendish Square and were forcibly removed, Flora wrote, 'The police should have protected them from molestation and left them to remove themselves.' Brought up among a Victorian Establishment which was mostly highly critical of the suffragette movement, Flora was no doubt influenced by it. She was an unexpectedly conventional person, and, although it was a principle she found hard to practise, she sincerely believed that men should dominate in all walks of life. 'The thought of a female Prime Minister makes my blood run cold,' she once wrote, and added that she shared the opinion of John Knox who denounced the 'monstrous regiment of women'.

In 1913 when fighting broke out in the Balkans, Hubert Walter had anticipated that Germany would declare war. When she did not do so, he decided that war was unlikely and accordingly started to build a family house in Chelsea at 19, Cheyne Place. It was a plan supported by Flora, for it was not a satisfactory arrangement for her to live permanently with her parents under the rigid routine of an invalid mother. Alice and Joan, to whom Flora now devoted much of her time, had lived in London, Brussels, Paris and Berlin, and their education, received from a succession of governesses, was rather mixed. A permanent home for them in London would provide an obvious solution.

Reginald MacLeod (now Sir Reginald) had been given his K.C.B. in 1905 in recognition of his public services to Scotland. He loved Scotland and the opportunity of serving her, but it was in business that he now reached the zenith of his career. He was the director of several trust companies, a director and eventually chairman of the Gresham Insurance Company, and, through Marcus Samuel (afterwards Lord Bearsted, chairman of Shell, and the MacLeods' nearest neighbour in Kent) he was offered and accepted a directorship in Shell. In 1914, Sir Reginald travelled to Canada, accompanied by Flora, where he visited all the branches of his insurance company. 'Just before we sailed,' wrote Flora, 'the Germans had sent their ship to Agadir on the coast of Morocco. It was a direct challenge to the French. Lloyd George made the great Guildhall speech in which he said that Britain stood with France and that any aggression would find Britain by her side. Germany withdrew the ship. We did not know until the paper came on board at Halifax, Nova Scotia, whether we should continue the journey or return home. It was a great relief when we read big headlines, "Will the West corner Hogs?" '

Sir Reginald and Flora landed at Quebec. 'We went up the St. Lawrence by river steamer to Montreal,' wrote Flora. 'The heat was overwhelming and we spent a lot of time lying in our baths, which we kept at a tepid temperature in an effort to keep cool. Canada was just at the beginning of her development and everyone was most commercial-minded.' Sir Reginald had great personal charm and was a shrewd businessman. He also had the advantage, in a country peopled predominantly by Scots, of being a native Scot himself, and the Canadians liked him tremendously. He had a passion for boats, and, in spite of the fact that Lord Strathcona had provided him with a free pass on the Canadian Pacific Railway, he determined to make as much of the journey as possible by lake or sea. 'We spent two days crossing the Great Lakes from Toronto to Fort William,' wrote Flora, 'and I was most impressed to find the waiters on board were university students paying their way through college. At Fort William we saw the corn, grown in Central Canada, assembled and loaded before its long journey to Europe. At each place we were entertained in the local country club where my father made his official speeches. We passed through Manitoba and Saskatchewan and stopped in Winnipeg, which was simply growing out of the ground like a mushroom.'

Sir Reginald so much enjoyed the journey that he decided, after visiting Vancouver and Victoria Island, to take Flora to the United States to see the Yellowstone National Park. 'My father, still full of passion for the sea, re-embarked at Seattle on a steamer bound for the Arctic Circle,' wrote Flora, 'and we sailed up the west coast of Canada to a place called Stewart which was the last port. It was completely virgin land and the only thing you could see on shore were a few bungalows and planks laid crosswise to make a road. All the bungalows were owned by real-estate agents. They were offering plots of land at absurd prices because we were inside the Arctic Circle. I was given a little gold nugget with A.B. on it, which meant Arctic Brother. I was told that when you lived in the ice-cold regions the rule was that you never put your light out and you never locked your door, so that people who got lost in the night and the snow could see a glimmer of light and know where to come for help.'

Sir Reginald was captivated by the vast space of Canada and invested in land for his granddaughters. 'It was during this journey,' wrote Flora, 'that I think I first realised that the power which Britain had so long enjoyed was destined to cross the Atlantic.'

When war broke out in 1914, Flora took Alice and Joan to Vinters, and Hubert Walter was virtually separated from his family for five years. He was employed by the Ministry of Information and lived almost entirely abroad, first in Brussels and Copenhagen and then in Switzerland, where in 1917 he was appointed *Times* correspondent in Bern. This was a world permeated with spies and intrigue and Hubert Walter was involved in some fascinating adventures. He used to recount the story of the German he heard in the neighbouring bedroom in Copenhagen, saying, 'Gott strafe England' each morning as he brushed his teeth. Although completely untrained in practical things, Flora, like all the other young women of her age, did her best towards helping the war effort. 'I signed on as a V.A.D. nurse in the hospital at Maidstone,' she wrote. 'I am sure I was an extremely bad nurse. I was once instructed to give Bengers to a patient, and it was to be cooked for so many minutes. I said to the Sister, 'Supposing I couldn't remember whether you had said eleven minutes or nine minutes, would it be better to over-cook or under-cook?' She said, 'If you couldn't remember that I had said ten minutes, you are not fit to make Bengers." '

The hospital had two wards, each of thirty patients, who were usually discharged before a new batch was brought in. 'The Matron had been the district nurse,' wrote Flora, 'and all the smart ladies of the neighbourhood became V.A.Ds. This little nurse bossed them in the most impressive manner. One day the Matron was late in arriving and one of the V.A.Ds made the tea. This was Matron's privilege and a terrible scene ensued when she came in and discovered it. When Hubert once came home on a few days' leave, I was on night duty and asked the Matron for a night off. "No, dear," she replied. "I am very sorry, but if you were not here who would boil Sister's egg?" '

In September 1916, work on the new house in Cheyne Place was finally finished and Flora moved to London with her two children. Alice now attended St. Paul's Girls' School and Joan went to a small school at Glendower Place. Flora was an entirely devoted mother, taking her children to the bus-stop every morning and walking home with them each afternoon. She followed their progress with a passionate interest and, in the absence of their father, made all the major decisions concerning their lives. Form-mistresses were invited to tea and questioned in depth both about their subject and their pupil. Alice thought this showed a remarkable interest and was pleased, but Joan, who was far more sensitive, found her mother's probing questions oppressive. In the evenings Flora often read poetry to her children and encouraged them to join her in reading Shakespeare aloud. Intellectually, there was a genuine meeting of minds between Flora and her daughters, for Alice and Joan were both intelligent girls, but otherwise there was often no such rapport. Alice was an ardent Pauliner and adored her famous headmistress, Miss Gray. She responded instantly to the discipline of the school and ultimately became head girl, but at home Flora found her exceedingly obstinate. 'She was perfectly happy to buy a pair of walking-shoes,' wrote Flora, 'but screamed with fury if she had to buy a pretty frock or dancing-pumps. She became a keen girl guide and used to wear a huge pouch by her side which contained compressed food, implements of different sorts, and a whistle. This was worn on her hip and when she put on her Sunday coat there was a large bulge. When I

F

protested about this she put the pouch on the outside of her coat.' Alice had inherited some of her mother's independent spirit and Flora had probably forgotten how obstinate she and Olive had once been, so it was not an easy relationship.

By 1916, London was faced with severe problems. Conscription was introduced and as more women enlisted in the Services, the need for replacements grew. Food was in very short supply as there was no rationing, but Flora adamantly refused to buy in stocks. 'I would have felt mean buying against other people,' she wrote. For the first time in her life she often went hungry, saving everything she could for the children and herself managing on a bun for lunch. 'As the casualty lists from the battlefields poured in,' she wrote, 'the unanimous country which had sprung into action in 1914 began to question. We realised that this was a war of stagnation and attrition, and victory was assessed by the numbers killed on either side. Our armies called for guns and ammunition which were in short supply, and the Government was blamed. When Lloyd George replaced Mr. Asquith as Prime Minister on December 6th, 1916, the war took on a new phase of life and munitions were supplied at utmost speed.'

The social needs of widows, wives and small children at home were acute, and Flora was an early recruit to the Infant Welfare Service, and subsequently became chairman of the Infant Welfare Centre in Chelsea. 'Our operation was primitive in the extreme,' she wrote. 'We hired a large room one afternoon a week and engaged an experienced sick-nurse. We bought some scales and some stationery. Then we invited mothers to bring their babies to be weighed and to consult the nurse. Every week we carried the scales and the case-records home. Each week we carried them back. We were successful beyond our hopes. It seemed no time before we had our own accommodation, a permanent nurse, and a doctor to examine the babies and advise the mothers.' The centre soon included a weekly sewing-class for women and a playroom for the children of working mothers. 'We initiated one of the first hire-purchase systems,' wrote Flora. 'The Committee bought material and the women worked on the garment, paying off the cost at sixpence a week. They were allowed to take the clothes home when they had completed the payment. I was sometimes soft-hearted enough, especially near Christmas, to let mothers take things home before they had finished paying. When they did not return I learnt my lesson.'

Young women with no previous experience of a welfare service were disinclined to leave home with small children in order to visit a clinic and it became the responsibility of volunteers to call on mothers in certain streets and make friends with them. 'At first I was very shy,' wrote Flora, 'as I felt sure they knew more about babies than I did. On my first visit the mother told me that she was worried because her baby never stopped crying. We talked about this and it finally transpired that she was giving the baby the same amount of food as it was having when the district nurse left. I felt I did know more than she did and that gave me great courage.' So urgent was the need for personnel that Flora was appointed medical secretary of a school in Battersea. 'My task was to be present at the doctor's inspection of the children,' she wrote. 'The mothers could attend but they did not. I took notes of what the doctor ordered and then saw that the prescriptions were carried out. I used frequently to have to take little bunches of children to have their teeth pulled out at the clinic. First of all I had to persuade the mothers to allow this to happen. They would say, "Well, I don't mind, if you can persuade her to go." I used to say piously, "Well, I take my children twice a year to the dentist." ' After the extractions, Flora distributed permanganate of potash to each child as a mouth-wash, and took them home. She was persuasive and successful in her job. She once managed to convince a mother who had consistently refused to take her child to hospital for treatment which the doctor had repeatedly recommended. The child had a discharging ear and a tin soldier was finally extracted from it.

Flora swiftly gained a reputation for being an able organiser. When the War Savings Movement began, Chelsea Borough Council asked Lady Phipps to help form a committee. Sir Edmund Phipps had been Hubert Walter's best man, and Flora was invited to become secretary. 'Margaret Phipps was the treasurer and responsible for the money,' she wrote, 'and I for the people. My duty was to see that there was a weekly collection in every street, and once a week the collectors brought the money to us in the Town Hall. We bought the fifteen-shilling war-savings certificates, which were handed over to each individual as they completed their total. We had fifty or sixty women working for us.' After the war, Flora asked the Borough Council if she might write in their name to thank each lady who had worked for the Savings movement. They agreed and Flora wrote to each one personally. The gratitude and pleasure these letters evoked touched Flora deeply and it was something she never forgot.

The war years which permanently transformed life in Britain had no less an effect on Flora herself. For the first time in her life she had seen how ordinary people had to live. 'I often felt guilty about my own good fortune,' she wrote, 'and the knowledge of it sometimes haunted me.' The arduous hours that Flora worked at three different jobs, on a poor diet and combined with her own home life, would have weakened a less resilient person. During the war Norman MacLeod was unable to let the shooting at Dunvegan Castle, and it was here each year that Sir Reginald took Flora and her children for the long summer holiday. The day war was declared Aunt Hanna flew both Austrian and British flags, in that order, outside her house at Uiginish and shortly afterwards said she was grateful to the war because her footman was interned and she had no expense in repatriating him. The large income she had inherited from her late husband, Count de Latour, virtually disappeared with the outbreak of war, and she was supported by the MacLeod estate until her death in the 1940s. Reginald MacLeod went to a great deal of trouble to save her from internment. Her hobby was skilled antiquarian research in the ancient duns of Skye and it was suspected that this was connected with petrol dumps for the enemy.

However, this was possibly the only sign of war which reached Dungevan, and the peace of Skye after the strains of London was a balm in itself. Flora could relax among the hills and waters which surrounded the castle and as the hunger and weariness began to recede, she became increasingly aware of her own deep love for Dunvegan. It was perhaps a coincidence that this transformation took place at a time when Flora once again became a possible successor to Dunvegan, but she would have been less than human if this knowledge had made no impression.

Ian Breac, heir to Dunvegan and the future chief of the clan, was a junior officer in the 2nd Battalion, the Black

Watch, and stationed in India when war broke out. He was at once ordered to France, and in the spring of 1915, while endeavouring to map the terrain between British and German trenches, he was killed instantly by a shot through the head. This grievous blow meant that Dunvegan would now become the home of the eldest daughter of the last survivor of three brothers. Although it was not until 1934 that Flora knew that she was the heir, the emotional effect of living in a castle where twenty-seven generations of her family had previously lived suddenly took on a new poignancy. 'Dunvegan has this extraordinary power of holding people,' wrote Flora. 'When I sit in the business room, I find it thrilling to think that I am sitting in the room built in 1500, by Alasdair Crotach, who fought in two battles in which the Fairy Flag was waved, who established the famous piping college of the MacCrimmons at Borreraig, and who built himself a wonderful tomb at Rodel in Harris which is looked upon as the finest piece of medieval sculpture in the Highlands.'

At the age of thirty-seven Flora, who had virtually spent all her adult life as an English-woman, suddenly discovered that, like every Highland Scot, she possessed the strong emotion of belonging to the past. This love-affair with the castle was to become a permanent part of her life, although if at that moment the belief was also born that she would one day own Dunvegan, it was a secret she kept to herself.

In 1918, when the war ended, the Belgian Government invited Hubert Walter, as *The Times* correspondent, to view the destruction of their country. They appointed an officer to accompany him and he was allowed to take Flora and his secretary with him. 'I remember Passchendaele with especial horror,' wrote Flora. 'It had been attacked again and again by our armies and blasted by artillery. It was defended heroically by the Germans. It was soaked in blood. Our poor guide showed us the plot of ground which was once his home—now nothing at all. The whole area was littered with shattered lorries, equipment, helmets and guns. The roads were a mass of pot-holes. We slept in a derelict pub and the three of us shared one bed. We saw people digging up treasures they had buried, and marvelled to watch men—returned to the site of their former homes—working through all the daylight hours to replace them exactly as they were when they last saw them.'

When Hubert Walter returned from abroad and was asked by the British Government which decoration he would like in recognition of his services overseas, he replied, 'Send me round a tray and I will pick the one I like best.' This was not considered the way to treat a serious subject and he received nothing. Flora was deeply disappointed in his lack of ambition. She could not understand it, for she herself had any amount. In recognition of their war service, women were now to be given the vote. 'The flower of our race, the young men who could least be spared, were dead,' wrote Flora. 'A whole generation wiped out.' She heard Lord Runciman appeal to the nation for women who must bridge the gap, and decided to devote herself to politics and to the political education of women.

Chelsea Politics, 1919

FLORA WAS BORN INTO POLITICS AND HAD ALWAYS ENJOYED the company of politicians, but until 1918 it was a scene from which women were barred. They now entered politics at a time of particular hardship. There was grave unemployment. Food was still scarce and the country was exhausted after the efforts and sacrifices of the war years. 'I think the situation was potentially more dangerous than most of us knew at the time,' wrote Flora. 'My future son-in-law, Robert Wolrige Gordon, who, as an officer in the Grenadiers, had marched out of Chelsea Barracks in 1914 and was one of the tragically small group who lived to return, told us many years afterwards that they had been brought home very soon after peace was signed, not because it was a mark of favour to a privileged regiment, but because it was necessary to have the most reliable at home in the event of trouble. And in London a company was kept under arms every night until the lamp over the House of Commons was extinguished and there was no longer any risk of riot. There was indeed much suffering and disillusionment. The sequence of demobilisation was not understood and a sense of unfairness prevailed which made 1919 and 1920 embittered and painful years.'

Sir Samuel Hoare, Conservative M.P. for Chelsea, wrote to Flora asking her to be the chairman of a Women's Auxiliary Branch he was forming in the constituency. This offered the ideal opportunity she was seeking. 'I realised the urgency of teaching the newly enfranchised electorate how to use the political power they now enjoyed,' she wrote. 'I invited some like-minded women to our home and we formed an association. I learned then what I think is a golden rule and that is, if you want to start anything off, you must have somebody who will give ten pounds for the stationery and stamps. Quite a lot of people would be excellent secretaries, but are not prepared to cover running-costs. I put up that ten pounds and we got a secretary. We held weekly meetings in different parts of the Borough, addressed by different speakers, and the work, duties and powers of our own municipal authorities were a frequent and absorbing topic.' One meeting of the women's branch was addressed by a brilliant young speaker recommended to Flora, but his theme was the abolition of the House of Commons and single-chamber government by the House of Lords. This caused great consternation among the Conservative women, who during World War II recognised the voice of their young speaker when, as Lord Haw Haw, he made his regular contribution on the radio from Germany.

When local elections were resumed, it was decided that the women's branch should petition the mayor and councillors of Chelsea to nominate women candidates. The four small wards, including Cheyne ward in which Flora lived and stood herself, each agreed to adopt one woman, but the large Stanley ward refused, on the grounds that the electorate did not want women or they would have already had them. 'The voters had naturally never had a chance of voting for a woman before,' wrote Flora. 'In the ensuing election the Conservatives retained two seats in Stanley ward, but seven Labour candidates were elected, two of them women. The four of us who stood in the other wards were all elected.'

Opposition to women candidates was strong in Conservative circles, but Flora and her friends obtained valuable male support on the Borough Council and made full use of it when the occasion arose. When there was a by-election pending in one of the wards, the women's branch enquired from the agent who the candidate was to be. 'No doubt under the instruction of their chairman, he refused to reveal the identity,' wrote Flora. 'We regarded this as a challenge and prepared to meet it. All our supporters who lived in Royal Hospital ward were asked to attend the adoption meeting, and I persuaded a young man (now Earl of Cranbrook) to take command. At first the opposition was gratified to see such a large turn-out for a usually ignored meeting, but their gratification did not last long. When the chairman asked for nominations, The Earl of Cranbrook proposed the high-powered lady candidate we had selected. The seconder followed amidst confusion and dismay in the enemy ranks. Their nominee was put forward, but there could be no battle, for our majority was overpowering.'

Flora took infinite trouble to train her women. 'They had a lot to learn,' she wrote, 'but they learned fast and taught their instructors a lot at the same time. They swiftly became a useful and efficient political group, and not unnaturally the men resented their encroachment upon territory which had recently been undisputedly their own. One lesson which women have taken time to learn is the obligation to accept the verdict of the majority and not regard a difference of opinion as a matter of quarrel and personal affront.'

So successful was Flora's performance that, within three years of her initial election to the Borough Council, she was not merely invited but pressed to stand in Stanley ward. 'I enjoy a fight, and was rather ashamed of a walk-over in my safe seat, so I gladly accepted,' she wrote. There were eighteen candidates for nine seats, and women on both Party tickets. Flora canvassed in every street. On polling day she asked one of her particular friends whom she had voted for and was dismayed when the lady replied, 'I voted for the first nine names on the paper.' 'Walter' was unfortunately almost the last. However, Flora need not have worried. The Conservatives swept home and Flora was one of the nine elected.

Following the election, the Borough Council received an application from the unemployed asking them to welcome a deputation to request either maintenance or employment. 'The time was fixed,' wrote Flora, 'and we sat round a long horseshoe table with the mayor at one end. Some of the important members of the Borough Council were absent and said they afterwards regretted it. Some of us wondered. The unemployed were brought in and seated in the centre to make their demands. We noticed that the balcony was crowded with an odd-looking audience. When the moment came for the council to consider and discuss their answer, the mayor asked the deputation to retire. They refused. The mayor said that the business could not be discussed while they remained in the chamber. The unemployed then became rather truculent and they called up to the balcony, "Do you wish us to go?" The crowd replied, "No, no! Stay!" We all sat still in our seats and the gallery threw down packets of food to the deputation. Soon they became abusive and started shouting

threats and hammering on the table. They said they had seen
rivers of blood flowing in France and were not afraid of
blood. A few of the councillors were frightened and wanted
the mayor to give in, but it was impossible to give way to
threats. At last in desperation, the leader of the deputation
shouted, 'Let the young guard of the Red Army come over
the top.' Sure enough they did. The crowd in the balcony
surged over the railing and dropped on to the floor below.
Once that had happened, the police were called in and the
drama ended rather feebly—the Red Guard and the
councillors jostling each other as we walked out sheepishly
together.'

However much Flora may have discounted this
demonstration, she did not discount the social conditions
which lay behind it. 'I became increasingly interested in the
housing conditions of Stanley ward and the slums which
stained it,' she wrote, 'and joined in forming a small group
which called itself the Chelsea Housing Improvement
Society. We succeeded in raising a modest sum of money,
partly in gifts, partly at a very low rate of interest, and we
applied to the Borough Council for permission to buy what
was perhaps the very worst slum and to rehouse the people in
four blocks of flats. World's End Passage was a group of
small, crowded, derelict houses huddled together against the
wall of a factory, thus with no through ventilation. The
Borough Council called a meeting at which all the parties
concerned could make their objections. Every one of the
tenants objected. They said poor people did not want baths or
modern sanitation.' The Borough Council overruled the
objections and the scheme went forward. In Flora's honour,
one set of flats was called Walter Block, and she made sure a
woman property manager was engaged, who collected the
weekly rents and became the tenants' friend and counsellor.

Resistance to change was strong, and it was an uphill battle
against public opinion to raise living-standards. When
pressure was put upon the Council to establish municipal
laundries, Flora visited homes in her area to inform herself of
the climate of opinion. 'Everyone said there should be
municipal laundries,' she wrote, 'but when I asked, "Would
you use it if there was one?" they replied, "No. We do not
want other people to know about the condition of our
washing."' Tenement blocks were supplied with only one

lavatory and when Flora complained she was told that the door of the second was invariably torn down and used for fuel. To help those who were short of food, the Borough Council ran a soup kitchen and Flora served on the committee with a Labour woman councillor. 'One day I received a 'phone call from the Town Hall to say the soup was poisoned and complaints were pouring in,' wrote Flora. 'I hurried down and discovered that a quantity of rice had been put in the saucepans, sunk to the bottom, and burnt. The taste was appalling. It later transpired that my Labour colleague desired to substitute a friend for the cook, and this was her crafty device for bringing about her dismissal. It miscarried. The only result was that all councillors were forbidden to go unaccompanied into the kitchen.'

Although local politics absorbed most of Flora's time, she was an enthusiastic supporter of the Conservative cause, and Sir Samuel Hoare continued to be returned with large majorities in Chelsea. Indeed, so wholehearted was Flora's political contribution that she was often told her zeal could have cost the member his seat. 'I once drove a poor derelict cripple, whom I had picked up on the street, to the poll,' she wrote. 'When questioned he said he had voted Labour, and no charge was made. Another time I was canvassing in Stanley ward and called on a house where the Labour committee were in conference session. Some of them were my friends and they invited me to come in and have a talk. They asked why I objected to their famous candidate, Bertrand Russell. I said I thought it was an insult to his recently divorced wife who lived in the constituency, where she was well known and highly respected. They replied that the issues of private life had no bearing on public life. I replied that I entirely disagreed and that it was essential and common-sense to enquire into the antecedents and personal records of every individual seeking an appointment, and a principle we should certainly apply to our own lives. We parted in friendship, but I was warned by Conservative Office not to discuss the character of the opposition candidate again. However, I was quite happy when Bertrand Russell was defeated at the election.'

The third occasion was more serious, but fortunately for Flora was not discovered. 'I canvassed in a large block of

council flats in which a friend lived,' she wrote. 'When I
called upon her I learned that misfortune had befallen her
family and they were in extreme need. Of course, all thought
of Sir Samuel Hoare and the purpose of my visit flew out of
my head and I did the little I could to comfort and help.
Naturally, this involved money. Central Office took a very
serious view of this offence and I decided I would in future
never canvass a friend.'

On election day, when Flora asked two elderly
Conservative ladies how they had fared in the polling booth,
they replied, 'Oh, we meant to vote for Sir Samuel Hoare, but
when we got there we saw there was a Communionist
candidate, and because we are Christians we felt obliged to
vote for him.'

Flora was caught up in the enthusiasm and hope which
followed the famous Peace Conference in Paris, and she was
an early member, and subsequently chairman, of the Chelsea
Branch of the League of Nations Union. Processions were
organised, and in spite of her father's strong disapproval,
Flora marched for peace. 'I was proud to have organised a
large meeting with an impressive panel of speakers presenting
every shade of opinion from extreme Right to extreme Left,'
wrote Flora. 'The latter was Mr. Houlihan, the leader of the
unemployed at our famous Borough Council confrontation.
He was to second the vote of thanks to the speakers at the
end. Lady Hoare took the Chair in the absence of our M.P. in
America. It was an agitating and disturbing meeting, but we
survived till the end when Mr. Houlihan, who had just
returned from a red-hot revolutionary meeting in the East
End, far from thanking the speakers, embarked on what must
have been a replica of the violent speech made by him earlier
in the evening. Ronald MacNeill, an extreme Right-wing
Ulster Unionist, gave him a push which sent him flying into
the body of the hall. Then rioting broke out and the timid
advised flight, but nothing happened. We just trooped out
disillusioned and dismayed. Lady Hoare was furious. She
said, 'You have forced me into the positon of having to
apologise to Mr. Houlihan.''

Throughout these years, Flora believed she was a good
mother to her children, and in many ways she was. She
avoided Agnes MacLeod's mistake and told her daughters
the facts of life at an early age. She introduced them to a

fascinating world through books and music, but she failed to realise that her driving ambition placed them under constant pressure. In September 1918, Joan joined Alice at St. Paul's, but within seven months she was forced to leave as a result of a complete physical breakdown and was sent to recuperate in Scotland as the guest of the Countess of Seafield. Admittedly, Joan was growing into an exceptionally tall person and this, combined with the difficult post-war conditions and the problems of settling into a large new school, may well have played a part in her collapse. Joan was an intensely sensitive girl and suffered far more than her mother realised from pressure of work and the sense that her home was not altogether happy. This was a subject Flora never discussed with her children and she could not understand how they knew. When questioned once about difficult human relationships she replied, 'It is important to pretend not to notice them,' and it was a policy she pursued for the rest of her life. Flora now lavished affection on Joan, who, she felt, needed protection and was less independent, and physically weaker, than Alice.

Meanwhile, Hubert Walter continued as a foreign correspondent for *The Times* and was able to fulfil various special assignments abroad, while Flora was absorbed in the political life of Chelsea.

The End of an Era

IN THE AUTUMN OF 1921, AGNES MACLEOD DIED AT VINTERS AT the age of seventy-one. She had been an invalid for thirty-two years and, although she had not suffered great pain, her creeping paralysis and partial blindness were bitter frustrations for a brilliant and active woman. Up to the last days of her life, she had carried through her daily programme, always strictly to time and never changing until unconsciousness finally forced her to relinquish it. When death came, the sorrow of her family was tempered by the knowledge that for her it was a merciful release and for them the end of a rigid and restricted home life.

Flora had not always appreciated how difficult life had been for her mother and later blamed herself for her indifference, but Agnes MacLeod had nevertheless been one of the strongest influences on Flora's life. Through her she had acquired not only her love of books and music, but also the hidden strengths of rigid discipline and an instinctive devotion to duty. It became an obsession with Flora never to be ill. If she had a cold she would insist that it was 'only an irritation of the nostril'. When Joan had barely recovered from her breakdown, Flora sent her to Queen's Gate School in September 1920, despite the doctor's warnings. She had to be removed again at Christmas. Flora determined that her daughters should not be subjected to illness at home and encouraged them to enter university, where she felt they would make friends and enjoy the company of younger people. Accordingly, Alice went up to Girton College, Cambridge, in the autumn of 1921, and her first letter from there was written to her dying grandmother. Agnes MacLeod was unconscious when it was read to her, but because they knew how proud she would have been of Alice, the letter was buried with her.

Flora now devoted herself to the care of her widowed
father. He moved from Vinters to the Walters' house at 19
Cheyne Place, and virtually made that his London home.
Norman MacLeod had finally decided not to return to the
Dunvegan he loved. It was an arduous journey for an old
man, and his wife had always disliked Skye, so he asked Sir
Reginald, his brother and heir, to take over the
responsibilities of the castle. Four times a year, at Christmas,
Easter, Whitsun, and for the long summer holiday, Flora
travelled to Dunvegan with her father and was his hostess for
the large summer house-parties. At other times father and
daughter shared the exhilarating freedom of having
Dunvegan to themselves and the first chance in their lives of
doing as they liked. This was the home Sir Reginald had left
as a boy, in all probability never to return, and now he
enjoyed entertaining his friends in the place he had always
loved and among people who were deeply fond of him. 'The
estate was still poor,' wrote Flora, 'but my father had
achieved great success in business and brought with him the
financial support which Dunvegan had not seen for
generations.' Dunvegan had never recovered from the
disaster of the potato famine, but a turning-point came when
the Government bought from Norman MacLeod a large
section of the land around Loch Bracadale. It was required in
order to settle newly demobilised war veterans and their
families from the densely populated islands of Lewis and
Harris. 'My father and his brother discussed this long and
urgently and with deep concern,' wrote Flora. 'They finally
sold. The money paid off the long mortgage on the estate and
it was a great relief to know the castle was free of debt at last.'
In the spring of 1921 a great storm swept Skye and 50,000
trees fell on the MacLeod estate in one night. Perhaps
remembering his mother's devotion to the garden. Sir
Reginald now spent the last years of his life restoring the
castle policies. He planted great numbers of flowering shrubs
and thereafter in spring the blazing display of rhododendrons
and azaleas gave him the greatest pleasure. At the age of
eighty, he worked tirelessly to replant the stricken woods and
forests and, when the plantations were a success, he loved to
walk among his trees.
In 1922, at the age of seventeen, Joan gained an entrance to
Oxford University. Her results were so exceptional that she

was advised to try for a scholarship, but with so much ill-health behind her it was agreed that she should spend the winter abroad. Sir Reginald took the family to Rome and Naples, and subsequently Joan spent the winter months in Paris. She went up to Lady Margaret Hall in 1924.

In April of the same year, Hubert Walter was appointed as *The Times* correspondent in Paris. Flora now travelled between London and Paris each week, managing both homes and journeying by night on the cross-channel steamer. She would arrive in Paris very early in the morning and, thinking it was an unwelcome hour to disturb the staff of her French home, she would make her way to a church in the city and sit watching the crowds pour in to Mass, enjoying the beauty and peace of Paris before it was awake. Then she would always walk, and never ride, through the lonely streets of the French capital to her home. It was a strenuous life for a woman of nearly fifty, but Flora's only sign of age was a head of silver grey hair. Her boyish complexion and youthful vigour otherwise gave an impression of great energy. She continued with her local government work in Chelsea. 'After the General Strike in 1926,' she wrote, 'I was much impressed by Baldwin's appeal on the radio to forget the unrest and turmoil of the previous days. At the time, Hubert was building a garage close to our house and it was to have three flats above it. The building trade union had ordered all public construction to cease and men working on private jobs to strike or not as they chose. Our team struck. I asked the foreman to pay each man a small sum to help tide over the gap until they received their next wage, and I invited all concerned to a dinner-party in an adjacent pub. It was most successful. Very appreciative speeches were made and I thought good relations were restored, but I served on a Borough Council committee which received reports from their health visitor of mothers and babies in special need of milk. She reported the case of a young, ailing mother whose newly demobilised husband was out of work. He was half-way through his years of training in the building trade when he was called up and he wanted to resume his training where he left off, but the union refused to admit him. Flushed by the success of the dinner-party, I said I thought I could get him a job and spoke to our foreman. He said, 'Tell him to come if you wish but I am very dubious.' He came and our team

With John welcoming HM the Queen, HRH the Duke of
Edinburgh and HRH Princess Margaret to Dunvegan

HM the Queen and HRH the Duke of Edinburgh meeting
the MacLeod national groups from all over the world

Outside the Castle with the people of Skye

walked out in a body. I was furious and visited the union headquarters. The secretary said he entirely sympathised with me and thought it very wrong but he could do nothing about it. At that time the Borough Council was advertising for one thousand workmen and stated that, if they got them, they would advertise for another thousand. This confirmed my view that trade unions did not always care for the working man as they did for their own political power.'

After the war, Olive had returned to England with her husband but the climate proved too much for him after the years in Africa and they bought a house in Spain and finally settled there. Sir Reginald paid them an early visit and was horrified to discover that the house was a two-roomed butt-and-ben. It was situated on the hills above Granada with a view over the richly irrigated plain and enjoying a marvellous climate. Using their collection of Arab treasures, Olive and her husband created an unusual garden and rebuilt their house, making it beautiful. They bought a vineyard and some more land. The annual visits which Flora and the family made to Granada were, in her own words, 'the heaven of our lives'. They would climb together on the lavender-covered hills and Flora was able to renew the deep affection for Olive which had been such a permanent part of their early lives. Olive had no children and was utterly devoted to her husband, something which Flora occasionally resented. Once, on a visit to the Balearic Isles, Olive received a telegram to say that Charlie was unwell. He did not enjoy good health and she at once left for Granada. Flora was dismayed. 'Our visit was a very sad one,' she wrote. 'It would have been so wonderful to have had Olive to ourselves for a week.' Olive was as socially conscious as Flora, and, with her husband, cared for those many hundreds of people in the district who suffered from extreme poverty. This help took the form of food and clothing as well as money. When, in 1929, Charlie Temple died from angina, the city of Granada presented the plot of ground in which he was buried. 'Olive remained so calm and dignified,' wrote Flora, 'and yet her heart had been torn out. The day he was buried crowds of poor people came from the neighbouring caves where they lived and made a great cortège. Many of them said their father had left them.' Olive now lived alone in Spain but she did not indulge in self-pity. Indeed, Flora often remarked that Olive was the only person she had ever heard 'laugh with such gay abandon in adversity'. When Uncle Olly's little granddaughter, Mary Northcote, was left an orphan at the age of three, she was put in Olive's charge and now became a part of the family. Olive would bring her on holiday to England and Dunvegan, and later with her governess, Miss Gallagher (Gally), she virtually lived at the castle with Flora.

Flora always looked forward to the holidays when her daughters would be at home and it was a sorrow to her when Alice decided to give up the whole of one summer vacation to visit Canada. Alice had what she described as 'a conversion to farming' at Cambridge and resolved to visit the land Sir Reginald had given her in British Columbia. It was a shock to her mother when Alice described her occupation as 'farm labourer' on her passport. Flora had wanted her to try for a first at Cambridge and encouraged her to pursue a worthwhile career, but Alice was without ambition, had no idea what she wanted to do, and was perfectly content with a good second.

On October 5th, 1926, before beginning her third year at Oxford, Joan became engaged to Robert Wolrige Gordon of Hallhead and Esslemont in Aberdeenshire. He had been an officer in the Grenadier Guards and fought courageously through the First World War. He was fifteen years Joan's senior, much shorter than her in stature and a man of considerable character who possessed great charm. However, Flora felt sure a soldier husband and the rigours of an Aberdeenshire climate were not ideal for her daughter. She had hoped that with her intellectual ability and social gifts, Joan would have taken her degree and married a diplomat or a politician. As it was, the Walters' Paris home made possible a French trousseau and Flora enjoyed shopping with her daughter. The wedding at Christ Church, Chelsea, in January 1927, was very quiet, and afterwards Flora wrote, 'It was a real knife through my heart when Joan left home. I had taken such care of her and she wasn't terribly strong. I felt it was going to be such a separation because, quite rightly, she had to be Robert's wife and not my daughter.'

Robert Wolrige Gordon found Flora's possessiveness overpowering and resolved to free Joan from it. Not surprisingly, relations with his mother-in-law were never good and they both failed to recognise each other's virtues.

Flora's strong personality was anathema to a man who had lived in a man's world and been brought up with a traditionally hostile attitude towards women. Although he had a hasty temper, no doubt increased by the strain of four years' front-line fighting on a man who was in no way robust, he was endowed with an excellent sense of humour. Once when Flora had been newly elected to a Health Committee in Inverness, he presented her with a first-aid questionnaire which he had prepared for the Boy Scouts and was delighted when she was unable to answer any of the questions. On other occasions he could be hurtful, and he once made Alice cry when he accused her of not knowing one tree from another, although this had been one of her subjects at Cambridge. Flora was equally hurt when, on her first visit to Aberdeenshire, she was not met by her daughter or son-in-law at the station or the front door. On the other hand, Sir Reginald found in Robert Wolrige Gordon a fellow Scot with whom he could talk and whose knowledge on Scottish subjects was as wide as his own.

Whatever doubts Flora may have had about the marriage, she had to admit that it was a deeply happy one. She had once told her daughters, 'Not everybody falls in love. It isn't necessary.' And it was now difficult for her to recognise that Joan had done so. In September 1928, Joan's first son and Flora's grandson, Robert, was born. When in 1931 Alice married her cousin, Archibald Corrie Macnab, in India, where he was a Commissioner in the Punjab, Flora's wedding telegram contained the three words, 'Are you sure?' It was not meant to hurt her daughter, but it perhaps revealed the true misfortune of her own married life.

In 1927, Hubert Walter left Paris and settled in London. The illness from which he suffered made steady progress but he continued to work for *The Times,* writing obituaries and articles from his home in Chelsea. In spite of increasing pain he refused to allow his disability to interfere with his work. He struggled to get out, going down to Printing House Square or to visit friends, first on crutches and finally in a wheel-chair. The task of nursing another invalid through the final years of life was daunting to Flora, but Hubert Walter did not enjoy the journey to Skye and found the castle stairs an unsurmountable problem, so he and Flora spent many weeks of the year apart.

In 1929, Norman MacLeod died and Sir Reginald became, at the age of eighty-two, the 27th Chief and owner of Dunvegan Castle.

Early Years in Skye

FROM 1921 ONWARDS, THE BALANCE OF FLORA'S LIFE HAD increasingly come down in favour of Skye. She shared her father's enthusiasm for the castle and immersed herself in the problems of the island. 'We used to travel to Skye by boat from Oban, which we reached by the night train from London,' she wrote. 'There was and still is no railway. The roads were primitive and tourism was unthought of, so our only visitors, apart from friends, were on yachts, or travellers taking a short holiday among the islands on the steamer which every ten days brought stores from Glasgow. They were warmly welcomed. There were no social services, no Department of Agriculture grants, and we were responsible for our own budget. A penny rate in Skye produced only a few pence. One evening the Chairman of the Council visited my father to tell him that a family in Glendale were all stricken by typhoid and the neighbours were afraid to nurse them. There was no option but to open the tiny hospital in Portree, but the father was required to pay all—more than he could afford—towards the cost and he eventually died. I was horrified.'

The primitive conditions on Skye made a deep impression on Flora, who had spent her life almost entirely in cities. 'Many Skye houses were just a butt-and-ben, with a mud floor and a thatched roof with a hole in it for the chimney,' she wrote. 'The people were very poor and the crofts were too small to maintain a family, so it was inevitable that the young people should seek work on the mainland, and many made their homes there. The father of a young family would seek a short-term job in Glasgow during the winter, or perhaps service on a merchant ship, or as a ghillie in the sporting season. The Dunvegan headmaster once told me how his family lived through the winter on bags of potatoes, barrels of salt herring and some salted meat. They wove their clothes and knitted their stockings and used the scanty cash to buy groceries, tea and sugar. The croft provided the potatoes, the cow some milk and butter, and the chickens some eggs. There was no industry.'

Flora felt that the need to encourage local industry was so urgent that she took matters into her own hands. 'I was distressed by the way the crofters were exploited by travelling merchants and forced to sell their eggs at unsatisfactory prices,' wrote Flora. 'The merchants operated a barter system where the crofters had no option but to sell their eggs in exchange for goods which were often of much less value. So I opened an egg depot in Dunvegan where the eggs were tested and graded, and each crofter received a regular weekly payment. I was thrilled by it all and worked hard at it, doing the accounts myself and seeing that the crofter was paid. We sometimes found most exciting eggs, even boiled eggs.' This venture lost Flora money. It was the price she paid for serving Skye, and she regarded it as entirely justified in her role as a benefactor.

Flora also developed a home-made tweed industry among those who had newly arrived from the Outer Hebrides and settled at Portnalong. 'The people of the Outer Isles were always skilled spinners and weavers and they brought with them their looms and installed them in or near their homes,' wrote Flora. 'About a hundred families settled in Skye and some sixty of them asked me to sell their tweeds to visiting tourists, and I became deeply interested in the trade. In those days the wool was dyed naturally in great caldrons, using rowan and elder berries, heather, seeds and seaweed. It was then carded and combed to remove the tangles, and spun on spinning wheels before being woven on hand looms. The final process of waulking and shrinking was done to music, and as the cloth was passed from hand to hand, the women sang a rhythmical waulking (labour) song. This is still a tradition among the islanders and their reaping, sowing, milking and rowing songs are famous. I was proud to show the skill of my clients and each had her range of patterns and some were imaginative and beautiful. I registered the name as Portnaskye and the cloth was stamped before being sold.'

In the interests of her workers, Flora visited the Outer Islands where she saw Harris tweed being made. 'Their name was copied as far away as Japan to signify high-quality cloth,' she wrote, 'and to protect the industry the Board of Trade imposed a trade-mark, a condition of which was that the work must be carried out in the weaver's home. I saw workers being brought by coach to the great modern mills which arose in Lewis and working there under excellent and hygenic conditions, only to be turned out at the end of the day to complete their cloth in dark, cold, airless little sheds, because the law stipulated that the work must be done in their homes. I recognised how a law, made with the best intentions and to protect local industry, worked, in fact, against it.' Flora had a flair for public relations and succeeded in getting some shops in London to buy her cloth, and once a famous Paris dressmaker came to Skye and placed several orders; but it was not a continuous trade. 'Even to my untrained eye the quality was uneven,' Flora wrote, 'and I knew the unreliability would inevitably reveal itself, for I could never guarantee an exact repeat of the original order.' Flora was totally untrained in business techniques. She had learned as a girl to keep her personal accounts immaculate, but her business records were, as one observer commented, 'an incomprehensible muddle'. Sir Reginald, whose business acumen would have been useful to Flora, was too busy and perhaps too old to train her. Although gifted in the world of high finance, he was not altogether practical himself. He once visited a hut in which tweed was being made, and ordered a length, believing in his innocence that it would make a man's suit. The weaver interpreted it to mean a full length, and when forty yards of material subsequently arrived at the castle, it was distributed to the family, who all had suits made. A coat of this tweed still survives.

In 1929, Flora was elected a district councillor for Skye and was at the same time co-opted as a member of the Education and Public Health Committees of the Inverness County Council and also of the County Nursing Association. Within two years she had firmly decided that her future lay in Skye rather than London. 'I determined not to be a ghost in a place where I used to live,' she wrote, 'and, therefore, gave up all my work in Chelsea and said goodbye.' Flora resolved that her complete break with things English should be seen to go deep. Once when staying overnight with Joan and Alice at a hotel, she signed her name in the register and firmly wrote

'Scottish' after it. Joan and Alice promptly wrote 'English' after theirs, for they said that, while they would have been perfectly happy to write British if their mother had done so, they were not prepared to insult their father.

Having been christened and confirmed an Episcopalian, Flora now joined The Church of Scotland, for she wished to share completely in the village life of Dunvegan.

Sir Reginald, had been a caretaker at Dunvegan for many years, but when in 1929 he became the owner, it made a profound difference. Instead of merely advising, he was able to take over the responsibility for administering the estate, and found many discrepancies which were an inevitable result of the years when there had been an absentee landlord. His authority was not always welcomed by those who had long been in positions of power, but he had an old-world charm which was difficult to resist. He installed electric light and central heating at the castle, but life there was still comparatively spartan. 'My father was a careful businessman,' wrote Flora. 'The petrol engine which supplied electricity was installed in the basement cellar and worked as long as any light was on. My father said all lights must be switched off at midnight. Frequently there would be an oversight and it was my business to find the light and put it out. The castle was a big place to search, carrying your own lamp. I sometimes crept into a sleeping guest's bedroom or into the humble corner where the boots were cleaned, to find the offending light.'

Sir Reginald believed that generous hospitality was in the tradition of his ancestors and he now surrounded himself with unlimited numbers of interesting guests, many of them young. Inevitably, much of the work of hostessing fell to Flora and she enjoyed it no less than her father. She had a generous approach to people and an unfailing interest in their lives which made for intelligent and amusing conversation at meals, and a dedication to the games afterwards. She had been brought up with the firm conviction that 'il faut payer de sa personne', so she abhorred pools of silence at meals, or those who did not pull their weight or add to the enjoyment of a house-party. It was something of which she herself could never be accused.

Flora and her father were both wonderful story-tellers and kept their guests enraptured with tales of the castle and its history. Perhaps their favourite story was of the Fairy Flag, which still hangs on the castle wall, and is alleged to have been given to the young 4th Chief by his fairy wife when she left him after twenty years to return to fairyland. When Sir Reginald inherited the castle, there was so little of the flag left that he made the decision to ensure its preservation by taking it to the great textile experts who had been working on the then recently discovered tomb of Tutankhamun. 'It left Dunvegan a tiny piece of crumpled silk,' wrote Flora, 'fragile enough to pass through a wedding ring. It returned, preserved under a sheet of glass four foot high and two foot wide, a ragged, tattered, battered, torn width of corn-coloured silk with beautifully executed darns in red silk. My father was amazed when he saw it. Mr. Wace, the expert, said the silk had been woven in Syria or Rhodes and he considered that the care shown in the mending proved that it had been something very precious, a relic, perhaps a saint's shirt. My father said in response, "But, Mr. Wace, I know it was given to my ancestor by his fairy wife." Mr. Wace replied, "Sir Reginald, I bow to your superior knowledge." ' Nearly eighty years later, Flora's six-year-old great-grandson, when asked if he believed in fairies, replied, 'Of course I do. My ancestor was one.' Although Flora herself believed the Fairy Flag* possessed magic powers and always looked upon it with reverence, she preferred to believe it was Harald Hardrada's famous viking banner Land Öde, which he lost at the Battle of Stamford Bridge in 1066 and which subsequently found its way to Dunvegan through Olav the Black, King of Man, vassal of the King of Norway and father of Leod, the 1st Chief of MacLeod. 'This appears to me as the probable and plausible history of the Fairy Flag,' wrote Flora. 'It thrills me, as it did when I was a child, to stand beside Land Öde and imagine what the Norsemen and English thought when they met at Stamford Bridge, when this victory-bringing banner was already famous.'

In 1933, Sir Reginald entertained at Dunvegan the Duke and Duchess of York, later King George VI and Queen Elizabeth. 'I am sure I was a very bad hostess,' wrote Flora, 'for I was far more concerned to see that their entourage was properly cared for than for the royal guests themselves.' Later in the same year, Flora helped her father to entertain a group

* For history of The Fairy Flag see Appendix 1, p206

of clansmen who came for the unveiling of two memorials to the MacCrimmons, one a cairn at Borreraig, where their College of piping was situated, and another a tablet in the wall of the old ruined church at Dunvegan where they were buried. So deeply did she immerse herself in the history of Skye and Dunvegan that Flora persuaded her father to give her a small house at Suardal, a few miles from the castle, so that whatever happened she might have a home there. 'I was anxious people should know, although I was living in the castle and running it,' she wrote, 'I did not regard it as mine.' Flora's cousin Brenda Osbaldeston-Mitford of Mitford Castle, Northumberland, daughter of Canon Roderick MacLeod, and the other possible successor to Dunvegan, had a house near Sligachan and was known in the district as the person who would inherit the castle. Had this happened, Flora's permanent presence a few miles down the road would no doubt have been an embarrassment. In her enthusiasm, it was a situation Flora failed to consider. In 1932 the people of Bracadale elected Flora as their representative on the County Council, and she had every intention of staying there.

On December 21st, 1933, Hubert Walter left London by car to spend Christmas with friends. He died peacefully and suddenly on the journey. Flora had already left to spend Christmas at Dunvegan and the telegram reached her as she was leaving the Vatten school hall after the children's party. 'It was with relief rather than sorrow that I received the news,' she wrote. 'I felt it was a liberation.' Within a few months Canon Roderick MacLeod had also died, and with his death Flora became the eldest daughter of the last surviving chief, and the future owner of Dunvegan. She therefore resumed her maiden name of MacLeod and from that time became known as Flora, Mrs. MacLeod of MacLeod.

Sir Reginald was now eighty-eight and suffering from failing health. Flora lived through anxious days. 'My father ended by having appalling cramps,' she wrote. 'I slept overhead and the night-nurse had a stick with which she could hit the ceiling and then I would come down and try to calm him.' In August 1935, while Flora's seven-year-old grandson, Robert, was staying with her at the castle, Joan gave birth to twin sons in Aberdeenshire. 'I remember the joy with which Robert ran into the room to tell me the news of

John's and Patrick's arrival,' wrote Flora. 'My father was only half-conscious when I told him of his twin great-grandsons, but he must have understood, for he dictated a telegram to Joan with the words "Great Joy".'

On August 20th, 1935, Sir Reginald MacLeod of MacLeod, Knight of the Bath, and 27th Chief of his clan, died at Dunvegan in the great four-poster bed in which he had been born eighty-eight years before. With his death Flora became, at the age of fifty-seven, the owner of the castle which had become the love of her life. It was a glorious summer day when Sir Reginald was laid to rest beside his father and mother in the old ruined church. The moors of Skye were purple with heather and MacLeod's Tables were wreathed in soft mists as the lone piper played 'The Lament for the Children' at the chief's grave. The warm sunshine enveloped the long line of mourners and gave brilliance to the summer colours, but for Flora a light had gone out. With her father's death she had lost one of the deepest attachments of her life.

In the weeks that followed, Flora was conscious of an increasing weariness. Perhaps the strain of incessant travelling and the years surrounded by invalids had finally taken their toll. In any case, she felt in need of a change. She had not seen Alice since her marriage, and in the autumn of 1935 she left to visit her in India. It was a different world from the bright lights of Government House thirty-six years before, but Flora enjoyed it. She lived for the first time in a bungalow. 'My most vivid memory was the journey through the Khyber Pass to the North-West Frontier,' she wrote. 'When we entered the Pass we had to leave our name and particulars at the entrance. There were two parallel roads for inward- and outward-going traffic, guarded by tiny forts opening only at the top and provided with ladders. Passengers were bidden on no account to get out of their cars and leave the road, as sporadic shooting could easily occur. Those were the days of the many small frontier wars, and the North-West Frontier Province was strongly held and guarded. We had to have a gun with us. Archie said this was stupid because the natives were not interested in people who were unarmed, but were most anxious to get a gun if they thought they could. From the top of the Pass we looked down into Afghanistan.'

Flora stayed with Archie and Alice for nearly three months, and on her way home in early spring 1936 she visited Olive in Spain. The weather was unseasonably bad and depressing and for some reason it was not the golden visit Flora had so often had. The two sisters talked of their father's death and of how they would live together when they were old. Olive was her usual gay self in spite of increasing pain from rheumatoid-arthritis, but the old magic was not there.

Flora now returned to Dunvegan after a long absence and began to pick up the threads of her life again. On May 14th, 1936, within a few weeks of her return, a telegram arrived to say Olive was ill. 'I cabled at once saying, "Shall I come?"' wrote Flora, 'but the answer was to the effect that it was not urgent. The next day I flew from Glenbrittle to London and on to Madrid. I did not arrive in Granada until early the following morning.' At Madrid airport Flora telephoned Granada for news and was told of a slight improvement in Olive's illness and was advised to come by train as there was no immediate hurry. 'I did not arrive in Granada until the following morning,' she wrote. 'I was met at the station by the manager of the little boarding-house, who told me that Olive had died twenty minutes before. When they tried to give her nourishment in the night, she said, "Oh, don't bother." She died very peacefully. She had no pain for the last day or two. She knew I was coming and had told somebody to light a fire in my bedroom. She looked so beautifully happy and asleep when I saw her. The funeral was next day. It was a lovely spring and there were masses of flowers.' Flora was deeply distressed and remained convinced that the delay in reaching Granada had prevented Olive from giving her a final message. 'Olive's death was the most cruel blow I had yet sustained,' she wrote. 'I was so deeply devoted to her, and had been from the beginning of my life. The sorrow was made worse by the knowledge that our last visit together had not been as happy as I would have wished.' Olive was laid to rest beside her husband in the plot of ground presented by the city of Granada and close by the home where she had known such happiness.

Flora began the inevitable task of clearing up Olive's possessions. The picture she loved was taken to hang in the library at Dunvegan. The Moorish treasures were packed up or discarded and the little dog was given its taste of poison and put to sleep. The faithful servants and friends, to whom Olive had devoted herself and who were about to pass through the agonies of the civil war, came to Flora and she did her best to help them, knowing how much they had meant to Olive. Mary Northcote now became Flora's responsibility and made her home at Dunvegan. Eventually, Archie arrived from India on leave to make the final arrangements and Flora left for home.

Within three years Flora had lost her husband, her uncle, her father and her only sister. These four deaths, following in quick succession and each in a different way deeply affecting her life, left her facing the future alone. It was at this moment that she needed and found a very great reserve of courage. The purging from her life of every deep relationship, except those with her daughters, was an experience which might easily have destroyed her spirit. The fact that it did not do so cannot be explained by any outside influence. She did not have a strong personal faith, for her religion was at most a formal affair. She did not have friends to lean on. One daughter was in India and the other deeply involved in Aberdeenshire, so it was within herself and alone that Flora found the courage she needed. Whether this courage was forged in the long, disciplined afternoons at Granton House when she read aloud to her mother, or whether it was the result of having to overcome the problems of her private life, there is no doubt that it represented a quality closely allied to sheer determination, as a result of which Flora changed from an able but not extraordinary woman of sixty into a personality of greatness and even occasional genius. 'I learned the hard way what it meant to live with chronic sickness and helplessness, incurable illness and terrible pain, which forty years ago the doctors could alleviate less than they can today,' wrote Flora. 'I believe in cycles—spring, summer, autumn, winter, nature and mankind—the natural God-given law for every human being. I accept it as profoundly inevitable, wise and right, to which one should adapt oneself as humbly, flexibly and graciously as possible.'

Although it may be said that Flora now experienced an immense sense of liberation from the heavy burden of duty and responsibility for others which so much family ill health had imposed upon her, she was not immune to grief and had indeed experienced her share of it. However, happiness more readily than sorrow brought tears to her eyes. The only occasion Mary Northcote was ever to remember seeing her cry was when she was listening to the music of Wagner. As gaily as Olive had laughed in the face of pain, Flora now pushed aside the shadow of death and faced the future with resolve.

Fire at Dunvegan

WHEN SIR REGINALD DIED IN AUGUST 1935, THE CLAN MACLEOD was faced with the acceptance of a female heir for the first time in its history. Although Dunvegan Castle and the MacLeod estate are recognised as the property of the heir or heiress of the last owner, the chief is not a legal office in Scottish law and is accepted or not accepted only by his clansmen. In the case of the Clan MacLeod the choice was between the descendants of the MacLeods of Talisker, who had long been established in Australia and were descended from the younger son of the famous Rory Mor (16th Chief, 1595-1626), and Flora, who was descended from the eldest son of Rory Mor and descendant of Leod (1st Chief 1200-80), who first started fortifying and building on the rock. The decision was by no means a *fait accompli*. Although Flora had lived at Dunvegan for a number of years, she had until now not been actively involved in clan affairs. The Clan MacLeod Society had been founded in Edinburgh in 1891 and Flora had regularly attended the *ceilidhs* with her father, but otherwise there was no organisation. The only overseas Society was in Australia and founded in 1912, but it was not until 1935 that the first clan magazine was published, carrying a letter from Sir Reginald and a portrait of Flora as Honorary President of the Society. Although Flora had long been interested in the castle and Skye, this nominal presidency was at that time virtually the only interest she had in the clan, except as acting hostess for her father to overseas clansmen during the First World War.

Sir John Lorne MacLeod, a famous Lord Provost of Edinburgh, and now President of the Clan Society, had been Flora's dancing-partner long ago and knew her well. He firmly believed in her right of succession and it was largely due to his influence that there was now so little questioning when the acceptance of a female chief became of prime importance. Nevertheless, it was not until March 17th, 1936—seven months after her father's death—that the Council of the Clan MacLeod Society, after careful consideration, passed a resolution accepting Flora as their chief. Their doubts were understandable. This was a break with tradition among people whose association was based on a reverence for the past. Flora herself sacrificed a long-held conviction that a man should be at the helm. 'I was deeply conscious that a male heir would have been preferable,' she wrote, 'but in my view it was better to have a woman who knew Dunvegan, lived there and was a dedicated servant of the community, than an absentee Australian whose nearest link with the castle stretched back 300 years.' It was clear to Flora, although probably not yet to her clansmen, that while a male chief would have been tied to his profession and the support of his family, she was now free to dedicate her life to Dunvegan and to the clan.

On February 4th, 1937, one day after her fifty-ninth birthday, Flora was welcomed in Edinburgh by over 200 clansmen at their first gathering since her appointment as chief. Telegrams were received from a thousand loyal MacLeods in all parts of the world, including one from the MacLeods of Talisker in Australia, which Flora read to the assembled crowd. 'This is perhaps the greatest day of my life,' she told them. 'Mingled with the pride and gladness of our gathering tonight, I cannot but remember that this is the first time I have attended one at which my father was not present. I recall the days of auld lang syne when my sister and I were both companions at these happy reunions.' Then speaking of the clan loyalties which bind Highlanders together, Flora continued, 'Anything that tends to weaken those links and break those chains is, I think, destructive of something that is permanent because of spiritual value. It is our duty to try and preserve them for the future. It is so easy to destroy, so difficult to build up. I think we as a clan are extraordinarily fortunate in having Dunvegan as our own home. We are really most blessed in having that wonderful castle with its wonderful Fairy Flag—that castle which has been lived in by MacLeods in an unbroken line for possibly 700 years. The castle is the link which binds the clan together.'

Flora spoke without notes, with hands clasped firmly

The royal party leaving for the landing stage

A royal farewell to Skye

together, and was obviously moved by the spirit of the occasion. In his reply Colonel Norman MacLeod reminded the gathering that 'the thing which has kept the clan together has been the chiefs we have had.' In speaking of the past, he had made a prophetic statement.

In the summer of 1937, the Government urged the widest possible welcome to overseas guests on the occasion of King George VI's coronaton. Flora took up the challenge and issued an invitation for visiting clansmen to a garden-party at the castle on three successive Wednesdays. Her initiative was reported immediately and transformed into a Dunvegan welcome for all MacLeods. 'Are you a MacLeod?' asked one national newspaper in bold headlines. 'If so, you are invited to Dunvegan Castle.' The letters poured in from all sides sending greetings, many saying it had been the dream of their lives to visit the home of their forefathers. Dunvegan was sufficiently remote automatically to restrict the numbers able to attend, but Flora sent cards of admission to all those requesting them. She filled the castle with flowers, and every Wednesday the guests were welcomed by the pipes and given a tour of the castle treasures, followed by a home-made tea. This included on each occasion a very large iced plum cake, surmounted by the bull's head in sugar and bearing the MacLeod motto, 'Hold Fast'. Flora entertained over 300 people and was so delighted with the response that she had notices hung up everywhere with the words, 'You are MacLeods, therefore friends. Please talk to one another.' This was the first time ordinary clansmen in such numbers had been entertained at Dunvegan since the ancient days of feasting in the castle keep. It gave Flora a surprising glimpse of the untapped support which Dunvegan and the clan could call on in all parts of the world. Many of Flora's friends abhorred the intrusion of the twentieth-century masses into the peace and privacy of their lives, but she did not. She loved the castle and felt it her duty to share her good fortune with others, often at her own expense. The years of family illness and the break with friends in Chelsea had made for a loneliness which was now reversed by this unexpected clan response.

Flora now filled the castle with her friends. She had long considered the most significant visit ever paid to Dunvegan was that by Dr. Johnson and Mr. Boswell in 1773. She loved to quote to her guests Boswell's famous words, when he described the castle as 'the jewel of the estate. It looks as if it had been let down from heaven by the four corners to be the residence of a Chief.' She once wrote, 'His visit is the one which has made the most difference to Dunvegan and to Skye. Ever since, admirers of Johnson and Boswell have made their pilgrimage to Scotland to follow the journey these two accomplished, and invariably it leads them to Dunvegan.' It was upon this road that, in the summer of 1937, Colonel Ralph Isham, an American and a passionate collector of Boswell papers, set out.

Ralph Isham was a man of considerable charm. Some years earlier, when Lord Talbot de Malahide had discovered in an old croquet box the unexpurgated manuscript of the much-published *Tour of the Hebrides,* a most valuable find of Boswell papers burst upon the world. Collectors cabled and wrote offering to buy, but the Talbots refused to sell. Isham quietly went to Ireland and managed to get himself introduced to the Talbots, who were so attracted by him that they invited him to stay. Lady Talbot soon started reading the manuscript aloud to him and when she came upon a passage she thought particularly discreditable to her husband's ancestor, she would tear the page out; to Isham's horror she even threw some pages on to the fire. He swiftly persuaded her to obliterate with indelible ink all the pieces she thought unsuitable, in order to preserve the manuscript. Isham made his way with the Talbots so completely that they finally agreed to sell him their collection, and the bulk of his fortune went into the purchase. The papers were subsequently taken to America and bought from Isham by Yale University, where they were given a place of honour. Experts immediately set to work to remove the indelible ink which had obscured the most exciting if somewhat bawdy passages.

By 1937, another collection of Boswell papers had been found in an attic at Fettercairn Castle in Scotland, and Isham determined to have it. This time it proved far more difficult for him and involved long legal disputes which caused him much anxiety. To alleviate his worries, and quite naturally for a lover of Boswell, he decided to travel to Skye. He wrote to Flora asking if he might visit her. She agreed and invited him to stay at the castle. 'We expected Colonel Isham to come from Inverness for dinner, driving himself by car,' she wrote. 'He was late. My mother had brought us up in such a rigid school of punctuality that we looked upon people who were late for dinner as being very guilty indeed. So when the bell finally sounded, I was prepared to receive him extremely coldly. However, when he came into the room with the most charming apologies and explanations (the car in front of him had stopped to admire the view and Colonel Isham had driven into it), this of course caused great conversations and all passed off very pleasantly. I found his intense interest in Boswell and in Dunvegan enormously delightful.'

Isham was without question a gifted woman-charmer. He was widely-read and a brilliant talker, both of which appealed to Flora. He lived in a large world which incorporated financial interests in New York and politics at home and abroad, but he was also sensitive. 'It was rather delicious to have somebody come and say, "I have brought you a shawl as I thought you looked cold,"' wrote Flora. Isham's unquestioned charisma worked no less on Flora than it had on Lady Talbot. His personal life was unhappy. He was worried about the Fettercairn papers and Flora felt deeply sorry for him. She swiftly agreed to be his guarantor with the Bank of Scotland in his legal negotiations, and was delighted when he suggested renting the Dunvegan fishing the following summer, and returning with his two sons. To the distress of her family, who regarded the relationship as far more than an ordinary friendship, Flora prepared the chief's rooms for her guests and determined it should be the holiday of their lives. 'I felt they had paid for their visit,' she wrote, 'and in any case Ralph deserved comfort and consideration in the face of all his difficulties.' The holiday was a complete success and as a result Flora became and remained devoted to the Isham family, who agreed to return to the castle the following summer. The friendship was entirely platonic, and many years later Flora discounted any suggestion of marriage by saying, 'I would never have become the fourth wife of a man so much younger than myself. It would have damaged both the clan and my family.' Those living with Flora at the time had no such confidence. She had always been an enthusiast and it was therefore difficult to gauge the depth of any relationship, but she corresponded with Ralph Isham for a period of over eight years from 1938 and her letters were deeply affectionate.

However, the greatest love of Flora's life was kept for her small grandsons in Aberdeenshire. She often visited Joan at Esslemont and was enchanted by Robert and later by John and Patrick as they kicked together on a rug on the floor, and thereafter christened them 'the heavenly twins'. These were the sons she had never had and who now received the full benefit of her affection. The situation was made poignant by the fact that their father, Robert Wolrige Gordon, was by now seriously and incurably ill. Flora's heart went out to Joan and her children, and she shared the increasing anxiety of their lives. It was during one of Flora's regular visits to Esslemont, on November 29th, 1938, that she received an urgent and horrifying telegram from Dunvegan.

The staff at the castle had lit a fire in Flora's bedroom in the south wing in readiness for her return the following day. It was a wild night of wind and sleet when fishermen on the Minch, battling against the wintry storms, saw a great light in the sky as if a city had suddenly grown out of the hills around Dunvegan. How the fire started nobody knew, but by morning it had gripped the entire south wing of the castle. The news spread rapidly on Skye, and islanders in their hundreds raced to the aid of the castle. The Portree Fire Brigade found it impossible to operate their hoses successfully. Immediately, chains of men working urgently and silently in the semi-darkness passed buckets of water from the burn. They dismantled the pictures and carried them out into the garden. The muniment room was emptied of its valuable documents, as a line of men stood on the stone stair-case and passed bundles from hand to hand, while others carried furniture to safety or threw valuables from the windows. The Fairy Flag was taken from the drawing-room and it was said by those who watched that as it passed the threshold the fire dropped. Whether this was true or not, there was indeed an element of magic about that night. In the rush and disorder which followed the fire, the love of the people of Skye for Dunvegan could be judged by the fact that next day not one thing was found to be missing. 'It is worth recording that after the fire had been got under control and the day being wet,' wrote Dr. Douglas Simpson in his short history of the castle, 'all the contents except some of the chief treasures, which had been removed to places of safety, were got back into it again that same night.'

A telegram was sent to Flora informing her of the castle fire and within a few hours the sad news had encircled the world on the radio, and even formed part of the daily news-sheets produced by passenger ships at sea. The wing built by Ian Breac in 1686 had been entirely gutted, but damage to the Fairy Tower was slight and only one picture had been destroyed. As Flora made her way swiftly and instantly across Scotland by car, her heart was heavy. 'For once I was unable to face the Press who had arrived in large numbers to await my return,' she wrote. 'I drove with lights out round the back drive and up to the back door of the castle. There a signal was given, a tiny knock, the door was instantly opened and I was thrust inside.' As Flora walked among the burnt ruins and saw how close had been the total destruction of her beloved castle, she was overwhelmed with a sense of gratitude. 'I shall never forget,' she wrote, 'nor will those who come after me forget, what we owe to the people of Skye. It was by their numbers and their courage the castle was saved from probably irreparable disaster.' Across the world MacLeods everywhere wondered if the castle would ever be habitable again, for they knew nothing of the extent of the damage, nor did they know that Flora would not rest until it was completely restored.

The following weeks were filled with visits from the insurance company and the surveyors. 'I have not made any plans on purpose,' wrote Flora, 'because the experience of a long life is that it is a great mistake to try and act too quickly. Poor castle, I have to see, though I hate seeing it, that it will be a very long time before it is habitable again.' Flora's pessimism did not last long. In May 1939, within five months of the fire, she had engaged the services of an architect and the rebuilding of the south wing had begun.

The Second World War

THE REBUILDING OF DUNVEGAN CASTLE BEGAN IN MAY 1939, AT a time when it was becoming increasingly difficult to obtain material, labour or transport for all building work. On March 15th, 1939, Hitler had invaded Czechoslovakia, and Britain lived under the shadow of war. Flora was undeterred. 'My whole thought and will has been set on bringing the castle back to life,' she wrote. 'It is a duty I owe to the past and to the future.' When war was finally declared on September 3rd, 1939, over a million people were moved out of the cities to places of safety and Flora immediately wrote to the War Office offering the castle as a rehabilitation centre for wounded soldiers. Her request was considered favourably and supplies of steel were made available for the reconstruction work to continue. Nevertheless, Flora was faced with constant difficulties and delays. 'The builders employed all the local men they could find,' she wrote, 'but had to import a great many more from the mainland. The work of the Skye builders was methodical, reliable and first-rate, but infinitely slower than the work of the men who came from outside. These men were living away from their families and, though they were paid more and given lodgings, they wanted to complete the job as quickly as possible. It was not easy to combine these two elements, both contending with the relaxing West Highland climate and the discouragement of constant rain and storm.'

Flora lived in The Cottage, an estate house some minutes' walk from the castle and made daily visits to the site, encouraging and urging on the workmen and providing unlimited cups of tea. 'I had a lot of fight in me then,' she wrote. 'The MacLeod motto "Hold Fast" is a very splendid one and has helped me and many others in difficult times to carry bravely on.' Having only the four walls of the south wing to limit him, the architect, Dr. Colin Sinclair, was able to build in an infinitely more comfortable manner than before. He regarded his work at the castle as the crowning achievement of his life, a conviction shared by Flora, if not by others. 'He is penetrated with understanding of the Celtic art and spirit,' she wrote, 'and with the skill which is able to combine a perfection of modern convenience with the preservation of ancient structure.' Slowly the new wing began to take shape. A modern kitchen was built, new central heating was installed bringing hot and cold water to every bedroom. The blind windows to north and south were opened out as Flora had long desired, 'for blind windows are like blind eyes,' she wrote, 'sad things.'

The summer months of 1939 were also filled for Flora with frequent journeys to Aberdeenshire, because of recurring crises in Robert Wolrige Gordon's health. 'It is possibly weeks before the end comes,' wrote Flora. 'No one who loves him or Joan can wish it, for the last months have been terribly sad ones. It is very tragic as he is so anxious not to die. Joan's day and night nursing have brought her to the end of her strength. She is magnificent.' On October 3rd, 1939, Robert Wolrige Gordon died, leaving Joan a widow after only twelve years, and her three small sons fatherless. It was a grief to Flora, who spent the following Christmas with them at Esslemont and wrote from her room on Christmas Day, 'Every hour is poignant with memories.'

Work at the castle progressed slowly through the winter months. 'It has been a constant anxiety in every way having to complete such a big task in wartime,' Flora wrote, 'but I shall sing my Nunc Dimittis when it is done.' The advent of spring brought a rapid improvement in the reconstruction, and by November 28th, 1940, Flora entertained to tea at the castle the thirty-one workmen who remained to complete the job. On December 26th, 1940, she wrote, 'My glorious Christmas news is that the castle is finished. It is lovely. How I wish you could see it in its fresh beauty. Nothing is as healing and refreshing and comforting as beauty.' To her clansmen she wrote, 'The castle is completely restored and I am once again living in it. That it should have been triumphantly completed I firmly believe is due to the magic of the Fairy Flag.'

By October 1940 the War Office had decided to make a

large area of north-west Scotland a prohibited area, for in such a comparatively small part of the country it was impossible for them to pin-point what they wished to keep secret. Skye naturally suffered under these restrictions and Flora was therefore officially informed that the castle would not be used as a rehabilitation centre. She was far from pleased. 'Skye remains a prohibited area to those not in uniform,' she wrote. 'Those who want to get in, can't get in. Those who want to get out, can get out but they can't get back when they want to. It is very hard to see how this can help to win the war, but the authorities say that it does, so we must not grumble. But it is sad to see our hotels and boarding-houses empty and be obliged to refuse hospitality to people from overcrowded areas eager to share our peace.' It would perhaps have been different if Flora had been able to share the trials and difficulties of war-torn London, but, as she could not, she felt cut off and frustrated. 'The Government announced there was to be no evacuation to any island because the sea passages would have been dangerous,' she wrote. 'I thought this was a great mistake, not only bad for Britain but also bad for Skye, because Skye was close enough to the mainland to provide food and services. As it was, we did not suffer at all. If evacuated families had been planted on us we should have had a lot of the discipline and hardship that ordinary people had to put up with. The Government said that people living in Skye on one particular day had free right to travel back and forth, but anybody else had to have permits unless they were in uniform or working. I thought this a complete farce. We might have had the most undesirable people in Skye on that day who would have been able to travel freely.'

Because there was so little hardship on Skye, Flora imposed disciplines on herself. 'We have reduced ourselves to one bath a week,' she wrote, 'because the grand new automatic boilers use a special fuel which is in short supply. So I feel I can look Mr. Bevin in the eye with a good conscience.' The conduct of the war was a constant source of interest to her. 'Churchill's speech is magnificent,' she wrote to Ralph Isham in December 1940. 'If you can keep us going with ships and munitions and aeroplanes we shall have victory within a year. I should love to hear what you think of it all—France, Italy, Greece, Spain, Russia and that abominable little Eire. It is tantalising to feel so far away from the great drama and not to be able to talk to people who think they know what the U.S.A. means to do about Japan.'

Each day the BBC played the national anthems of the allied countries before the 9 o'clock news and Flora always tuned in and stood to attention throughout. After the fall of France, Mary Northcote, who was being educated at the castle during the war years, noticed that Flora remained seated for the 'Marseillaise'. 'The defection of France was a stunning blow,' she wrote, 'and yet it made us all feel more braced and resolved.' Although Flora's mind moved over the battlefronts of the world with an almost Churchillian vigour, her life at the castle was sadly mundane. She formed a National Savings Association in the village, but her heart was with her friends in Chelsea, who were suffering under heavy German bombing and many of whom were killed. 'I am terribly proud of the way Britain is carrying on,' she wrote, 'especially London. I get perfectly calm, normal letters from tradesmen who have been bombed out, assuring me of their best attention at all times.'

Perhaps the only aspect of the war which reached Skye was an endless stream of red tape. As in the urban areas, the Dunvegan school-children were issued with gas-masks which they were required to carry to school. In Skye, with its unusually heavy rainfall, the cardboard boxes in which these were stored were soon sodden and useless and the practice had to be abandoned. The Home Guard was organised under the enthusiastic command of a retired Indian Civil Servant, Sir Godfrey Fell. He was a neighbour and friend of Flora's, and trained his men arduously and almost nightly. His first call for volunteers was answered by Flora's chauffeur, John MacLeod, and the local banker Mr. Hope. MacLeod was given the responsibility for listing and reporting casualties, and his colleague for checking the blackout. 'Obviously, they both had nothing very much to do throughout the war,' wrote Flora, 'and I considered they were being trained in entirely unnecessary accomplishments.' When the Home Guard erected a block on the Sligachan road in order to forestall a possible German advance, Flora commented crisply, 'Can you imagine the Germans landing in Skye? Their first action would be to get off it.' Flora was herself responsible for the distribution of food in the Dunvegan area in the event of a German landing. Emergency stores were kept in the castle basement and had to be checked regularly. Flora supervised her team for the periodic turning of the sacks of flour to prevent deterioration, and emerged at the end hot and covered in flour. 'When I was informed that we must all wear steel helmets for this job, it was the final indignity,' she wrote. 'I sent an embittered letter to Sir Godfrey Fell saying that I wished it could be remembered that the Home Guard were people exempted from conscription because they were doing essential home service as shepherds or because they were physically unfit.' Sir Godfrey Fell wrote an equally angry reply in which he pointed out that it was his duty to carry out instructions. In the event, the Government needed the steel for more important purposes and helmets were not available.

Flora found two important outlets for her energies during the war. The first was as a county councillor at Inverness, where she fought determinedly on behalf of her part of Skye and was prepared to accept almost any allies when she was engaged in a battle in which she believed. Over the years these included the provision of modern sanitation in primary schools, new roads, and an independent water supply for Dunvegan. 'I saw on the County Council how the influential member has his little road put right,' she wrote, 'while the bigger community of crofters is never put down on the list.' Flora was almost invariably on the crofters' side. However much she may have criticised other councillors for promoting their areas, she saw nothing incongruous about the fact that her interests were centred on Dunvegan. 'I did not stand to benefit personally,' she wrote, 'and I felt it my duty to fight for the rights of those who had elected me.' Inevitably, this brought her into conflict from time to time with her fellow councillors. The feud with her near neighbour, Lord Macdonald of Sleat, who represented Broadford, was famous and occasionally reached proportions reminiscent of the feuds of her ancestors. Once in a council meeting Flora referred to a concession made by Lord Macdonald as 'the crumbs from the rich man's table', and was later quoted by local Skye wits as having said that Dunvegan was feeding on 'the crumbs from the Lord's table'. A fellow councillor who worked with her at the time wrote, 'She was charming and much loved but far more political than any of us. She was always taking people into corners and working on them in the most delightful way. With a touch of the hand or a sparkle of those very blue eyes, she would turn them round to her point of view.'

It was, however, in her role as chief at Dunvegan that Flora found her second and more long-lasting satisfaction. On November 28th, 1940, she welcomed ten shipwrecked fishermen who turned up at the castle gates with the bedding they had managed to salvage from their boat. Flora dried their equipment, provided ten hot baths, and tea out of her own ration. Although civilians could not go to Skye, many overseas servicemen spent their leaves there, and they were often MacLeods. For some it was the last holiday they would ever have. They were lonely and far from home and Flora was in every sense a mother to them. She invited them to stay at the Castle, and afterwards corresponded with their parents. They in turn treated Flora as a mother, sharing with her the smallest details of their daily lives and providing her with an overseas correspondence which by the end of the war was very large indeed. 'It is good that these young men should find the mother country a real mother country,' Flora wrote. 'I was astonished to find that many of them knew quite a lot about Dunvegan. They had been taught its history by their grandfathers and had always wanted to come. It was a tremendous privilege to me to be able to say to them, "This is really your home—your very oldest home where your roots are planted. When you come here and climb the staircase hewn in the rock and pass through the postern gate, you are climbing the stairs that your forefathers climbed. When you are in the drawing-room, which used to be the one great living-room of the castle in ancient days, you are in the room where they feasted, where the pipes were played and where the clan life was lived. This belongs to you as well as to me. Dunvegan is ours. It is a clan home.' Flora then took her guests to stand beneath the Fairy Flag and gave them each a signed picture of it. 'They looked upon it as a protection,' she wrote.

Among the immediate pre-war visitors to the castle had been Mr. and Mrs. Jerzy Machlejd from Poland. An agricultural merchant by profession, Jerzy Machlejd was also a Member of Parliament in Warsaw and a descendant of Rory Mor, a branch of whose family had settled in Poland.

The Machlejds travelled to Skye with two Polish friends, bringing with them a scroll bearing the names in Polish and in English of all the Polish MacLeods. The scroll was given a place of honour at the castle, and hangs there to this day. Throughout the war, Flora followed the fortunes of her Polish clansmen with the deepest concern. Jerzy Machlejd was imprisoned by the Germans and later shot. His young niece, Wanda Machlejd, was a courier in the Polish Resistance movement and also imprisoned by the Germans. After the liberation of Poland, her plight was brought to the attention of clansmen in Britain, and she came to Scotland to complete her further education. Her widowed mother subsequently asked her to come home and Wanda returned to the hardships of Warsaw. It was a great moment for the clan and for Flora when Wanda was given permission to attend one of the first Clan Parliaments, and the link with her was never thereafter lost.

It was not uncommon for MacLeod prisoners-of-war in Germany to use their one letter home to write to their chief, and their letters, often written on scruffy little pieces of paper marked with their prison number and the stamp of the Nazi censor, contained moving accounts of how their memories of Dunvegan and Skye sustained them throughout their captivity. One of those who spent several leaves at Dunvegan and came under Flora's spell was a young bomber pilot from Australia, Squadron-Leader Lewis MacLeod. Every night thereafter, before taking off, his crew would pass the picture of the Fairy Flag from hand to hand, and they survived the required thirty bombing raids without casualty. To Flora's sorrow, Lewis MacLeod then volunteered to be a Pathfinder and was shot down and killed. His only brother was also killed in the Pacific and Flora corresponded with his old parents in Australia, who in their bereavement chose to adopt two young British settlers and treat them as sons. Flora met the parents on her three subsequent visits to Australia.

The letters Flora received from the young men she entertained were always enthusiastic. 'My visit to the castle was without doubt the grandest experience of my life,' wrote one. 'It was like a dream I never thought would come true,' wrote another. 'It made my leave the best I have ever had or hope to have.' Gunner D. J. MacLeod, stationed at Gibraltar, was moved to write a poem after his visit. It was called 'A Soldier's Hope' and appeared in an Edinburgh evening newspaper. The last verse read:

I shall raise my eyes to Heaven
And the stars shall be my friends,
And my soul shall wander freely
Until my sunset ends,
In that blessed isle of peace
Where the earth communes with God
In my isle across the sea.

The servicemen wrote home in their hundreds telling their families about Dunvegan and Flora. Their letters created a reserve of affection and loyalty across the world which encouraged the BBC in January 1943 to put out a programme on their overseas service entitled 'Dunvegan calling all MacLeods'. Flora was invited to take part and in her first broadcast displayed a professionalism which was to become the envy of many commentators. 'Whether you are the citizens of this country or of the great Dominions or of the United States of America,' she said, 'you are the child of Leod whose home was upon this rock washed by the sea. Here your fathers and mine feasted and fought, loved and laughed, lived and died. Here they listened to the famous MacCrimmons, nine generations of them, piping to the chief and clan. Here still hangs the Fairy Flag with its eternal magic. They made island history in the olden days. You are making world history today.' On the most mundane level, Flora was perhaps the best castle guide there has ever been. Many years later, when she was being filmed for television in the castle drawing-room, she leant forward and suddenly remarked, 'This is real living in the past. You see, here the past is alive.'

Until the London blitz was at its height the clan *ceilidhs* in Edinburgh and London continued annually and Flora travelled down to be present at them. The clan magazine struggled to survive against acute paper shortages and the loss of subscriptions from overseas members, but Flora never lost heart. In June 1942 she wrote, 'Surely the end of the nightmare must soon appear in sight and one feels proud and thankful for the steadfastness which has faced nearly three years of trial without faltering, and that with America we know there can be no question of exhaustion, and that not only the war but the peace to follow it will soon be won. It was, however, not until November 1945 that Flora travelled to London to attend the first post-war clan gathering, at which she welcomed her MacLeod servicemen home from the battlefields of Europe. She had always believed in making friends with the Press and had, therefore, personally sent an invitation to a reporter from the *Daily Mail*. 'All I said was, "May I speak to Mr. MacLeod, please?"' he wrote in his column the following day, 'and a dozen gentlemen in tartan kilts tried to shake hands with me at the same time. "We are all Mr. MacLeods," they said. "All of us." "But I want to see the chief, Mr. MacLeod, the one who sent me this." And I waved an invitation card hailing me to a *ceilidh* of the Clan MacLeod in Northumberland Avenue, London. Twelve pairs of MacLeod eyes twinkled humorously. "Now, if you had only made yourself plain," said the kilts. "The gentleman you want is Mrs. MacLeod." So I was introduced to one of the most charming ladies in Scotland. The clan had gathered in their sashes and crests, kilts and sporrans to bid farewell to Canadian and American clansmen before they returned home from the war of many MacLeods. For on all fronts and in all services, kinsmen·who made Mrs. MacLeod's turreted Dunvegan Castle in the Isle of Skye their first shrine after Buckingham Palace—had fought shoulder to shoulder.'

That evening Flora danced the 'eightsome reel', the 'petronella' and the 'dashing white sargeant' with the servicemen for whom she had cared. She was sixty-seven years old, an age when most women might consider their active lives had finished, but hers was virtually about to begin.

Canada—
the First Clan Tours

IN THE SUMMERS OF 1947 AND 1948 TOURISTS POURED INTO SKYE for their first taste of the Highlands in ten years, and for many their first holiday since the war. Thousands came to Dunvegan Castle, which at that time was ill-equipped to cope with them. Tickets and literature were sold to holiday-makers at the front door and all the proceeds were placed in a red cardboard box. At the end of the day the remaining literature was counted; the number of brochures missing was automatically assumed to be the number sold, and this amount of money was subtracted from the cardboard box. The change that remained provided the figure of the number of visitors at the castle on that day, and was frequently, if not always, misleading. Flora's genius was much better directed at making tourists welcome than at charging them a fee.

Archie and Alice, who in 1943 had taken the name MacLeod, returned to Dunvegan from India to assume their role as Flora's successors. It was not easy for them. They had not been at the castle for ten years and throughout that time Flora had held the reins alone. Archie offered to help his mother-in-law in some of the practical needs at the castle. He suggested making a catalogue of the pictures, but she did not want one. He offered to help in the management of the estate, about which Flora knew little, but she was not enthusiastic. He noticed that the castle water was blue and thought this could be due to the copper piping. When he asked Flora if she had ever had the water tested, she told him to do it himself if he was interested. Archie, who was anxious to please, collected a water sample and sent it to Inverness. When Flora later attended a County Council meeting and was told the sample had arrived, she was furious and told her astonished son-in-law to mind his own business in future.

Archie did not enjoy good health, something which Flora

always found difficult to forgive. When he once waited for several hours at the foot of the castle stairs in order that Alice, who was out on a boating-trip, should help him climb them, Flora's irritation knew no bounds. It was almost impossible for a woman who had become so much of a one-man-band to share her responsibilities with others. Although Flora was patient and charming to MacLeods, even of the most vague origin, she could be horribly rude to people she disliked. When Alice once invited her husband's sister-in-law to stay at the Castle and paint her portrait, Flora made her disapproval so much felt that after a few days the poor woman remarked despondently, 'If only I could think of one thing to say to her that I knew would not bore her to tears!'

Flora had longed for a male heir but she believed the entail on the estate was unbreakable and that her eldest daughter had to succeed. The entail was a tedious and expensive restriction, necessitating large numbers of signatures and consequent legal costs every time the smallest business transaction was concluded with Dunvegan property. It was during one of these negotiations that Flora discovered she could break the entail with the approval of the three direct heirs. Alice was now over forty and had no children, so Flora's mind turned to her grandsons in Aberdeenshire. Robert was to remain at Esslemont and inherit his father's estate, so Flora resolved to make John, her second grandson and the elder of the twins, her heir. Although nothing had yet been decided, she told Archie and Alice her plan. It was a bitter blow. It was galling enough for a man to change his name once at the request of his mother-in-law, but it was a real indignity to have to do it twice. For this Flora blamed her lawyer who was, in her view, too old for the job, and who, she felt, should have informed her earlier that it was possible to break the entail. It is certainly true that had Flora known this she would probably have made John her heir from the start, and although the lawyer could hardly advise her to disinherit her elder daughter, he probably should have informed her of this fact. Flora believed her decision was in the interests of Dunvegan, and it may well have been. Her political judgment was seldom wrong, but the way in which she pursued it—inflicting wounds without thought upon Archie and Alice—revealed a ruthlessness worthy of high politics. To help ease the situation, she suggested that Alice should have the running of the crofting estate in her lifetime, while John inherited the castle. It was an arrangement singularly unattractive to both parties.

With the future of Dunvegan still unresolved, a letter arrived from the Revd. A.W.R. Mackenzie early in 1947 inviting Flora to attend the Ninth Annual Gaelic Mod, and the first since the war, at St. Anne's, Cape Breton, Nova Scotia. As a Highland chief, Flora was an absent patron of the Mod and was one of the various Scottish Chiefs whom A.W.R. Mackenzie invited in turn. The Mod was to last for four days from July 30th to August 3rd, and include a special MacLeod Day. 'When I opened the letter and told Archie and Alice,' wrote Flora, 'they said, "Very interesting but absolutely impossible." I said, "Yes, of course it is. It is out of the question." In bed that night I asked myself, "Why is it out of the question? Why is it impossible?" I could not answer.' The young Canadian servicemen, who had been at Dunvegan during the war, and their parents, to whom she had written, gave Flora her answer. She came down to breakfast the next morning and told her astonished daughter and son-in-law, 'I have decided it is not impossible and I am going to accept.'

Alice and Archie's ten-year absence in India was felt by some of the family to explain their reluctance to accept that it was now common practice in Scotland for the youngest heir to succeed. There were clearly misunderstandings on both sides, for Alice was under the impression that she had reached a *modus vivendi* with her mother about the future of Dunvegan before her mother's departure for Canada and she received a body blow when, within a few days of parting, a letter arrived from the lawyer in Edinburgh informing her of the decision which had been reached since Flora left the castle and before she flew from Prestwick—namely that she was no longer the heir to Dunvegan. Flora had also decided that, as Alice was under no obligation to hand over the crofting estate to John, it could not be separated from the castle. The decision was made all the more painful, coming as it did from a third party.

Alice and Archie had already decided it would be uneconomic to manage the crofting estate without the revenue from the castle, and now their continued presence at Dunvegan would, in any case, be an embarrassment. They

I

changed their name back to Macnab, and later Archie realised his claim as chief of Clan Macnab and bought back the family home and estate at Kinnell in Perthshire. Flora had achieved her ambition, but in a manner which cast a shadow over her family relationships which was not easy to erase.

Flora was now most anxious lest John, born a Wolrige Gordon, with a mother born Walter, would be at a considerable disadvantage when his claim was considered. She rejoiced when his succession was secure, and when at the age of fifteen and still a schoolboy at Eton, he took the name of MacLeod of MacLeod. 'I am confident that my grandson, who is proud to bear the name of John MacLeod younger of MacLeod,' she wrote to her clan, 'will follow me worthily at Dunvegan, and I hope and believe that you feel you do well to welcome him in God's good time as 29th Chief.'

Flora now put the difficult business of breaking the entail behind her, and concentrated all her energies upon the clan. Her invitation to Nova Scotia came from what is possibly one of the most Gaelic-conscious areas in the world, and a country where the name of MacLeod is one to be conjured with. The first settlers were led by a pioneer and a man of great force of character, called the Revd. Norman MacLeod. In the early nineteenth century, Norman MacLeod led a band of some three or four hundred emigrants from the Highlands who wished to go to America. During the voyage a storm arose and blew them north and west and they landed and established a settlement at St. Anne's, Cape Breton. Norman MacLeod ruled them with a rod of iron. So great was his influence that after thirty years, when he decreed they should leave Cape Breton, and ordered them to build six little ships, they did so without hesitation. Half the community sailed with MacLeod on a perilous journey, first to Australia and then on to Waipu in New Zealand, which subsequently became one of the historic sites of the country. It was, therefore, a considerable event for the people of Cape Breton to receive a Highland chief, particularly the chief of MacLeod, from a country which many still regarded as their homeland and with which there had been no contact throughout the war.

In late July 1947, Flora flew from Prestwick on her first

trans-atlantic air journey in a Constellation bound for New York. 'How I enjoyed the flight over the calm summer sea in an air-conditioned plane,' she wrote. 'I was so thrilled when I first saw Gander after the thousands of miles of ocean. As a child I had been instructed that Newfoundland was the land of bogs and dogs and fogs and logs, and it lived up to its reputation. Fog at Gander delayed the landing for several hours and there was no connection to take me to Sydney (Nova Scotia) by five o'clock in the afternoon. The next flight to Nova Scotia was not until 10 p.m. I sat in the airport in my tartan and in stifling heat. When at 10.15 p.m. the flight had not been called, I went to the desk and asked the reason for the delay. I was told my plane had left twenty minutes earlier. Wireless conversation ensued between the pilot and the ground staff. Yes, my luggage was on board. Yes, they had the right number of passengers. It was finally established that an unbooked passenger had inserted herself in my place. I demanded that the plane return. I said it had got to come back as there was a reception waiting for me at Sydney.' Flora's desperate appeal impressed the ground staff, and the plane did return, but it did not eventually land at Sydney until past midnight. It had been a long journey and Flora emerged from the door of the aircraft hot, dirty and dishevelled. Her arrival was heralded with a blaze of photographers' flashlights, and on the tarmac she could see the outline of an escort of Canadian Mounted Police. There were speeches of welcome, including one in Gaelic from the local mayor and a touching reunion with her host, Captain Donald D. B. MacLeod, whom she had last seen during the war, on leave at the castle. After the emotion of the initial welcome, Flora was suddenly conscious of a great crowd of people in the darkness behind the barriers, and they were cheering her. They had been waiting nearly eight hours for this moment and their hands stretched through the railings towards her. Flora walked over to them in amazement and clasped their hands in hers. Many of those who had made their way to Sydney airport on that hot summer evening in 1947 were directly descended from the band of emigrants who had landed with Norman MacLeod over a hundred years before. Others had letters from sons who would never again return to Canada, but who had spent the last and happiest days of their lives with this 'silver-haired dynamic little lady'.

Their outstretched hands were for Flora part of the castle and its heritage, part of the Scotland she loved and part of the new world which appeared to love her with a depth she had seldom before experienced. 'I was tremendously moved,' wrote Flora, 'by the enthusiasm of these strange people who seemed so happy to see me.'

From the airport Flora was driven with police escort to a hotel room laden with flowers. The following morning she was driven to Baddeck and the home of Captain MacLeod, over which now fluttered the battered flag which had long waved over Dunvegan Castle when the chief was in residence. It was now famous as 'the first time the flag of a Highland chief has flown in Canada'. Flora now made a grand tour of Cape Breton, and each little township gathered to prepare a feast of welcome, with pipers and tartan-clad dancers. The ship's bell of the corvette *Dunvegan* was presented to Dunvegan school, and as the Premier of Nova Scotia, the Hon. Angus L. MacDonald, had been a pupil there, he was an honoured guest. Flora described him as 'that most beautiful speaker and great Highlander', and was his guest at Keltic Lodge. Clansmen in all parts of the Province gathered to hear their chief speak, and in their turn presented her with countless bouquets and tartan gifts.

In brilliant sunshine and in a crowded arena, the Gaelic Mod opened on July 30th. Among the thousands present were three elderly MacLeods who had travelled thirty-six hours by train in gruelling heat from Glengarry, Ontario, to welcome their chief to Canada. 'Things were much less formal than with us,' wrote Flora. 'Highlanders gathered together from all parts to dance and sing and listen to the pipes. Judging was done on the spot and there were no set competitions or serious appraisements. It was much more a grand social gathering combined with a real *ceilidh* spirit. The welcome given me was wonderful.' The story of MacLeod Day, when Flora was presented with an exact replica of the chief's flag, went all over Canada and America. The blue cloth had been woven by students at the Gaelic centre, and then embroidered by a clanswoman, with the castle depicted in white and the door and windows in crimson.

On Sunday, August 3rd, Flora unveiled a memorial to the Revd. Norman MacLeod on the site of the first settlement. The inscription bore her name as well as his, and those who took part in the open-air Gaelic service which followed were all MacLeods. 'I should become sentimental if I tried to tell you what a living sense of the oneness of our big clan family burned in me,' wrote Flora, 'and the pride of knowing that we still belong to each other because of the past which, consciously or unconsciously, is bone of our bone and flesh of our flesh.'

From the moment Flora had stepped on to Canadian soil, a disciplined, erect little figure with a straw hat perched firmly on her head, she had drawn the affection of the crowds. It could not altogether be explained by the immense love of ancestry which dominates Nova Scotia, or entirely dismissed as an upsurge of Celtic emotion, for it was, as one observer put it, 'the sheer blaze of her personality' which made an impact on people. Flora visibly shone when she was at the centre of a host of admirers. Her skills as an actress may not have been great in Wagnerian opera as a girl, but she possessed those two qualities essential to a person at the centre of the stage—she enjoyed it immensely and she gave her audiences something worth waiting for. Her speeches were from the heart and extempore. 'Underneath I suppose I am very simple in my tastes,' she wrote, 'and I like simple people.' She meant it and they knew it, but it was a strange admission from a woman who was a dedicated reader of *The Economist* and an advocate of all things intellectual. However much the publicity and the autograph hunters might have dismayed others and would certainly have shocked her parents, for Flora they were the bread of life. They filled an emptiness or perhaps fulfilled an ambition which had long been there. Overnight Flora had become a queen. In a farewell broadcast the C.B.C. described her as 'the guardian of the Fairy Flag, mother of Dunvegan and queen of hearts.' It was the last part of the description which pleased her most. 'I had a queen's welcome,' she wrote, 'and it was as a queen I flew away. It was as an ordinary passenger I landed at Prestwick, but contrasts make the savour of living.' Flora humped her own bag from the airport to the Inverness train, unnoticed by the Scottish crowd to whom she was then hardly known.

In 1947 there existed in Canada only one rural Clan Society, and Flora's visits were made to individual friends or limited to official engagements like the Gaelic Mod.

However, in no time enthusiastic and highly successful Clan Societies were formed whose members subsequently made the arrangements for Flora's many visits to Canada. 'They were heart-warming and deeply rewarding,' she wrote, 'but of course could not, and did not, attempt to recapture the "first fine careless rapture" of the first transoceanic reception after the separation of the war.'

When she left for Canada, Flora had written, 'I should dearly like this to be the first of other visits to my clansfolk in other parts of the world,' and she did not long delay. In November 1947 she was the guest of honour at the St. Andrew's Day banquet of the Caledonian Society in Paris, their jubilee and the first since the war. 'I flew there for three gay, giddy days,' she wrote. 'It was a very fine affair and I was in an illustrious line which included our present King and Queen when Duke and Duchess of York. The clan and I felt ourselves much honoured. Unhappily, it was a time of considerable unrest and provision was made to light the hall with torches should a sudden strike cut off the electricity from the many brilliant candelabra. However, the only casualty was the haggis, which got involved in the railway strike and which the most imaginative and Herculean efforts failed to locate and retrieve in time.'

After the war, Flora was invited to serve on the Scottish Tourist Board. She had long regarded tourism as the most important Highland industry and together with her neighbour and fellow county councillor, Major Iain Hilleary, she initiated in 1950 a special Skye Week. At that time what has since become a commonplace event in almost every small town in Scotland was nearly an innovation. The dates were chosen with considerable care to coincide with the best weather conditions and the traditional carpets of wild flowers for which Skye is famous in early spring. The events of the six-day programme depicted different aspects of the island's history. The opening ceremony and the Portree Games on Saturday, May 20th were attended by the Lord Provosts of three of Scotland's major cities. Monday was Trotternish Day and celebrated on the north end of Skye, mostly associated with Flora Macdonald. Tuesday was MacLeod Day, and Flora entertained 300 guests to tea on the lawn of the round garden, and afterwards showed them the castle. Those who came commented on the family spirit and the sense of gaiety which surrounded the occasion.

On Borreraig Day, which followed, the interest moved across Loch Dunvegan to the place where for centuries MacCrimmon pipers had their home and college. Flora crossed the loch by boat and a ceremony was initiated which has continued ever since. 'A great concourse of people with General Martin* at its head was waiting on the rocky shore to greet Mrs. MacLeod of MacLeod,' wrote one reporter. 'MacLeod stalwarts, according to ancient custom, waded out knee deep and carried their Chief ashore, and then General Martin, a magnificent figure standing well over six feet with an ancient plaid thrown over his shoulder, given to his family one hundred years ago, welcomed the chief and her retinue to his domains.' The procession moved in solemn silence up the hill to the memorial cairn and the music of a lone piper. 'There are few more moving experiences,' wrote Flora, 'than to stand on the rocky headland and listen to a great piper playing one of their immortal pibrochs and look upon the panorama of sea and mountain and islands which inspired their music.'

In later years, Borreraig Day became a far more solemn and formal celebration, with the piper required to pay a rent to General Martin on behalf of the Glasgow College of Piping, for the lease of the land—the rent being one penny and the playing of a pibroch. It was on the occasion of Borreraig Day that Dame Flora first met and admired the fine piping of Seumas MacNeill and John MacFadyen, founders of the Piping College in Glasgow, with both of whom she enjoyed a lasting friendship.

The first Skye Week had been an outstanding success. When Flora and her party embarked and sailed back across the water to the Castle, those on board began to sing 'Over the Sea to Skye'. To the west across the Minch the dim outlines of Uist and Harris shone in the evening light and to the east the jagged peaks of the Cuillins rose in all their power, silent and enveloped in the haunting melody which floated across the water, and not surprisingly Skye Week was born and proclaimed a permanent feature of the Island's year.

In July 1951, accompanied by her daughter, Joan, and her twin grandsons, Flora set off on another clan tour of Canada.

* Major-General J. S. S. Martin of Husabost 1888–1973

This time it was not limited to Nova Scotia, but included the great cities of Ottawa and Toronto. The welcome was no less enthusiastic than the one she had received at Sydney Airport four years before, but it was on a much larger scale. 'She received a warm greeting to Canada from every man, woman and child with a drop of Scottish blood in their veins, and that included almost everyone,' wrote one newspaper.

The bridgehead which Flora had successfully established in Nova Scotia encouraged her clansmen to expand their operation. Two hundred MacLeods were invited to meet their Chief at a reception in Toronto given by Mr. Donald MacLeod and his sister, Mrs. Reeve. The names of the guests had been gleaned from the Toronto telephone directory and they were entertained in a room decorated with heather and thistles and to the accompaniment of the pipes. It was an example followed by countless cities across the world in later years and prompted Flora to reply whenever she was asked the number of MacLeods in the clan, 'Look in your local telephone directory and you will discover how numerous we are.'

Flora visited the Gaelic community in Glengarry, Ontario, where more than a thousand clansmen welcomed her when she appeared outside the village of Dunvegan. She was given a great ovation and was deeply touched, speaking to the crowd in Gaelic, a language in which she was by no means fluent. 'It has been my dream to come here,' she said, 'and here I am. Now you must visit me at Dunvegan Castle.' In Prince Edward Island, Mayor Earle Macdonald, forgetting ancient feuds, spoke from the steps of the City Hall before the multitude and said, 'We welcome you to our city and to our hearts. And not alone do we welcome you, but we welcome too that tradition of nobility of all that is oldest and best in Scottish history, which is so dear to very many of the people of this island.' The waitresses in the hotel at Niagara Falls were specially dressed in MacLeod tartan to welcome Flora and her family. The twins were about to celebrate their sixteenth birthday and a great fuss was made of them. One newspaper described them as 'these two young princes of a noble family', and this inappropriate regal tag was not entirely fallacious, for their reception in Canada would have done credit to a minor royalty. Flora was immensely proud of them and admired their poise. 'They charm people to pieces,' she wrote, and she was possibly the most vulnerable.

Throughout her tour Flora forged links between Britain and Canada which were considered of international value in the post-war years. She was humbly and unfailingly grateful for Canadian generosity to Europe at a time when there was much ingratitude and hostility. In Ottawa a large reception was held at the Château Laurier, Canada's premier hotel. Flora's speech that evening, in which she suggested that Canada would play an important part as intermediary between Britain and the United States, was widely reported in the Press and on the radio. The following day she was received by Mr. St. Laurent, the Prime Minister, and afterwards attended a lunch given in her honour in the Press Gallery of Parliament House.

The concept of the clan tour, which had started in Nova Scotia in 1947, had now assumed proportions of national and even international significance. However, it was in the small communities, dependent on the spirit within them for their survival, that the Clan Society remained at its most attractive. Here it was inclusive of, and of service to, the whole area in preserving traditions of value in people's lives, and it was once again at Cape Breton that Flora ended her tour in 1951. Nobody had forgotten her earlier visit and she was considered a 'natural' for the celebrations marking the departure of Norman MacLeod for Waipu. The public turned out in force to welcome her family. The procession of cars from Sydney airport was more than a mile long, and, preceded by pipe bands, moved along streets lined with cheering crowds. During her visit Flora was the guest of Dr. and Mrs. Gilbert Grosvenor. He was the Director of the National Geographic Magazine of America and she was the daughter of Graham Bell, the emigrant Scotsman who invented the telephone. They were both deeply interested in the Gaelic College and the Highland population of Nova Scotia, and had their summer home in Graham Bell's house on Cape Breton, a place he had chosen as being most like Scotland within reach of New York. The friendship which ensued between Flora and the Grosvenors was mutual and permanent. Flora invited them to be her guests in Skye, and they in turn suggested doing a feature on the island for the National Geographic Magazine. In July 1952 the beautifully illustrated article on Skye was published, and 2,100,000 copies were distributed throughout the world. 'The impact was immediate,' wrote Flora. 'Skye enjoyed its busiest tourist season for years, and the castle had its largest number of visitors.' Flora received letters and cables from every continent. The clan movement which she had brought to life now assumed gigantic proportions. 'I think we are doing our bit to help Britain at home and overseas,' she wrote, 'by welcoming strangers to share our scenery and our magic.'

America

In 1938 AN AMERICAN, JOHN H. MACLEOD FROM WALLINGFORD, Vermont, came to Skye with his wife and children. Flora invited them to the castle, and they had tea together in the drawing-room under the Fairy Flag, and were thereafter forever captured both by its magic and by that of their chief. John H. MacLeod had corresponded with Flora throughout the war and had sent her food parcels, roses for her garden, and a treasured folding table for her business room. He was a descendant of the early Scottish settlers in Nova Scotia, and news of Flora's successful tour there had naturally reached him. He wrote and asked her if she would consider making a similar visit to MacLeods in the United States. She at once agreed.

Flora's links with America were strong. Mary Northcote's relations, the Stuyvesant Fishs—one of whom had married Uncle Olly—offered Mary refuge with them during the war, and although Flora had refused their invitation on the ground that the sea passage was too dangerous, she responded by saying that she would welcome them or any of their friends at Dunvegan. Among those who took advantage of this offer was a young doctor from New York, Dr. Yale Kneeland, and there ensued a life-long friendship with the Kneeland family.

In 1952 Flora visited Ralph Isham at Cape Cod. It was the first time they had met for fourteen years and Isham's health was failing, but the friendship survived, and he was responsible for introducing Flora to a wide circle of friends, most of whom shared his interest in Boswell and Johnson. When, in 1959, Dr. I. F. Grant, the historian and scholar, had completed her book, *The MacLeods—the History of a Clan,* Faber and Faber were anxious to publish it and after much negotiation agreed to print 2,000 copies at £2 if Flora contributed £1,500 towards the cost. It seemed probable that the castle tourists could provide £500, and Flora resolved to seek an American publisher and literary contacts, with the assistance of Ralph Isham. Among Isham's friends were Donald and Mary Hyde, leaders of an artistic and intellectual society, in whose New Jersey home Flora was often a guest. Flora had lunch with Donald Hyde, his friend Lauder Greenway, and a representative of the publishing firm of Doubleday. The Doubleday representative said that, although he thought the book deserved to be published, his firm could not undertake it, but Donald Hyde and Lauder Greenway volunteered to guarantee £1,000 towards the cost of Dr. Grant's book. 'I walked on air,' wrote Flora afterwards, 'and I do seriously attribute this to the magic of the Fairy Flag.' It was Mrs. Hyde who retorted with the classic remark that 'it was not so much to do with the Flag, but more to do with the Fairy.' It is probably true that Flora now enjoyed some of the deepest personal relationships of her life with intellectual east-coast Americans. They in turn found her company fascinating, for not only did she share their interest in books, music and stimulating conversation, but also her presence at a dinner-party ensured its success. It was unusual to meet the only female Highland chief and particularly one who had been born at 10 Downing Street. Flora did not, like so many upper-class British people, look down on everything American. As a child revels in the excitement of Christmas morning, she revelled in the luxury, dazzling materialism and vitality which America first revealed to her.

From 1939 onwards, Flora had recognised that America would emerge at the end of the war as the dominant power of the free world, and power was a subject in which she was an expert. It was, therefore, inevitable that the clan movement, which had been launched so successfully in Canada, should now proceed to the United States, but Flora was inwardly apprehensive about her American debut and perhaps afraid of failure. She wondered if the glories of Canada could be repeated in a larger setting, and questioned whether the close family links which existed between Scotland and her descendants in Canada could possibly be as strong in the powerful and totally independent U.S.A. With hindsight, it is possible to see that the stage was set for an unparalleled impact. The post-war emotions which prevailed in Canada were no less strong in America, and had been reinforced by the climate of the cold war. The fear of Communism was great, Senator McCarthy was in the midst of his now famous investigations in Washington, and America was in the mood to respond to traditional values, and in search of friends who offered a sense of security.

In 1952 Flora made an exploratory visit to the United States with her daughter, Joan. It confirmed her view that there existed a large untapped source of support for the clan. The correspondence with America had been growing steadily since the war. In their letters several clansmen addressed Flora as 'Dear Mother', and this strangely intimate relationship between people who had never met was evident in other ways. One clansman wrote giving his height, weight and colour of eyes 'so that you may know me when we meet'. Flora had herself quoted in the clan magazine from the letter of a seventeen-year-old American boy, who wrote, 'We are so glad to hear of our race in Scotland. We are so afraid that our customs will die out here that we are beside ourselves. You who live in Scotland, the Mother of us all, have no idea how easy it is to lose a precious heritage such as our own. You can take the Scot out of Scotland but you'll never take Scotland out of the Scot. Ever since I can remember, the sound of the pipes has filled me with such pride that I thought my chest would burst.' In 1952, John H. MacLeod wrote to clansmen in the major cities of America asking whether they would welcome a visit from their chief. The response was immediate and overwhelming, and an important tour was planned for the following summer.

On June 1st, 1953, three months before she set sail for America, Flora was made a Dame Commander of the British Empire in recognition of her social and public services to Scotland, and was thereafter known to her clansmen and friends as Dame Flora. A deluge of congratulations poured in from all corners of the world and the clan felt itself honoured. No doubt Dame Flora was equally pleased, but on the day following the investiture, upon her leaving Mary Northcote's flat in Onslow Square, where she had spent the night, the medal was discovered to be the one object she had overlooked in her bedroom drawer. The importance of Dame Flora's proposed visit to the United States was acknowledged

in government circles at a moment when Britain was hoping
to increase her overseas trade, particularly her tourist trade,
with America, and the tour was, therefore, sponsored and
supported by the British Travel Association. The twins' visit
to Canada had made a great impression, and it was agreed
that John and Patrick should again accompany their
grandmother.

On September 16th, 1953, Dame Flora set sail for New
York on board the *S.S. Caronia*. It was a journey for which
she had prepared herself over many months. The discipline
which had been so much a part of her life since childhood
equipped her with a mental alertness and physical strength
which belied her seventy-five years. She had aged very
little—indeed many people said she looked younger than
before. It was probably true. One doctor who examined her
after her eightieth birthday remarked that she had 'the heart
and skin of an eighteen-year-old girl'. The forcefulness, which
had been a feature of her face in middle age, now gave way to
a delicacy and grace which was singularly attractive. Her
hair, which had been tied back in a bun, was now softly
curled, and she was more clothes-conscious than she had ever
been in her life; but although her physical appearance was
more feminine, she had lost none of her masculine
determination. 'The weather has been cheerless until today
which has been lovely with a spanking breeze,' she wrote to
Joan from mid-Atlantic. 'Our captain deftly evaded a fierce
storm which engulfed the *Queen Mary,* by rushing north on
the Canadian route, and having reached Newfoundland
turned south. There are a lot of rich people on board,
including British who have diverted their activities overseas.
then there are two nice Enders from California. He is
extremely intrigued about Clan MacLeod. 'You've got
something there,' he frequently says, and I think envisages us
as a sort of shade of Aimée Macpherson. I have read *Digby*
and loathed it, and *The Loved One* and laughed aloud, but I
have been very stern and rationed my pleasures brutally.'

At 7 a.m. on September 22nd, the *Caronia* sailed past the
Statue of Liberty towards her berth in the harbour of New
York. Wearing a trim dark suit, a white blouse and a tartan
hat perched jauntily on her head, Dame Flora was piped
ashore by the pipe band of the New York National Guard
and greeted by assembled clansmen on the quayside. 'I could

not detect the slightest evidence of the ageing process,' wrote
Yale Kneeland, who was on the dock to meet her. 'She was
still as light on her feet as thistledown, and as effervescently
gay as always. Her schedule for the next two months is
quelquechose formidable. I honestly don't think I'd be capable
of living through it myself, but the blood of a thousand
Highland heroes courses in her veins and I presume it won't
let her down.'

Dame Flora posed for photographers, sailed through a
host of interviews, and made a radio broadcast in which she
invited 22,000 American clansmen to visit Dunvegan. The
following morning newspapers from coast to coast of the
United States announced the landing of 'a great Clan chief'.
When she was entertained to an official dinner by the
MacLeods of New York the following evening, she was
already almost a national figure. 'Here I am, well launched
amid scenes of unparalleled enthusiasm,' she wrote to Joan,
'pipe band, twenty photographers, Press, Travel Association,
clan, friends, all too fantastic for words, and all this at 8 a.m.'
John and Patrick, who flew into New York the following day
to join their grandmother, were somewhat surprised to be
welcomed at the steps of their aircraft by a correspondent of
the *New York Times* and invited to change into their kilts for
an official photograph. In the three months which followed,
306 newspapers, with the total circulation of twenty-two
million, heralded the arrival of 'the little lady from Scotland'.
At one press conference a group of cynical journalists
bombarded her with questions about fairies and what her
ancestors wore beneath the kilt. Dame Flora capped their
jokes and dispelled their cynicism with a dazzling
performance, which gave her, the following day, one of the
best press coverages of her life.

North Carolina is the state which possesses one of the
largest and most ancient of all Highland settlements, and it
was here that the tour began. Tom Johnstone, Labour
Secretary of State for Scotland, had once delighted Dame
Flora by publicly comparing her to Flora Macdonald, and this
was Flora Macdonald country. On Sunday, September 27th,
fifteen hundred people of Scottish descent filled the Old
Bethesda Presbyterian Church, and after the traditional
picnic in the grove, which followed the service, Dame Flora
spoke to them. With confidence and poise she talked of the

past and of the links which bound together America and
Scotland. The following day, standing on the stump of the
oak-tree under which, it is said, Flora Macdonald addressed
the Highlanders on their way to the disastrous battle of
Moore's Creek in 1776, Dame Flora spoke again. 'It is quite
remarkable,' she said, 'that nearly 180 years after Flora
Macdonald's speech from this very spot, another woman
from Skye should stand here and address the descendants of
those Highlanders to whom Flora Macdonald spoke.' Dame
Flora then toured the battlefield, and for many the image was
complete and Flora Macdonald lived again.

The audiences to whom Dame Flora spoke were not all
Scottish. She was the guest of President and Mrs. Woodson
and spoke to the student body of Flora Macdonald College.
This was one of the many occasions when she had an
audience composed entirely of young people, and they were
not always sympathetic. At one high-school a large crowd of
gum-chewing bobbysoxers assembled unwillingly to listen to
her—a seventy-five-year-old lady whose world was totally
alien from theirs. Dame Flora groped her way through the
first agonising ten minutes of her speech to an
accompaniment of shuffling feet, rustling papers and discreet
sniggers. She searched for a thread which would capture the
imagination of these young Americans and quite suddenly
she found it. For threequarters of an hour, without a note
and without a pause, she spoke to an enraptured and silent
hall and at the end they stood and cheered her to the echo.

The tour gained momentum, and with unrelenting pace
Dame Flora moved through Virginia, into Canada, to Rhode
Island and Connecticut, where she spoke to a gathering of
1,300 people at Hartford. This was known country, where she
had friends and where the clan loyalties were strong, but
when she moved west she entered virgin territory as far as the
clan movement was concerned. In Cleveland, Ohio, she was
welcomed at the airport by Troop 28 of the Eagle Scouts
dressed, with her consent, in MacLeod tartan. From Chicago
and   Palmer   House,   which   she   described   as
'grand—grander—grandest of hotels', she wrote, 'We have
enjoyed a very delightful two days in Lake Forest about
thirty-five miles from Chicago, in houses lived in by gracious
people, spacious and very English, some very large and all in
their private grounds. The twins amaze me by their acumen

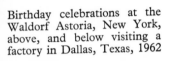

Birthday celebrations at the
Waldorf Astoria, New York,
above, and below visiting a
factory in Dallas, Texas, 1962

Above, Dame Flora with Malcolm MacLeod of Napier and Alison MacLeod Mac-Gibbon of Christchurch, when she was presented with a painting by New Zealand artist Austen Deans in Wellington, 1955, and right, the farewell reception in Auckland

Dame Flora welcomed to an Australian MacLeod Week in 1957 by Mr and Mrs Bruce MacLeod

and penetrating remarks. They revelled in finding themselves
in the atmosphere more nearly resembling their own past,
though they establish themselves with the utmost virtuosity
with all sorts and conditions. The Boy Scouts of Canton
adored them and they were boys with them, and men of the
world here. Our success here is considered quite phenomenal
and unheard of in McCormick-isolationist-ridden Chicago. I
understand that his paper is so good that everybody takes it
and the enlightened read only the back pages. I will send you
a leaderette in the *Daily News* entitled "MacLeod of
MacLeod." Our reception by pipers and battalions of
photographers took all our backers and sponsors by
surprise.' British officialdom was not slow to recognise that
such publicity was worth money. The British Consul in
Chicago arranged for Dame Flora and the twins to appear on
the N.B.C. television programme *Welcome Travellers,* which
at that time commanded the largest viewing audience of any
day-time show in the country. It was a blatantly commercial
exercise. 'The sponsor or advertiser pays 55,000 dollars for
half-an-hour,' wrote Dame Flora, 'so we will contribute
about 10,000 dollars.' Although this was something of which
she disapproved, the British Consul was most persuasive in
telling her it was in the national interest, and a wonderful
opportunity to advertise Scottish goods. Dame Flora,
therefore, agreed to take part. 'We were invited to the
television studios at midday,' she wrote, 'and we confidently
hoped that we were going to be given lunch, but far from it.
We had a few sandwiches and then the promoter came and
told me that he was going to ask me on the programme what
gift would please me most, and I was to say, "I have visited
the Scottish old people's home and would very much like a
gift for the old people." I said that would be all right. He then
disappeared and presently came back and said, "I want to
make quite sure that you understand what I said." I told him
that he need not be anxious. He finally came back a third time
and repeated it.'

'At last we were taken to the stage and in the left-hand
corner there was a chair for me, and the twins were told to
stand behind it. On the right of the stage, and seated on a
long pew, was a very large family from a mother down to
quite small children. A little woman sat at a table close to us.
The compere had invented a silly story about the MacLeods

K

and the Frasers. I objected to the Consul and said I did not want to take part in this nonsense. He advised me not to make a fuss about it because this was a very important opportunity and could not be thrown away, so I submitted to that. When the programme began, the camera was switched on to our corner and we made our modest contribution. Then the lights turned from us to the family on the other side of the stage and the compère said something like. "Now friends, this is a great day for us. I feel very proud to be able to present to you this most remarkable family and that you should share this moving story with me." The story was then told of the bereavement, poverty and anxiety in the family. "Now what can we do to make this family happy?" asked the compere. "I believe a kitchen range would be wonderful." Whereupon the curtain in the centre of the stage opened to reveal a magnificent kitchen range and an enchanting saleswoman. The curtain closed. "Now," said the compère, "what can we do for the younger ones? I think the daughter could do with a washing-machine." Eventually, the whole family was equipped. Then the lights focused on the little woman seated at the table. "I feel guilty," said the compère. "I feel as if I was doing wrong in having persuaded this lady to come and tell you her story. It is a piteous story." Then the lady told of the degradation into which her life had drifted. There had been the most wonderful rehabilitation and she now felt hope and happiness again. The compère thanked her and she was presented with a luxurious set of flying luggage which we would have given worlds to have. As we walked out feeling somewhat disillusioned by the whole affair, somebody rushed up and thrust a pink blanket into Patrick's arms. There followed a great controversy about the ownership of the blanket. We said that as Patrick's part had been minimal he had absolutely no right to it, and he said as it had been given to him it was his blanket.' The saga of the pink blanket thereafter became a standing joke in the family and helped to dispel the aura of commercialism into which the tour occasionally fell.

From Kansas City to San Francisco, from Dallas to Detroit, from New York to Los Angeles, Dame Flora was now wined, dined and lionised on a grand scale. St. Andrew's Societies, Caledonian Clubs, and university women all vied for her attentions and she seldom refused an invitation.

However, when the St. Andrew's Society of New York, an entirely male organisation, invited her to attend their annual dinner unofficially, she wrote to Joan, 'They have decided they cannot break their 168-year-old rule against women guests, in which decision I whole-heartedly sympathise. I am saying that I am very happy that John should represent me, but that I am establishing the new tradition of sex equality between chiefs, and I cannot therefore accept their kind invitation to be a spectator, adding that I am sure they will appreciate my position as understandingly as I appreciate theirs.' It was understandable for Dame Flora to cherish the genuine interest of Scottish Americans, but it was far less easy to understand how she could enjoy the unpalatable and occasionally vulgar display of phoney adulation to which she was now subjected, but she did. 'I found it most amusing because it was so undeserved,' she explained, and added, 'it interested me to hear the American women discuss their housekeeping problems and I admired the comfort and luxury in which they lived. I was fascinated to see their husbands conveyed across the golf-course in their mechanical cars.'

In Washington, Dame Flora was received by the Senate and at Fort Ord she was the guest of General Robert B. MacLure and took the salute as the officers and men of the 63rd Infantry Regiment, in full-dress uniform, marched past and provided a glittering display in her honour. 'Fort Ord really was an unbelievable experience,' she wrote afterwards. 'The twins were assigned to different companies and John returned unable to say anything except, "I have fired a bazooka. I have fired a live bazooka." It is a terrific place—35,000 troops in training for sixteen weeks. The training is very severe and thorough; the feeding, accommodation and equipment superb. There is very little I have not seen—barracks, Naafis, recreation rooms, classrooms, dining-rooms, living accommodation for officers, married quarters, an adorable school, and everything else you can think of. The Presidio (administration buildings) and the Army Language School are in Monterey, and the MacLures themselves live in a small, almost self-supporting, house. The language school has 148 Russian teachers and before the course is finished the pupil will have been to each one of them and will find himself able to talk to all kinds of people in every part of Russia. There was a dinner for 1,200 in our honour and an Army pipe band from San Francisco.'

In the midst of her success, Dame Flora did not forget her ordinary clansmen. She travelled to Louisiana to be the guest of a small boy who had written a letter addressed to the Lord High Justice of Skye, saying he would like to know something about his Clan. Dame Flora had corresponded with Bill MacLeod* ever since, and she now became close friends with his family.

In October 1953, 300 MacLeods from North and South Carolina gathered to form a Clan Society. Their example was repeated right across America in the wake of Dame Flora's journey, and thirteen societies were formed and later incorporated into an official Clan MacLeod Society of America under the Presidency of John H. MacLeod. It was the greatest organisational success the clan had ever enjoyed and was to give the United States the largest membership in the world. Dame Flora was the feudal figurehead who ruled her empire with the affection of a mother and the expertise of a politician. Her clan was, by and large, a classless society, but certain clansmen stood out above others. John MacLeod of Newport Beach, California, was one of a large family born in a croft on the island of Bernera, Harris. He had left for North America at the age of seventeen and eventually risen to become the founder and manager of Macco, one of America's great construction companies. He and his wife were Dame Flora's hosts in Los Angeles, and the rock upon which the fortunes of the MacLeods in California depended. Angus and Mary MacLeod of Dallas, Texas, both successful business administrators, collectors of fine antiques and objects d'art, and the owners of a beautiful house called *Dunvegan,* in which Dame Flora was often a guest, provided another pillar of support in the south. The Sayre MacLeods of New York and the Lamar MacLeods of Chicago were among others of wealth and influence who in their turn provided a backbone for clan activity; but it was a young man, Donald B. MacLeod, who gave it the solid organisation which made survival and growth possible. He gave it an address—a box number at Grand Park Central Station—and he gathered round him the enthusiastic workers and organised the activities of the new association. He lived in a

* Later a State Senator

tiny house in Greenwich Village, which he called *Casa Dunvegan,* and there he welcomed travelling clansmen with traditional hospitality. In the first flush of enthusiasm following Dame Flora's visit, John H. MacLeod launched a membership drive to enroll 50,000 MacLeods in the American Society and a bi-annual clan newsletter was instituted, edited first by Maybelle Luman, and later by Margaret Zerwick, to keep members informed.

Dame Flora returned to Dunvegan elated with the efforts of her journey. Other clan chiefs had travelled abroad but none had achieved such impressive results. Within weeks of her return her spirits were damped by news which seriously affected the castle. The roof was in a dangerous condition. In the fierce Hebridean storms, water had seeped through the outer harling and penetrated deeply, rotting the beams and endangering the very fabric of the building. It was a bitter blow, following within fourteen years of the fire, and making the future of the castle uncertain at a moment when its fame was world-wide. Dame Flora was driven into a state of real anxiety. Her concern was for the future. A Labour Government had convinced her that large estates would be penalised, and she had a continual fear of death duties or even confiscation. In 1947 she had approached the National Trust in Edinburgh with a view to entrusting the castle to them, while safeguarding the rights of the family to live in it. She rejected the idea. Later she considered forming a clan trust, with each trustee a president of the Associated Clan Societies, but the idea was not pursued as the family was against it.

Dame Flora had always set herself against begging for money, either in the clan magazine or on her tours abroad. She knew it would be fatal to the clan fellowship for which she cared so much. She paid her own travelling expenses, which over the years amounted to several thousand pounds, and accepted the lavish hospitality and generous gifts of her clansmen and friends, but she remained bitterly hostile to the concept of fund-raising, and when in later years some clan chiefs made journeys for these purposes, she wrote angrily, 'Let it be remembered that it can be counter-productive, when important commercial interests promote great tours in order to exploit the Highlands. Highlanders may be poor, but they are proud'.

It was, therefore, an unexpected and astonishing surprise
to Dame Flora when in 1954 the American MacLeods,
having heard the news of the castle repairs, formed the
Dunvegan Foundation. 'Gaelic history tells us of the
"calpa",' wrote John H. MacLeod to American clansmen, 'a
tax paid by clansmen to the chief of the clan to help him
maintain his headquarters and to uphold the dignity of the
chiefship. To ensure the continued occupancy of the castle by
John the younger, chief-designate, and his successors,
MacLeods the world over are binding together to share the
expense of repair, maintenance and upkeep of the castle, its
gardens and surrounding grounds.'

It was a brave idea and one in which Dame Flora herself
could hardly believe. 'I still think I shall wake to find it a
glorious dream,' she wrote, 'for I have carried with me night
and day for many years a gnawing anxiety about the future.
How could it be possible to hold fast to Dunvegan and
preserve it for the clan in the teeth of heavy taxation? Is it
really possible that clansmen who live thousands of miles
from Dunvegan and from one another should yet in dreams
behold the Hebrides and conceive it their privilege, their
pride and their pleasure to maintain the castle with which
their name has been associated for 700 unbroken years?'
Dame Flora's tour of America had made it not only possible
but also a reality.

Australia and New Zealand

IN 1953 DAME FLORA HAD WRITTEN, 'I AM THE MOST AMBITIOUS woman in the world and I ask myself whether next year I cannot visit Australia and New Zealand.' Following her reception in America and the response it evoked, she viewed the countries of the southern hemisphere as a challenge that must urgently be met. 'I must hurry, hurry, hurry,' she wrote. This urgency was in no way because of her age or because she felt time was running out, but because of an innate sense of timing. 'If there is such a tide of support in America,' she wrote, 'where Scottish descendants compose only a small proportion of the total population, I am convinced that in the Dominions, where the population is largely Highland, it will be overwhelming.'

Dame Flora viewed her campaign as a general might view a battlefield. 'What would you do if you had to invade a continent?' she asked herself, and this passion to rally the clan now became the deepest ambition of her life. 'We MacLeods are entering upon a new chapter in our history,' she wrote, 'and are pioneers in a movement which may well extend to other clans and even, dare we hope, lead to a rebirth of the Highlands.'

She was so captured by this vision that in September 1954, within nine months of her return from America, and leaving Joan as her representative at the castle, she was on her way to the Antipodes. Dame Flora had no contacts with Australia, but her clansman, Bruce MacLeod, lived in Sydney and was a member of the Edinburgh Society. 'I wrote to him,' she said later. 'At that time he held a modest position in the Bank of Australia and New Zealand and was proud of being a descendent of Sir Rory of Talisker, the senior cadet branch of the chiefs of Dunvegan, whose family had emigrated to Australia in the early eighteenth century and played an

151

important part in its history. Bruce MacLeod advertised in a Sydney newspaper asking clansmen who would be interested in my visit to meet him. Seventy came, each subscribed £1, and the plan was launched.'

On this journey Dame Flora was accompanied by Hopeton Kneeland, the twenty-four-year-old daughter of Dr. Yale Kneeland of New York. Hopeton was an ideal sparring partner for Dame Flora. Throughout the journey she kept a complete diary which would have done Boswell credit, and which was frequently and perhaps suitably unprintable.

Dame Flora's arrival in Australia marked the first visit of a Highland chief to that country since the war and was, therefore, of great public interest. The one Clan MacLeod Society which existed in Australia was founded in 1912 at Melbourne, but was no longer active. This presented Dame Flora with the challenge she required. She apparently blossomed under the exhausting regime of a clan tour, which now took on an established pattern and varied only with local colour and tradition. On October 2nd, 1954, having visited clansmen in Hong Kong and Manila, she landed in Sydney. 'We arrived about midnight,' she wrote, 'after such a journey and such outstanding welcomes. The airport crowds continue to amaze and thrill me.' From the smallest township to the great cities, people stood at their windows or in the street to watch Dame Flora go by, often marching disciplined and erect behind a pipe band. Every Sunday it became part of the ceremonial for her to read the lesson in church, and clansmen in their thousands came to hear those clear, ringing tones proceed from behind an enormous lectern, which frequently left her entirely hidden.

The press conferences continued to be occasions at which she excelled, and news of her visit reached a wide public. 'This illustrates the marvellous loyalty and enthusiasm of the clan,' she wrote. 'A young man called MacLeod Robertson flew 1,400 miles from a huge sheep station in the north-east, which he has not left for six years, to see me. Papers only arrive once in three weeks. That is how he heard somewhat belatedly of my visit—left all and came. He manages 800,000 acres with a staff of twenty-seven whites and eighty Aborigines. Most of the men work in the bush, rain or shine, sleeping on the ground with a tarpaulin in case of need.'

In New South Wales one thousand envelopes were

addressed to every MacLeod on the electoral roll, notifying them of the visit of their chief. By the time she arrived, a new society of 500 members had been formed, which afterwards rose to 750, and an Adelaide newspaper reported in bold headlines, 'Mother of thousands wins Adelaide hearts.' The train which made the all-day journey from Armadale to Sydney, normally called the Northern Table-land Daylight Express, was renamed the Tartan Express on the day Dame Flora travelled on it. It stopped eleven times on the twelve-hour journey. 'This is the most intriguing train trip I have ever taken,' wrote Hopeton from on board, 'and every time the train stops a horde of Scots-Australians dashes up, sometimes with bagpipes and at others with just the town mayor, and for the allotted time—usually about two minutes—Dame Flora shakes hands, kisses babies, poses for photographers and waves a ten-foot yellow tartan sash from the carriage door. She has been given so many bouquets of flowers that the train hostess has filled two iceboxes and is working on a third. You cannot imagine what this trip is like, but one lady told me last night that in shaking hands with Dame Flora she felt as if she had met the Queen herself "for she is the queen of the clan, you know." '

Dame Flora was physically strong, never suffered from travel weariness, and invariably arrived in a place feeling as fresh as a Highland morning. It was incomprehensible to her that an American of twenty-four should not do the same. She was considerably annoyed when Hopeton arrived in Sydney completely exhausted and retired to bed with a cold. 'Hopeton is in bed today,' she wrote to Joan. 'I don't believe in lots of aspirin and mysterious green pills. I don't think she has a temperature and I think I have taken the greatest care of her. I am hampered by not understanding American methods and techniques. She is so charming and completely glamorous in the eyes of the clan that she must get well. The success of our visit is really breath-taking. They had a garden-party yesterday raising £2,000, and turned away applications for the evening reception and for the farewell banquet.' To commemorate Dame Flora's visit to Sydney, a MacLeod Week was held and subsequently became an annual event in the Sydney calendar.

At every *ceilidh* and at every tea-party Dame Flora's message seldom varied. 'Mac is the Gaelic word for son,' she

would say over and over again. 'Clan is the Gaelic word for
children. We say we are the children of the son of Leod. We
must be members of a family.' This approach never failed. She
was an ideal mother for her family of Australians and she
brought them a gaiety, dignity and world perspective for
which they loved her. In turn, she was intensely loyal to them.
Bruce MacLeod now became the leading figure in Australian
clan affairs. He and his wife were socially gifted, and Dame
Flora so much appreciated the arrangements they had made
for her that she called specially on the manager of the bank
where Bruce MacLeod worked to tell him her high opinion of
her clansman.

In complete contrast to the affluent Americans, most of the
Australian clansmen lived simply, and often moved out of
their own rooms to accommodate Dame Flora. 'Of course, it
is all very different from America, where we lived in high
luxury with plutocrats,' she wrote. 'Our experiences have
been in a very different world here. Apart from half-a-dozen
completely enchanting visits to sheep and cattle stations with
folk of our own sort—immensely energetic and hard-
working—we have lived in small suburban homes and
associated with our hosts and their passionately loyal friends.
These homes range from great comfort, though usually
insufficiently provided with sanitary accommodation, (all the
work being done by the hostess, as almost quite literally
nobody has any domestic help) to the simplest.' Hopeton
was, as always, more explicit. 'The apartment which adjoined
the wash-house in the garden,' she wrote of one home,
'contained in addition to the W.C. a stepladder, five old tyres,
a pile of newspapers, a lawn-mower and three old shoes.'
Dame Flora did not mind. 'I think it is really a very good
thing to be living as we do,' she wrote, 'for, after all, the
influence and strength of the clan depends on numbers, and
each one of seemingly unimportant contacts may produce a
series of reactions. Launching the clan here on the right foot
is terribly important.'

Dame Flora perhaps enjoyed most of all her visits to the
Australian farms and countryside. 'The rural areas are
tremendously Scottish,' she wrote, 'and quite literally
MacLeods travel sometimes many hundreds of miles just to
shake hands. Many of them are sentimentalists with tears in
their eyes and husky throats. At Bendigo a man brought his

two tiny daughters ninety miles to an evening party and returned home the same night.' In Queensland Dame Flora was the guest of the MacLeod Walkers at Glenlyon. 'We learned the terrifying risks of the sheep-farmer when the rains fail,' she wrote; 'vast burned paddocks and empty water-tanks. We made a visit to the great wool store where we watched buyers from all over the world appraise the value and then buy at incredible speed and good prices.'

At every stage of the tour Dame Flora visited her elderly clansmen in hospital or the young clansmen in school. On one such occasion, with children and parents in their Sunday best, she horrified the crowd by inviting them all to sit on the floor, and then proceeded to do the same herself before launching into a story about the Fairy Flag. At a glittering evening reception when the electricity failed, she told Highland stories in the dark to the extreme delight of her audience who groaned with indignation when the lights came on. In Adelaide a champagne dinner was followed by a reception at the Royal Caledonian Society, and the BBC decided to film it for British television. Dame Flora was exceptionally keen on her television appearances and invariably performed well. 'Bands and dancers as guards of honour,' wrote Hopeton. 'Cameras trained on the first Scottish chief to visit Australia and the silver high-heeled slippers wobbled violently, causing her to lurch to one side, not the champagne but the vanity which caused her to wish to appear taller.' Dame Flora found her feet and proceeded to captivate her audience by telling jokes and cutting a fifty-pound cake in the exact shape of Dunvegan Castle.

On November 16th, she arrived in Western Australia. 'Perth really is a heavenly city,' she wrote, 'partly because of its huge Swan River and the adjacent sea, partly because it is not too large, and full of gardens and parks. One of my first exploits was to place a wreath on the cenotaph (I have done this many times now) which is stately and simple in itself and horrifyingly impressive because of the many thousands of Western Australians killed in the First World War—each name cut in bronze on tablets which ring the base of the building under cover. I shall never forget the impression this memorial made on me with column after column bearing the names of the young dead, a whole generation sacrificed from this vast, sparsely populated state.' Dame Flora was visibly moved whenever afterwards she spoke of this occasion. They were tears not just of sentiment, but of gratitude that young people, so many thousands of miles from Britain, should have sacrificed their lives for the nation she loved.

However, it was the week in Canberra which gave her possibly the greatest pleasure of her tour because it provided the political interest which was largely missing from the intensely Scottish gatherings she attended, and politics was a subject never far from her heart. She and Hopeton were received by the Prime Minister, Sir Robert Menzies. 'We were interviewed for half-an-hour by the P.M.' wrote Hopeton. 'Great fun, and then promenaded round the House by his charming little wife, Dame Pattie. We were shown an original Magna Carta, a hundred years younger than No. 1, and Captain Cook's diary describing the discovery of Botany Bay.' The next day, after attending Question Time and tea for lady senators, Dame Flora was the guest of honour at a dinner given by the Speaker, the Hon. Archie Cameron, and attended by the Prime Minister and ten other eminent Scottish-Australian statesmen. 'As their political views as well as their religions differed widely,' wrote Hopeton, 'conversation was like walking a tight rope. It could not have been more fun. The Prime Minister said that all sorts of enemies were dining together peacefully, thinly disguised as Scots.' Dame Flora walked the tight rope with considerable poise. She was at her exuberant best when surrounded by men who spoke knowledgably on political subjects. 'The dinner was so extraordinary that I am overpowered when I think of it,' she wrote afterwards to Joan. 'We were sixteen, including twelve of the most distinguished members of both Houses. It ended with a speech from our host who called on the Prime Minister and President of the Senate to propose and second the toast of my health, and they did so in terms which overwhelmed me.'

Dinner conversations in Australia did not often rise to the level of Canberra. 'I wish we could hear more real big world talk,' she wrote. She frequently complained about the lack of international news and was infuriated that her favoured *Economist* reached her several weeks late. It was a paradox that a woman who was so dependant upon hearing the latest political reports from London should at the same time devote her energies to rallying a clan united by an ancient heritage, whose eyes were, therefore, predominantly focussed on the past; but she did not find it incongruous. 'I am a passionate believer in the British Commonwealth,' she explained. 'It is my conviction that Scotland has contributed more than any other country to its creation, and Scottish pioneers have settled in Canada, Australia and New Zealand, bringing with them a common language, united by a common love of the mother country, and endowed with a courage and resilience of which their descendants should be proud. I believed my clan movement was a valuable element in sustaining loyalty to Britain and binding people to their past and to each other. In return I was convinced it would benefit Scotland.' In 1954 these convictions proved exactly right and Clan MacLeod enjoyed a great upsurge of support. Five new Australian Societies were formed as a direct result of Dame Flora's visit.

In 1953 at Invercargill, New Zealand, the Southland Clan MacLeod Association was formed and although not the largest it was the first of its kind in the country. Some New Zealanders, including Alison MacGibbon of Christchurch, were life members of the parent Society in Edinburgh, and after the reports of Dame Flora's tour of the United States, had written, urging her to visit their country. However, it was a remarkable clansman, Malcolm MacLeod of Napier who finally arranged Dame Flora's first tour of New Zealand in 1954. Malcolm MacLeod was a Lewis man, a post-office engineer, with a host of friends and relations scattered across the country, and a house decorated with enough tartan to put Queen Victoria's Balmoral in the shade. He had an undisputed flair for organisation, and the arrangements for Dame Flora's visit, which was to cover both North and South Islands, were left in his hands.

On December 2nd, Dame Flora launched her New Zealand tour with a visit to Christchurch. 'We arrived here to find the customary pipes, Press and welcome from fifty clansmen,' she wrote, 'and such a green, smiling, happy, radiant, prosperous country—a town of parks and gardens and flowers and water with big hills which can be seen at the end of streets, and sufficiently small to make you feel you can walk into the country if you want. You will gather that I have already lost my heart. One has the feeling that New Zealand has arrived and is content, whereas Australia is vast and fighting to conquer its vastness and achieve the potentiality of power and greatness. And this reflects itself in the people here who seem serene and happy. We are living with a family of only two—Mr. and Mrs. McGibbon—in a comfortable, two-storeyed house with a lovely garden. The clan garden-party yesterday was perfectly organised and the day was perfect. In the morning we drove up hills two thousand feet high and drove along a saddle-back looking down on the estuary and port of Lyttleton, with the sea a different blue from any I have ever seen. On the other side we could see the town of Christchurch and the verdant plain which produces their famous mutton and Canterbury lamb. The plain itself ends in their southern alps, rugged volcanic mountains seven thousand feet high. The past became strangely alive as we imagined the immigrants who landed at Lyttleton staggering up the steep hill carrying all their belongings.' It was a suitable beginning for a tour which was to relive the past. The entire journey throughout New Zealand was accomplished by car, and only once, when she crossed Cook's Straits, did Dame Flora abandon her drivers. These were all either clansmen or friends of Malcolm MacLeod, and the memory of their service is preserved by a small cross made from some of the woods for which New Zealand is famous. On each piece of wood the name of a driver was carved, and at the end of one of the cross-beams the wood was charred, whilst at the end of the other Malcolm placed a rag stained with his own blood. This represented the fiery cross with which Highlanders were summoned to war in the past.

Dame Flora attended a *ceilidh* at Waipu in the far north, the settlement of Norman MacLeod, the centenary of whose departure she had celebrated in Nova Scotia in 1951. The only survivors of that great emigration were two old ladies of 102 and 98, Mrs. Jessie Mackenzie and Mrs. Joanna Macrae. Dame Flora met them both. 'It really is impressive,' she wrote, 'to talk to people who actually lived through the migration. One was born on the little ship, and the other left at the age of six on one of the later boats. She could remember something of the Old Cape Breton, the voyage and the landing—a little girl she had evidently knocked off the swing they had on board, and the girl thought she had done it on purpose. Funny little bits and pieces. They had a cup of tea at the baker's on landing. There was this baker's shop and a butcher and a doctor, and her grandfather had come out two years earlier and had built a house.'

At Gore Dame Flora stayed with Jim MacLeod, another of her wartime guests at the castle, and later the President of the Clan Society of New Zealand. It was here she attended a children's picnic and came third in the grandmothers' race, for which, in spite of all her protests, she was awarded the first prize. She was seventy-six, and a lady in the crowd remarked loudly that she had the figure and ankles of a girl. It was fortunate she had. 'This has been an extremely interesting and strenuous week,' she wrote, 'and I have just emerged from the fifth consecutive night in a different bed. We spent two nights on a launch at Tauranga and were wafted on a stormy sea to Moor Island where swordfish are found. We were transferred to a swordfish-hunting boat and harnessed to a mighty heavy rod with base attached to the deck, and roped into a seat and so trawled assiduously with no result. Yesterday morning I witnessed top-dressing from the air and flew in the tiny Cessna plane which does it and afterwards was taken on an aerial 'See the Country' flight. Old Mr MacLeod believes this fertilising from the air would be the making of Skye, and he knows Skye. Expense, of course, is the problem. Every inch of this amazing Manawatu country, hills and valleys, is treated, and the farmers cannot say enough for it. In the afternoon we had a garden-party in Palmerston, and a crammed Scottish Society's "do" in the evening. It is wonderful that this venture should so much have caught the public imagination and be reckoned so highly.'

The adulation was intense. At one church service the minister in his sermon compared Dame Flora to Jesus Christ, which prompted her to write, 'It is an accepted convention that I am of enormous importance, a leader, an inspiration, an example and a marvellous speaker. And now you know.' This undiluted diet of praise which at first may have seemed exhilarating was not easy to live with. 'I dread the thought of two speeches today, for I feel myself getting stale,' she wrote. It was not difficult to understand why. The combined tour of Australia and New Zealand lasted for nearly six months from September 25th, 1954 until March 1st, 1955, and Dame Flora worked without a break, often in severe heat, and making new friends at every town and village. Those who took part in a single section of the journey cannot easily have understood the physical stamina it must have required to complete the course. By the end, Dame Flora depended heavily on being revived by occasions which particularly interested her. At Helensville she received a traditional Maori welcome. 'The evening was undoubtedly one of the most colourful of our whole tour,' she wrote. 'The Haere-Mai was followed by Poi dances and hakas, and action songs mingled with our own Scottish music. Part of the ceremony was that the chief came and laid a stick (tiki) at my feet and I had to pick it up. This happened three times and then we touched noses in a ceremonial manner. Maoris have tribes and Scots have clans and both have chiefs, and so we felt very close. Chief Mosan was good enough to say that rain was the sign of a great chief. It was rather wet and I was very grateful to him.'

At Napier, Dame Flora was the guest of her famous clansmen. 'This is a modest home—Malcolms, she wrote, 'the great organiser to whom I owe this tour. Living conditions are excellent and I think almost completely normal. There is first-rate meat everywhere, usually hoggett, which they esteem better than lamb, which is what the British market prefers. There is always a roast, usually cold at lunch and hot at night. In most houses grace is said. Today morning tea of 280, a broadcast, dinner and dance tonight and farewell broadcast tomorrow. It has been wonderful but it is time to go.'

The Clan MacLeod Society of New Zealand, founded in 1953, was suitably launched and within three years Dame Flora had succeeded in bringing to birth a clan movement which now encircled the world.

The First Clan Parliament

ON AUGUST 10TH, 1956 DAME FLORA'S TWIN GRANDSONS CAME of age. To celebrate the event and to repay the hospitality she had received from her clansmen overseas, she decided to open the doors of Dunvegan Castle for a week from August 11th to August 16th. This was a coming-of-age party for staff, tenants and friends, but it also gave the opportunity to invite clansfolk from abroad to join with those in Britain in acclaiming John as heir of Dunvegan and the future chief. Dame Flora decided that it should include a Clan Parliament. This parliament was an innovation, the first of its kind to be held in clan history and, therefore, necessarily an experiment. It was perhaps unsuitable that the word 'parliament' was chosen, for none of the delegates who crossed the oceans to be present at the first gathering was elected or even delegated by his clan Society. They were instead all dedicated MacLeods and, most important of all, admirers of their seventy-eight-year-old chief. She was by now their close friend and the common link which bound together a diverse collection of people who shared the same name and blood and possessed a common heritage, but the majority of whom had never been in Skye or, indeed, met each other.

Dame Flora had long been aware of the importance of the castle to her clan movement, and stories of its history had been told at *ceilidhs* and gatherings on all her journeys. It was where her heart lay and where she returned after her long absences abroad, to the comparative peace of her own room, her correspondence and her friends. Perhaps the greatest pleasure of her life was being able to entertain those she loved at her castle, where she was indeed queen and where she always resolved to make each visitor feel this was the most memorable event of his life. She planned, therefore, to entertain her clansmen to a week of unsurpassed festivity.

The preparations for this historic week were detailed and thorough. The previous two years had been difficult ones for the castle. Damage to the roof was far more extensive than had first been realised, and was referred to by Dame Flora as 'the castle nightmare'. It was a moment when Dame Flora had needed professional advice. She had not taken it. Employing a building firm from Edinburgh, she too much enjoyed climbing the ladders and encouraging the workmen herself to appoint a clerk of works. It was a decision for which she was to pay dearly and which she later described as 'my disastrous failure'. The anxious weeks during which crumbling cross-beams had been lifted from the roof by giant cranes were now over. Dame Flora had watched the operation closely. At one point, a beam had slipped and hung perilously balanced over the dining-room, threatening to crash and destroy everything beneath it. In the moments of panic which ensued one of the castle staff saw Dame Flora run and stand, pale and silent, before the Fairy Flag until the danger was past. This solemn visit to the Flag on her arrival and departure from the castle was observed by Dame Flora through many years and often imposed upon members of the family in a manner which one of them described as 'something akin to spontaneous religious emotion'.

The problems of financing the initial repair had been immense, but they had been resolved. The new copper roofing which now covered the castle was light and considered modern and ideal, but it had never before been tried under the weather conditions which prevailed in Skye. However by 1956, and in time for the first Clan Parliament, the work was finished and appeared satisfactory.

Dame Flora now turned her mind to the organisation of her celebration week. She was totally unskilled in practical gifts, and, having never cooked in her life, she found the ordering of stores and the planning of menus an anxiety. By instinct a Victorian, she believed in serving large quantities of food and having plenty left over. She once ordered a crate of thirty-six dozen eggs to feed four guests for a fortnight. The kitchen staff was eventually reduced to selling them off in the local village shops. She disliked old soap in a bathroom, and every guest was treated to a new tablet. There was the problem of finding extra staff for the castle at the height of the summer tourist season, and of accommodating her guests in the local hotels and boarding-houses. She enjoyed personal power to such a degree, and had organised her own life for so long, that she found it virtually impossible to delegate responsibility to others and even harder to trust them with it when she had. Those who worked closely with her, including her family and most loyal castle staff, had to accept without complaint sudden changes of plan about which they were seldom consulted. They did so because Dame Flora was an enthusiast and a charmer, able to pour oil on troubled waters and to call on deep wells of loyalty in those around her. Although she insisted on giving her guests the greatest comfort, she herself lived in comparative discomfort—a tiny bedroom with a bathroom some distance away, up several stairs.

Some weeks after the arrangements had been completed, Dame Flora had been told that Her Majesty the Queen and other members of the Royal Family were making one of their annual cruises up the west coast of Scotland, aboard the Royal Yacht *Britannia*. After landing at Kyleakin and paying an official visit to Portree on Monday, August 13th, they would like to drive to Dunvegan Castle for lunch. This was the same day as the coming-of-age banquet and the castle would be full of clansmen. As her personal guests at the castle, Dame Flora had already invited two clan members from Canada, two from Australia, two from New Zealand, and John H. MacLeod from America. She now shared her life so completely with her clansmen that it seemed inconceivable to her to think they should not be present at the royal lunch. Dame Flora, therefore, asked and was given permission for her house-guests to be included. A week of unparalleled family celebration now had the honour of a royal occasion.

Newspapers from all over the world were naturally eager to report the event. *Life* magazine sent two photographers to cover the week, and Dame Flora entertained them, together with other journalists, at the castle. Her reputation with the Press was excellent and she took great trouble to preserve it. Clansmen arrived and found their way to the various hotels within reach of the castle. Transport had been carefully provided, together with an agenda of the week's events. It was an exciting moment, the culmination for Dame Flora of many years' work and incessant travelling.

On Saturday, August 11th, 1956, the week opened with a children's party for tenants and clansmen at the castle. 146 children of all ages assembled at the castle gates and were piped down the drive to be received at the front door by Dame Flora herself. Children responded to her as they might to a fairy godmother, with a mixture of awe and excitement. She never failed to compliment a child on a pretty frock, or to give credit for a well-mannered handshake, and it went a long way to create the family spirit of which she was so proud. On Sunday, dressed in her tartan, and accompanied by her family, she made her ritual one-mile walk to and from Duirinish parish church for the two services for which she played the organ. The church was packed with visiting clansmen and that evening she entertained them all in the castle drawing-room where she outlined the week's programme and gave her own inimitable account of the castle's history and its treasures. It was a memorable evening for those who had made the journey of a lifetime to be there.

On Monday, August 13th, Her Majesty the Queen, accompanied by Their Royal Highnesses Princess Margaret and the Duke of Edinburgh, were entertained to a simple and entirely Skye-produced meal, prepared and served by the castle staff under the careful eye of Charles Heron, Dame Flora's butler and a friend of the family for many years. It was the first time a reigning monarch had visited Dunvegan since King James V anchored his fleet at Portree and was subsequently alleged to have been entertained by the chief to a feast on MacLeod's Table Mountain. After lunch the royal guests were taken to the drawing-room where the banqueting tables for the evening were already set. Rory Mor's horn, traditionally quaffed by the young chief at his coming-of-age 'without setting down, (putting down) or falling down', was placed in readiness for the feast. This, together with the Fairy Flag and other castle treasures, was shown to the royal party, who then visited the bottleneck dungeon before being taken by Dame Flora to meet her visiting clansmen in the gun-court and to plant commemorative trees in the round garden.

It was only by chance that this royal visit coincided with the Clan Parliament, but it was perhaps another piece of castle magic. Clan delegates, who had already felt themselves swept into the spirit and beauty of Skye, now felt themselves royally honoured. As the young Queen walked slowly down to the castle jetty with Dame Flora to board the launch which was to take her out to *Britannia* at anchor in the deeper waters of the loch, several hundred people clustered on the rugged shore to cheer her. As the launch moved away, the Queen, a solitary figure, stood in the stern and waved farewell, and suddenly from the crowd there floated across the water the haunting music of 'Will ye no come back again'. Dame Flora, an erect, silver-haired figure, stood beside her grandson and heir and watched the launch pass out of sight. Dunvegan Castle had been singularly honoured and for those clansmen from small places many thousands of miles away, it was a deep emotional experience and one which they owed, like so many other important things in their lives, to Dame Flora.

That evening in the castle drawing-room, the keep of ancient times where the MacLeods had feasted for generations, the great banquet took place. Clansmen enjoyed salmon and venison together in the spirit of conviviality which centuries before had been part of that same room. At the end of the meal, in the presence of family and clan, and to a battery of photographers' flashlights, John quaffed the horn which contained a bottle and two-thirds of claret. He had practised in advance with water and finally with claret and had torn out the false lining, inserted by his grandmother, for he was determined to do what he had promised. He quaffed the horn impeccably and the united clan declared that he had proved his manhood and was indeed worthy to be called a chief. It was the climax of Dame Flora's dream. She, who had so much longed for a son, had found in her grandson a male heir, making the future of the castle and the clan secure.

The Clan Parliament itself was held the following day. With Dame Flora in the chair, issues were discussed which ranged from the organisation of Clan Societies to pen-friends and personal and circular letters from the chief. These were hardly world-shaking parliamentary issues, but it was their very parochialism which, although uninteresting to those outside the clan, gave the Society a practical programme for the future. The most important issue on the agenda was unquestionably the preservation of the castle. Dame Flora submitted to Parliament a balance sheet of the repairs, which revealed that out of a total sum of £32,000 expended, £15,000 had come from the Historic Buildings Trust, £4,600 from clansmen, and nearly £10,000 from her own resources. leaving an outstanding debt of only £2,500. She told the assembled delegates that if the castle ever had to be sold she wanted the branches of the Clan Society to be given an opportunity to buy it. She read a statement which she admitted was not binding in law, but which she hoped could hardly be disregarded. 'I wish to place on record,' she said, 'my earnest wish that this historic association which has existed for over 700 years between Dunvegan Castle and the Clan MacLeod should not be brought to an end. If it should ever become necessary for the heir who succeeds to Dunvegan Castle in terms of my trust disposition and settlement to sell or dispose of Dunvegan Castle, that the Presidents for the time of the Clan MacLeod Societies in Scotland, England, Canada, Australia, New Zealand and the United States of America shall be given an opportunity of acquiring or purchasing the castle at a price to be mutually agreed, and that the said Presidents shall on behalf of the members of Clan MacLeod form a trust for the preservation and upkeep of the castle and for its use for the benefit of the members of Clan MacLeod.'

The most important feature of the first Clan Parliament was without question not the speeches or the debates which followed, but the social contacts made between overseas clansmen. Five national Clan Societies, who had hitherto never known each other, were welded into an international body during that week, and this silent transformation made the MacLeods into an organisation of strength. This was partly achieved by the atmosphere of the castle itself, partly by the expeditions to Borreraig and Trumpan, and, in later years, a journey to the Outer Islands, partly the sense of sharing in a common past, which had been emphasised by the royal visit, but above all by the personality of Dame Flora herself. The week ended with a garden-party, *ceilidhs* and a firework display. Nothing of great importance may have been decided, but its undoubted social success led to a decision to hold a Parliament at Dunvegan every three years. Although the first one was numerically the smallest, no subsequent Parliament at Dunvegan could compete with it. The clan was then at its zenith and perhaps in her inner thoughts Dame Flora knew it, but it was something she would never admit.

Dame Flora's life now took on an added interest. She had not only her clan journeys but also a Parliament to plan for at regular intervals, and one had no sooner finished before she was preparing for the next. As the years passed she referred to each Parliament as her last. It never was. Circular letters poured forth from her to all corners of the world. Writing annually in the clan magazine, opening with the words, 'My dear clan family', and ending, 'Hold Fast, your friend, Flora MacLeod of MacLeod', rather in the style of a mother to her children, she urged her clansmen to visit Skye, encouraged those who wanted improvements in the agenda before Parliament, and advised her world family on topical political issues. To the distress of Scottish Nationalists, who had long hoped to include her among their supporters, she remained a convinced Tory. 'To me Scottish Nationalism should mean devolution emphatically "Yes", Home Rule and an independent parliament emphatically "No",' she wrote. The Clan Parliament, whose delegates she hopefully referred to as M.P.s, met at Dunvegan in 1959, 1962, 1965, 1968 and 1971 and evoked an ever greater response from clansmen. The agenda was not much changed, but in 1965 a group of younger MacLeods met separately in the north room of the castle and became known as the North Room Group (N.R.G.—Energy). To these Dame Flora gave her particular attention, for she regarded them as future leaders. She hoped that delegates to Parliament would increasingly be less those who could afford the journey or enjoyed the trip than those who were of value to the organisation, if necessary supported financially from their national Society. 'I believe the clan has started a movement,' she wrote, 'which will mean something to the world. I foresee the day when we shall have an international Clan Parliament at Inverness with two representatives from every country and clan.'

Dame Flora had a vision, and like many people who dream dreams, she did not ask questions or observe the difficulties which lay in her path. She entertained relentlessly at the castle at a pace which made her guests feel like royalty and often left her family and staff exhausted. Her visitors were taken on boating expeditions and walks over the moors, and included in a welter of after-dinner games. Four-course meals, amply laced with whisky and wines, became the daily routine in the summer months, and for thousands of Scots who had never been visionaries Dame Flora became the vision and the dream, for she made each one of them feel he was the most important person in the world.

It is impossible to avoid asking the question why she did it. After the initial excitement of the first tours, the return visits inevitably lost some of the glamour and must often have been monotonous and exhausting. Although she had many devoted friends among her clansmen, the vast majority of those she met did not share her interests, and many did not regularly support the clan. The ceaseless diet of worship to which she was subjected no doubt had an effect. It was possible for her to describe one evening as 'a most festive and memorable occasion', and for Hopeton to write, 'Incredible illiterate speeches and toasts, alternated with items such as yodelling cowgirls, morose baritone, and our host tapping and shaking his stick covered with loose beer-bottle tops.' As a mother looks with blinkered eyes on her child, Dame Flora refused to look with anything but pride on her clan. While she spoke about family and fellowship, and no doubt for many these words had meaning, the feuds between her clansmen were often violent. She was once deposited at the bottom of her host's drive and compelled to walk to the front door because her clansman driver was not on speaking terms with his MacLeod neighbour. When confronted by such facts she would reply firmly, 'I do not wish to tarnish the image,' and like a ship riding out the storm she sailed on her way. She possessed an infinitely sympathetic and loving heart, which was given generously to her clan. One Scottish MacLeod serving a long prison sentence as a convicted murderer received regular letters from her throughout his years of imprisonment.

The clan tours to America continued almost annually after 1953, and culminated in a yearly celebration in February of her birthday in New York. This was a banquet she regularly attended until she was over ninety, and several hundred MacLeods across the States made it their Mecca, and assembled in her honour to the music of the pipes and the flow of good whisky. Young debutantes in white dresses were presented to their chief, in much the same way as British debutantes of the past were presented to their Queen. For a day before the banquet in an upstairs room of the Waldorf Astoria, the MacLeods still gather to discuss their affairs and debate their finances. It is a practice which has continued for nearly twenty years and, whatever disappointments and difficulties there may have been, the Americans have emerged at the end of it as the most successful Clan Society in the world. Their membership exceeds that of any other country, including the United Kingdom. Their delegations to the triennial Clan Parliaments are always the largest, and while this may be due to a combination of proximity to Scotland and the money to afford the fare, they have contributed to the image of the MacLeods as the most highly organised clan in the world.

Anthony MacLeod, whom Dame Flora first met in Manila, subsequently transferred his home to New York and became president of the Clan Society in 1967. He instituted the principle that a president should serve for three years—a principle which has been one of the reasons for the American success. He was succeeded in 1970 by C. Anderson MacLeod and it was during his period of office that the Dame Flora MacLeod Silver Trophy was presented by the clan to the best pibroch player at the Grandfather Mountain Games in North Carolina. In 1973, under the presidency of Milton MacLeod, the clan has endeavoured to increase its activity between the annual gatherings in New York.

Dame Flora places great faith in the MacLeods of America. She believes that their vision and the magnitude of their aims correspond with her own, and that in financial difficulties they would save the castle. She hopes that under their leadership the clan will survive and flourish even after her death. Perhaps with the magic of the Fairy Flag, upon which she is alleged to depend so greatly, this may be so. In 1970, when interviewed by the *New York Times* and asked about her clan, she replied, 'We are a family. We belong to one another. It is a living thing. We meet each other as friends. We visit in one another's homes. It is the fellowship which draws us together.' She then turned for support to a fellow MacLeod. 'Isn't it?' 'No,' he replied with obvious affection. 'It's you.'

After 1954 Dame Flora returned twice to visit her clansmen in Australia and New Zealand. These tours lasted six or seven weeks and were of necessity based on the provincial state capitals and their close proximity, with visits only to special friends. They were streamlined and conducted at high pressure. Within a decade Australia and New Zealand had changed rapidly. The sense of isolation which had permeated Australia disappeared as travel became easier. Trade with America and Japan increased, and in 1964 Dame Flora wrote, 'How Australia is growing in stature, and not only materially, for she is growing into a great nation.' Similar changes were apparent in New Zealand. Perhaps few of Dame Flora's clansmen realised as early as she did the need to modernise the organisation. 'Wonderful *ceilidhs* and loyalty and enthusiasm, but little growing life,' she wrote in 1964. 'Apart from social gatherings and travelling hospitalities, we must grow or stagnate and ultimately fade away. There is far too much dead wood at the top which re-elects itself regardless of service rendered and regardless of age and health.' On her last visit to the Antipodes in 1970 she vigorously pursued and encouraged young MacLeods to take responsibility for their clan and its future. She was delighted when New Zealand drew up a new constitution, providing for the election of a president alternately from North and South Island and a deputy to succeed him.

At home, the Clan Societies of Edinburgh and London provided a stable foundation for the whole clan movement. Although they were numerically smaller than the American Society, social contact between their members was far greater. Here Dame Flora was a friend as well as a chief, regarded with affection by clansmen, some of whom lived in Skye and knew both her and Scotland too well to idolise either. Among her neighbours at Dunvegan were the Norman MacLeods of Suardal, her cousins Charles and Caroline Stewart, the granddaughter of Norman Magnus 26th Chief, and Kenneth (Coinneach Mor) and Toni MacLeod of Harlosh. These clansmen among others were a real support to their chief at Clan Parliaments and throughout the year, and without them the reception of overseas MacLeods would have been more difficult.

Dame Flora felt genuinely at home with her clansmen of whatever distinction, but she had a particular regard for those who achieved fame. The Rt. Hon. Iain MacLeod was her guest at the castle and she followed his political career with passionate interest. She greatly admired him as Colonial Secretary and invited him to become Honorary Vice-President of the Edinburgh Society, but when in 1963 he began to write hostile articles in the *Spectator* about the Prime Minister, Sir Alec Douglas-Home, she was extremely annoyed. It was during this period that she was interviewed on French television and when asked 'Est-ce que vos sujets vous obéissent?' (Do your subjects obey you?) made it very clear in her reply that at that moment Iain MacLeod was 'un mauvais sujet'. Ultimately she relented and invited the MacLeods to stay with her at Dunvegan where all was forgiven. It was a bitter blow to her, and she felt to Britain, when in 1970 Iain MacLeod died, shortly after his appointment as Chancellor of the Exchequer in the new Conservative Government. She thereafter never allowed the slightest criticism of his performance to pass unchallenged in her hearing, and she treasured the letter he wrote her from 11 Downing Street shortly before his death. Lord MacLeod of Fuineray, Founder and first leader of the Iona Community, was another clansman similarly placed in her esteem.

Dame Flora always regretted that she could not speak Gaelic, but she says, 'I was either too old or too lazy to learn when Dunvegan became my home.' She supported piping in all parts of the English-speaking world and believed in the Mod as a great annual Scottish event, but she was a realist. 'Where Gaelic is the living language of the people,' she once wrote, 'it is right that it should be taught in the schools, but the area in which this remains true is increasingly restricted to the remoter Islands and Highlands. I am a convinced democrat, and consider it unfair that Gaelic should be required as a second language if another language is preferred by the parents of the pupils ... The simple music of past days, the rhythmic mouth music to which the people danced, the labour songs, whether reaping, milking or sowing, are gems of beauty in their own environment but become incongruous on a public platform.'

The children at the village school at Dunvegan found in Dame Flora their greatest admirer. Each year she gave prizes to the school and often presented them herself. Although her choice was usually classical books in English, the achievements of Highland children remained her pride and joy.

Throughout history the chiefs of MacLeod have been remembered for particular things. Some are remembered for an addition to the castle; others for a great victory on the field

of battle, or as patrons of Highland art and music. Norman
MacLeod, the 25th Chief, will long be remembered in Skye
for his devotion to her people during the potato famine.
Dame Flora, in her turn, has created a world-wide clan
organisation, the first of its kind, upon which other clans
have endeavoured to model themselves and which has
contributed to the binding together of the English-speaking
world.

Politics

BETWEEN THE AUTUMN OF 1958 AND THE FOLLOWING SPRING, three events took place in Dame Flora's life which were of particular importance. On November 20th, her youngest grandson, Patrick Wolrige Gordon, won a by-election in his home constituency of East Aberdeenshire and became, at the age of twenty-three, the youngest Member of Parliament in the House of Commons. Patrick was in his second year as an undergraduate at New College, Oxford. He had long wanted to make politics his career, an ambition encouraged by his grandmother, and East Aberdeenshire was the only constituency in which he wished to stand. When, in 1958, Sir Robert Boothby, who had represented the constituency for twenty-four years, was given a peerage, Patrick put his name forward and was subsequently adopted as the Conservative candidate.

The campaign which followed was an exciting one. A local Liberal, Mr. Maitland Mackie, was believed to present a strong challenge to the youthful Tory candidate who appeared vulnerable and inexperienced after the ebullient Boothby. Dame Flora hastened from Skye to support her grandson. She always loved a political fight and politics was part of the fabric of her life. The campaign like that of all by-elections, was the subject of comment in the national Press. Much to her annoyance Dame Flora was generally restrained from speaking in the campaign. Patrick acknowledged her unlimited gift for hitting headlines, but believed that once she got upon the hustings it would be extremely difficult to get her down. However, on one occasion it was agreed she should speak to a gathering of old-age pensioners. Dame Flora was over eighty and did not qualify for a pension herself, but even if she had she would on principle not have drawn one. 'I was convinced that the British Government made a great mistake in sharing all its privileges and pensions with rich and poor alike,' she said. 'I would have liked to have seen the rich receive much less and the poor receive much more. In an egalitarian society it is the poor who suffer.' It seemed unlikely, even accepting Dame Flora's radical views on the pension, that this meeting would give her the opportunity for a controversial speech. However, that morning a national newspaper had printed a large photograph of Field-Marshal Lord Montgomery going to draw his old-age pension. Dame Flora set off for the meeting with a head of steam. 'I felt very hot about it,' she wrote. 'It was not so long after the end of the war. The country was immensely grateful to Monty, and I would willingly have voted him a large sum of money from the nation as a thank-offering, but that Monty should advertise himself by going to draw an old-age pension, I thought repellent.' Dame Flora not only thought so but said so from the platform. It was a sensation. Montgomery was a national hero and the following morning Dame Flora's attack upon him appeared in banner headlines. It was a memorable performance and caused considerable amusement, but she was not invited to speak again.

On November 21st, when the poll was declared, Patrick had won East Aberdeenshire with a handsome majority. Dame Flora basked in reflected glory and went down to London to listen to his maiden speech. She always made a point of standing in the central lobby under the statue of her famous grandfather and dreaming ambitious dreams for her grandson. To her clansmen in her annual letter she wrote, 'I like to think M.P. transposed is P.M.' It remained her undying ambition.

It was at this moment that Joan Wolrige Gordon left Aberdeenshire where she had lived since 1926. Her eldest son, Robert, and his wife were returning to live at Esslemont, and she now decided to make her home with her mother at Dunvegan. For Dame Flora, who had probably felt closer to Joan than to any other member of her immediate family, it was a welcome decision. Since 1936 she had lived at the castle virtually on her own, and, although she had large numbers of visitors, they did not entirely compensate for the loneliness of day-to-day living. Joan was an able administrator, and had given valuable public service in Aberdeenshire. With her she brought experience which was to benefit both castle and clan at a time when it was greatly needed. It had been a bitter shock to discover during the winter months that the newly-installed copper roof at the castle was inadequate and that damp had once more invaded the walls and ceilings. Dame Flora had never asked her clansmen for help, and, only two years before, they had raised £5,000 for work which now proved to have been a failure. It was her mistake. She now knew to her cost that she should have taken professional advice, and when asked whether it was obstinacy or ignorance which had guided her, replied with humility, 'Both.' The copper roof was replaced by a new lead one, and without complaint Dame Flora met the cost herself.

In 1960, Dame Flora was being driven to Kyleakin ferry on her way to New York for her annual birthday party. It was a fine, sunny winter day, but on rounding a corner an oncoming car drove straight into hers, and both she and her chauffeur, John MacLeod,* were injured. She was taken at once to Broadford Hospital and later transferred to Raigmore Hospital, Inverness, with a broken hip. At eighty-two it was considered doubtful whether she would walk again. She had no such fears. Mary Northcote reached Broadford the day after the accident and arrived at Dame Flora's bedside before she had been transferred to Inverness and was greeted with the words, 'Darling, you must be tired. Have you eaten anything?' Joan's telegram from Australia suggesting she should return home was answered by a forceful command to continue where she was. At Inverness, Dame Flora was horrified to discover that the radio was forbidden to patients on a Sunday. Although she had her own wireless and was not personally affected, she organised a protest with as much skill as a well-trained shop-steward, and the public radio was duly reconnected.

Recovery was rapid. The physio-therapist at the hospital confided that she gave Dame Flora only half the exercises normally prescribed, as she always insisted on doing double what she was told. On her discharge from hospital Dame Flora walked with the support of crutches and was later advised not to put pressure on her leg and to walk with the regular support of a stick. Each afternoon she could be observed stumping out from the castle, with her stick

---

* John MacLeod never fully recovered from the shock of this accident and died a few months afterwards.

hovering two inches above the ground which it never touched. She was determined to walk again and within a year she was in New York for her birthday with no stick and with only the trace of a limp. Joan now undertook several clan journeys on her mother's behalf and was welcomed both as the chief's daughter and as the mother of John. The clan appreciated her gifts, not least among which was her ability to foster her mother's interests without usurping them.

In 1959, Patrick Wolrige Gordon, invited by his former headmaster, attended an international conference for Moral Re-Armament (MRA) at Caux in Switzerland. He knew nothing of MRA except that it occasionally provided excellent dinners for M.P.s at its headquarters in London. Caux was the meeting place of some of the leading statesmen of the world. Adenauer and Schuman had both been there and regarded MRA as having contributed to Franco-German unity after the war. They sent representatives regularly to the summer conferences, who met with leading figures in industry and the trades unions. The magnitude and international impact of Caux impressed Patrick, but the most important feature of his visit was a personal one. Although he was young and successful, he was disillusioned with the quality of his own life. At Caux he found a vital personal faith and as a result became convinced about MRA.

Dame Flora, like many British people, felt a marked hostility towards MRA. She admits that she knew nothing about it, but shared the general belief that it was alien to the reserved attitudes of the British. When she heard of Patrick's decision she lamented the fact that a grandson of hers, whose career was most important to her, should have taken such an uncompromising stand and felt it was a grave mistake. 'Patrick was like the woman in the Gospel,' she wrote, 'who found the piece of money in her house and called in the neighbours to share it. He just had to share this glorious new gospel with all of us, and of course we were extremely unreceptive. Patrick was ostracised to a great extent by people who had previously been his best friends.'

It was a painful and divisive issue in the family circle, but Dame Flora, in spite of her reservations, stood by her grandson. 'Because I was so sorry for Patrick I held very, very tight to him,' she wrote. 'I was not converted but I was extremely fond of him and had the greatest admiration not

Visiting Japan, the Yawata Steel Works and the Sofukuji Temple, with the author in 1963

In India with Rajmohan Gandhi on the 4,500 mile march

only for his character, for his uprightness, for his courage, but also for his very great ability.'

Opposition to Patrick's beliefs was not limited to his family and friends. His colleagues at Westminster urged him to abandon MRA. A Government Whip took him to lunch and advised him that his future prospects in the Party would be damaged unless he renounced his convictions. He refused. Dame Flora, who was far more interested in his success than in his principles, thought it was a mistake. 'He could have lived the Christian life,' she said, 'without anybody knowing why, and it would have been just as effective.' Like all new converts, Patrick was probably over-zealous and made mistakes, but he was only twenty-four and faced a barrage of opposition. In order to please her grandson and because she was both curious and adventurous, Dame Flora accompanied him to Caux for a weekend in 1961. 'We flew together to Geneva and a car was waiting,' she wrote. 'Patrick and his friend drove me up that beautiful drive to Mountain House. I was impressed with the perfection of the surroundings—the beauty of the scenery and the flowers. That weekend was a revelation. I particularly remember three little Buddhist monks dressed in their saffron robes, with their tiny hands hidden in their long sleeves. When the time came for them to pay their tribute they came and recited. It reminded me of the prayer-wheels one used to hear about in one's childhood. There was a remarkable Italian woman, a trade-union leader, the arrival of a monster plane from South America—all of whom had come to thank Dr. Buchman for his life and his tremendous work. I felt he was very tired.' Dr. Frank Buchman, the American initiator of MRA, was that summer celebrating what proved to be his last birthday. During a morning session of the conference on June 4th, Dame Flora became aware of Peter Howard. 'He was a totally dynamic figure,' she wrote, 'and made a first and indelible impression upon me. He kept spilling on to the platform like Hermes, the god who carried good news. He read telegrams. He introduced delegations. He brought messages, and he did it all with tremendous vitality.' Howard recognised in Dame Flora a personality of genius. He had been schooled in a worldly environment which appealed to Dame Flora. As a boy he had overcome a crippling disability in his leg to play rugger for Oxford and eventually to become

captain of England's Rugby Football team. He had then
worked as a political journalist in Fleet Street on Lord
Beaverbrook's *Daily Express,* which he had left in 1942 to
work with MRA. He accepted Dame Flora's reservations
without argument and found her criticisms bracing. In turn,
she found him an unexpectedly sensitive person with a world
vision which exceeded her own. She at once liked him and
there ensued a lasting friendship both with him and his wife,
Doë.

At a breakfast party with young people, Dame Flora met
Rajmohan Gandhi, the twenty-four-year-old grandson of
Mahatma Gandhi, who was responsible for the work of
MRA in India. They talked of the Indian Empire and the
fight for independence and India's future. Dame Flora wrote
afterwards that she thought Gandhi 'a very great young
man'. However, it was the practical side of Caux which
impressed Dame Flora far more than the speeches. 'The
whole running of this house is done as their contribution to
MRA by the people staying here,' she wrote. 'In answer to
my questions I am told of the gifts to Caux which have made
this magnificent welcome possible. The Ruhr miners give coal:
Denmark gives butter and eggs; others give meat or milk;
Thailand gives rice. It is a vast tribute paid from around the
world. A group of ladies told me they were planning tea for
the next day. I asked, "How many people do you expect?" I
think they said five hundred.' Dame Flora was so impressed
by her meeting with a delegation of British dockers that she
ordered and subsequently read each week their newspaper,
The Waterfront Pioneer. At Geneva airport, waiting for her
plane to London, she was introduced to the man in charge of
printing at Caux. 'What is the biggest job you have on hand
now?' she asked. He replied, 'We are printing a quarter of a
million leaflets for the Japanese students,' It was a statement
which left Dame Flora breathless, and she at once asked how
it would be paid for. The man replied, 'We have received a
gift of a thousand tons of paper from Scandinavia.' This was
Dame Flora's last recollection of Caux, and perhaps best
describes her attitude to MRA. She was moved by the
sacrifice of people's lives and the outreach of a world idea;
she was captivated by certain great personalities; but she was
totally unconvinced by the personal aspect of MRA and the
idea of seeking God's guidance, to which she referred as
'absolute twaddle'.

On August 6th, 1961, Frank Buchman died and the world press announced that Peter Howard would succeed him. Dame Flora wrote from Dunvegan Castle:

Dear Mr. Howard,
My thoughts are much with you all at Caux today. I am sure you knew when I was with you that the earthly parting could not be long delayed. I am privileged to remember at his tremendous birthday celebration, Dr. Buchman found time to spare a kind thought for me. I should indeed like to make my humble contribution to breaking down the wall of prejudice and hostility and ignorance which is terribly prevalent in Britain. I hope it will not break Patrick's career of service in Parliament.
Yours very sincerely,
Flora MacLeod of MacLeod.

In October 1961 the Executive Committee of the East Aberdeenshire Conservative Association carpeted Patrick for his MRA activities and made him promise that he would not mention MRA in the constituency in future unless specifically asked to do so—a promise he kept both in the spirit and in the letter. However, life was made increasingly hard for him. Dame Flora was deeply distressed, and throughout these anxious months she corresponded with Howard, who shared her concern. It was an honest exchange, and Howard was equally open with her about his own difficulties and burdens in the wake of Buchman's death. The poignancy of the situation was increased by the fact that for two years Patrick had been in love with Howard's daughter, Anne, and in January 1962 they became engaged. Howard was about to leave for India. 'Dear Peter,' wrote Dame Flora:

Little did I think that my next letter to you would be on a subject so close to our hearts. I am happy and so I think are you and Doë. I think the young ones are very happy.
I believe there is God's blessing in this marriage and that Anne will give the support and comfort and wise comradeship which will mean everything to him, for he is lonely and unfulfilled. I think they are both very lucky for I am sure Anne will have a loving and utterly loyal husband and, I hope, a great statesman. I am very happy to think

that we, the families, are already friends and can pray and plan and rejoice together.

God bless you and your Indian journey.

For certain members of the East Aberdeenshire Executive Committee, Patrick's engagement to the daughter of the leading figure in MRA was the last straw. They resolved to get rid of him. The political battle which followed and which attracted national publicity for several weeks is not relevant to Dame Flora's life except for two reasons. Firstly, because she stood by Patrick throughout the ordeal, and was the only member of his family to support him publicly, and secondly because she provided at Dunvegan Castle an oasis of peace which her grandson and his fiancée were to enjoy nowhere else throughout their engagement.

Shortly after his engagement was announced, Patrick was invited by his local chairman to resign his seat 'like a gentleman'. He refused. At an Executive Committee meeting, summoned while he was in hospital, it was decided by nineteen votes to fifteen to recommend withdrawal of support from him. Members who had not attended the meeting on the understanding that it was to decide on a suitable wedding present for the Member, were dismayed. A full Association meeting was called and support for the M.P. in the constituency began to mount.

Dame Flora prepared for battle. When questioned by the Press she replied, 'I love a fight, especially a political fight. I think I may join in myself.' She must have known this would infuriate the Scottish Establishment, most of whom opposed Wolrige Gordon, and of whom her own family was a part. Her clan campaigns and political action on the County Council had in any case not endeared her to the Establishment. On April 23rd, 1962, two days before the vital Association meeting in Aberdeenshire, she issued a statement to the Press:

I stand behind Patrick, because I respect his courage, his ability and integrity, and because I believe in his political future.

The attack on his service in Parliament has collapsed and degenerated into a smear on his personal beliefs. Patrick believes in uprightness, honesty, unselfishness and the good life. Can anyone deny that our public life would be better if more young men and women in Parliament lived fearlessly guided by these principles?

I deplore this painful and unnecessary dispute at a time of unprecedented importance in our national life. It has damaged the Government which it is our purpose to sustain. I hope it will prove to have united members of all parties in support of Patrick. It could not have been expected that he should accept the verdict of a majority of seven taken at a meeting without an agenda and attended by sixty-seven, of whom thirty did not vote. He could not have crawled away like a whipped dog with his career blasted. He had to fight.

The statement had an immediate effect. It reinforced Patrick's supporters, most of whom were ordinary people battling against a phalanx of big names and whispered innuendo, and brought outraged protests from their opposition. Dame Flora was delighted by both reactions. On April 25th, at a packed meeting of his Association, Patrick received a massive vote of confidence. It was a personal triumph which was reported far beyond the bounds of Aberdeenshire. Dame Flora had passed through the fire with her grandson, and, like that of all people who share persecution, their relationship was immensely strengthened.

On June 2nd, Dame Flora travelled down from Skye with her clansmen and friends to attend Patrick's wedding in the parish church of Lavenham in Suffolk. Peter Howard met her at the station and as they walked arm in arm up the platform to the music of the pipes, the sun shone, the anxieties melted and hurts were healed. 'It was wonderful,' she wrote afterwards. 'It was perfect. An atmosphere of love and joy and peace so universal that the bitterness was obliterated in the glory and the wonder. Do you remember the glorious scene in the *Walküre* and Brünnhilde's "submissive justification"? This was a triumphant vindication.'

It would be wrong to underestimate the trauma through which Dame Flora had passed. Her life, for all its difficulties, had never before been exposed to personal in-fighting within the family which had been part of the Aberdeenshire battle. For many years she had been at the receiving end of considerable adulation, and she had risked it all in a moment. In return, she found herself surrounded by new relationships, among which was a lasting and close friendship with Patrick's wife. The correspondence with Peter Howard continued and covered a wide variety of subjects, including world politics, Scottish history, journalism and the clan. It cemented a friendship between two visionaries. Howard's vision was for humanity and Dame Flora's was for the clan, but their dedication and commitment were not unalike. Both lived and thought in a world context and yet enjoyed family life. Both had a flair for capturing an audience or planning a campaign, which instinctively united them. In the autumn of 1962, Peter and Doë Howard were Dame Flora's guests at Dunvegan. This was a rare holiday in the year during which Howard worked an eighteen-hour day, and was repeated only twice. 'These visits were a revelation to me,' wrote Dame Flora. 'It was a joy to know that Peter really cared for the Highlands and was able to identify himself with the castle—its age and strength—and accept it as his Highland home. I always hoped he would spend a long holiday and relax. I closed the doors to other visitors with that intention. But, of course, it never happened like that. For Peter it was the opportunity to write still longer hours while the rest of us were asleep. His only requirements were an electric fire, a kettle and a tea-tray. I like to think that a little of the power which fired his plays was inspired by Dunvegan.

'There were long tramps over hill and moor, days in the boat; sometimes we caught baskets of mackerel off Dunvegan Head, or went on expeditions and picnics. Whether it was walking, boating or fishing, or talking, or eating, or playing "Oh Hell" or "Careers" round the library fire in the evening, Peter threw himself into whatever it was with such keen enjoyment that he made it tremendous fun for everybody. He made friends of and with our staff. He integrated himself completely into the simplicity of the centuries-old tradition of hospitality and friendship of ancient Dunvegan. Was it ever stormy? Did it ever rain? I do not remember.'

The sun shone for Dame Flora in Howard's company. She enjoyed discussing politics with him and it was a subject on which he was well informed. She said she was sometimes tired and at eighty-four was beginning to feel it was time to slow down. This was not Howard's conviction, and he at once invited Dame Flora to travel with him on one of his Asian journeys. It was an invitation which pleased her, but she was concerned for her strength and particularly what would happen if she died thousands of miles from home. Howard replied simply, 'I will put you in a box and bring you home.' It was on that cheering note of reality that Dame Flora agreed to visit Japan and India with Howard in April 1963.

Meanwhile life at Dunvegan continued uninterrupted. The third Clan Parliament was successfully accomplished in the summer of 1962 and hundreds of visiting clansmen were made welcome. In October 1962, King Olav V of Norway made a private visit to Dunvegan. 'We were very happy to bid King Olav welcome in the ancient Norse Castle,' wrote Dame Flora 'We are a norse clan—our first chief, Leod, was the son of Olav the Black, King of Man, under the Crown of Norway. These were the days when the sea was a highroad and not a barrier as it is today. We showed King Olav the dungeons, the sea-gate and the Fairy Flag which we believe was brought from the Holy Land by Harald Hardrada. He was a delightful and appreciative guest and we gave him a simple Scottish tea. Afterwards in the company of many Skye people, who had come from many parts of the island, we watched him depart in a bright red helicopter.'

In January 1963, Dame Flora underwent an operation for cataract. By late February she was reading books on Japanese history and preparing her wardrobe for the flight to Tokyo in April. 'I cannot tell you how much I am looking forward to it,' she wrote to Howard. 'It will be wonderful from every angle. The thrill of a strange new world, meeting people who strive to build a new and better world, and being with those for whom I feel great love and respect. How thrilling to see a glimpse of modern India through the eyes of Mahatma Gandhi's grandson.'

This visit to Asia was the first of four journeys between April 1963 and February 1965, during which Dame Flora travelled with Peter Howard through many countries. They were journeys which were to affect her life deeply.

Peter Howard

JAPAN WAS A COUNTRY DAME FLORA HAD LONG WISHED TO VISIT, but she had dismissed the idea as impossible. In April 1963, at the age of eighty-five, as Peter Howard's guest and accompanied by his daughter, she flew over the North Pole to Alaska and on to Tokyo. Howard had been invited to Japan by two former Prime Ministers, Mr. Yoshida and Mr. Kishi; Governor Sogo, the head of the Japanese Railways; Mr. Yamagiwa, Governor of the Bank of Japan; and Mr. Chiba, a former Minister of Labour, for the opening of a new MRA centre at Odawara, eighty miles from Tokyo.

On board the aircraft plans were discussed and briefings given with the care and precision which marked Howard's work. A competition was held during the flight. The airline asked passengers to guess the number of miles it flew in an average day. The prize was a magnum of champagne, and Howard won it. As he did not drink, he told Dame Flora he was going to present the champagne to a racehorse owned by Mr. Sohma, one of his friends in Japan. A year earlier the horse had been entered for an important race, when it was taken ill. Sohma was dismayed. He was a man without great faith, but Howard told him he would pray for the horse to recover and win. Sohma replied, 'It is most unlikely but if it does I shall give you half the prize money.' Much to everyone's surprise the horse recovered and ran an astonishing race to victory. With the proceeds Howard bought a car for the work of MRA in Japan. It was an unusual scene on that warm spring afternoon in Tokyo when Howard emerged from the aircraft, with a magnum of champagne on one arm and Dame Flora on the other, to be welcomed by the Sohmas and Mr. and Mrs. Masa Shibusawa, his hosts in Japan. 'We drove to Yokohama for tea,' wrote Dame Flora, 'and we saw the great harbour filled with ships. I thought of Gilbert and

184

Sullivan who record Yokohama in the immortal *Mikado*.'

Dame Flora was by now a seasoned traveller, but surprisingly unspoiled by her experience. For her Japan was a magic world, studded with people of her own size with whom she could, therefore, for the first time in her life talk face to face. It was admittedly a world to which she was not at once accustomed. On the first evening she did not come down to dinner, not because she was tired but because she was suddenly overcome with shyness and fear at the prospect of using chopsticks. 'I showed the cloven hoof,' she wrote, 'and afterwards I felt I had been a worm. I hate thinking of myself as a coward.' Thereafter she was never once late for an interview or an outing, always immaculately dressed and invariably outgoing and interested in those she met. She was intensely independent, starting with morning exercises in her bedroom and insisting on a good walk every day. She always packed her own bag and cleaned her own shoes. Howard, who often had difficult companions among the delegation of twelve who travelled with him, regarded her in the same light as he did the magnum of champagne.

Dame Flora's performance was no mean achievement. It was not like her clan tours: she was no longer the central figure in an adoring crowd. Howard was not interested in numerical success and social contact alone, but in meeting people's deepest spiritual needs and bringing change into the areas of conflict in the nation's life. Inevitably this meant he was a man of controversy—loved by some and hated by others. He was the guest of rich capitalists and bitter Communists, of Conservative ladies and revolutionary students, and for all his message remained the same. After a decade of living in a world dominated by things Scottish, Dame Flora found this new experience a breath of fresh air.

Peter Howard's first speaking engagement in Japan was to the students of Waseda University. These were the students whose violent demonstrations had caused General Eisenhower to cancel his visit some months before, and who had refused to give Robert Kennedy a hearing. This was a hostile crowd and it was questioned whether Howard would be able to speak. He invited Dame Flora to accompany him to the hall. 'I felt immensely privileged to be in the hall when he spoke,' she wrote. 'It was crammed full. He spoke in English, translated into Japanese, literally as he spoke, by a wonderful

interpreter. There was an almost magnetic stillness. You could
have heard a pin drop. Every word that Peter uttered went
straight to the heart of those turbulent young people.' Howard
took Dame Flora to meet some of the leading political figures
of Japan. Mr. Yoshida, then eighty-three, entertained them in
his beautiful home overlooking Mount Fuji, and indulged his
passion for Skye terriers by enquiring about the island from
which they came. When world politics was discussed Dame
Flora was a lively contributor. The emerging role of China;
future political patterns in Asia; Macmillan and the Common
Market were subjects raised and debated in depth. 'It was an
honour to meet that great old man who guided Japan through
those terrible years of war and peace,' wrote Dame Flora. 'He
was not the least like Winston Churchill and yet reminded me
of him. I saw them both as great personalities, as great
people.' Yoshida said afterwards, 'Only four people I know
from the Western world have come to Japan and won the
hearts of the Japanese people, and one of them is Dame Flora
MacLeod.' This was a man's world, in which Dame Flora felt
completely absorbed. She was deeply disappointed when
Howard left for Hokkaido with an entirely male delegation.
Thinking it would please her, Howard arranged for her to see
some of the traditional beauty of Japan in his absence. It was
clearly a mistake. Although she was charmed by Kyoto with
its beautiful gardens, and found the 'poise and pace of the
acting' at the Kabuki Theatre 'deeply impressive', she was not
a willing tourist. The Japanese food and the flower arrangements gave her little pleasure. 'I do prefer our own great
bunches of roses and gay masses of tulips,' she wrote. Escorted
on each side by Japanese ladies in their kimonos, she visited
countless temples and climbed everlasting stairs. 'My sweet
companions counted beautifully until they got to seventeen,'
she wrote. 'After that the numbers became rather involved,
particularly at one temple which had one hundred steps.'

It was when Dame Flora was put to work that she was most
content. She was one of the first women to be taken through
the Yawata Steelworks. Wearing a black coat and peaked cap
she walked many miles past the great furnaces and assembly-
lines, with a word for each workman and an energy which
surprised the Board of Directors in a nation where women
were not fully emancipated. At Nagasaki it was not the garden
where *Madame Butterfly* was written which appealed to her,

but the thriving shipyards. 'For Britain it is a most alarming sight,' she wrote. 'The speed, the efficiency, the devotion of the workers is indeed something we have to fear. There is only one Union in the whole shipyard so that men can be transferred from one job to another without a moment's delay. They have an order book which will keep them busy for a year. Wages are much lower than ours, but their output is frightening.' Dame Flora wrote that she found the Japanese 'immensely hard-working, courageous, industrious and self-confident but rather hard and pitiless,' and that she regarded these characteristics as 'praiseworthy'. 'I think it is good to be ambitious and self-confident,' she said, 'but I do not think they are very tender people.' When the Shibusawa family came later as her guests to the castle, their six-year-old son was captivated by the seals in Loch Dunvegan. He told Dame Flora that the tourists could be invited to contemplate the seals through a telescope and be charged sixpence for each look, and that he, Masa, should have threepence because he was the person who thought of it. Dame Flora was permanently impressed by the financial expertise of this child—the great-grandson of the founder of modern industrial Japan, but she was at the same time deeply shocked by a military camp she visited. The soldiers had given an excellent jujitsu and sword display, after which Howard and his friends were invited to lunch in the barracks. 'I was considerably amused that we were given a small table in the corner of the big refectory,' Dame Flora wrote, 'and every man had his lunch first. The women were the last people served. How badly dressed the soldiers were! How slovenly they walked! Not one of them stood up when the National Anthem was played. I was horrified to think that this wonderful, precise, military nation should have allowed this.'

Dame Flora's political perception was matched by a curious naiveté. At a luncheon party with a wealthy director she continually asked the Geisha girl who served the meal what she did for a living. With Japanese modesty, the girl put her hand over her mouth and giggled quietly, for her relationship with the man in question was clear to everyone present, but Dame Flora persisted. The director laughed until the tears ran down his cheeks, but she never understood why. At another official party, seated on the floor in Japanese style, she drank three glasses of what she described as 'the most delicious water'. It was, in fact, *saki* and highly alcoholic. She left the table at the end of the meal firmly unmoved, to the considerable amazement of her Japanese hosts.

In Japan, where age is revered, Dame Flora was a formidable figure, but she was also loved. The Japanese are not people who easily show affection, but they did so openly to her. She was made a leading guest among others at the wedding of the Sohmas' daughter, Fujiko, and sat at the same table with the bride and bridegroom, the Crown Prince and his equerry. 'It was utterly amazing,' she wrote, 'and acutely embarrassing.' Another evening she sat next to a cabinet minister at dinner. He spoke no English and she spoke no Japanese but she gave him the best of her attention. The next day he sent round his most treasured possession, a stamp collection, as a gift for her.

It is difficult to know why she stirred such shy and reticent people in this way, but much of it can be explained by her own unselfishness and self-discipline. After a day of total giving of herself she would collapse into bed exhausted, but she was always up on time the following morning, ready to start again. She did not once miss reading a daily newspaper or finishing a chapter of her book. Howard laid down a strict code of discipline for his travelling companions and she observed it religiously. She said, 'It would be so selfish to get sick.' She felt complete contempt for one member of the delegation who deliberately broke the rules, and was delighted when the offender was 'punished' by suffering from dysentery in Hong Kong. They later became good friends, but the back-sliding was not forgotten.

Dame Flora was the guest in Hong Kong of Heyward Isham, the son of Ralph Isham, now serving in the American State Department, and from there she flew with Howard to India. Of all the Asian nations, India was perhaps the closest to Dame Flora's heart. It was here in 1900 that she had lived during the glittering era of the British Raj, and it was here she had returned to visit her daughter when she had first inherited Dunvegan. It was now a new India. 'We flew to Calcutta,' wrote Dame Flora, 'and landed in a monsoon storm. For several days Calcutta airport had been closed and we were only the second plane to land. It was torrential rain. To my amazement a number of people had gathered to welcome Peter. Rajmohan Gandhi was, of course, there, but what most impressed me was the Chairman of the Dockers

who had come in his working-clothes at the end of a hard day
in blinding rain and wind to greet Peter and ask his guidance.
I was very moved.'

As Dame Flora drove through the streets of Calcutta that
afternoon, an India was revealed to her about which she had
previously heard only through Kipling's books and the after-
dinner conversations of her British friends. 'That drive was a
staggering experience,' she wrote. 'I had never conceived or
imagined that human beings should live in the ghastly conditions of squalor that we passed through. I asked myself what
one could attempt to do with such horrifying conditions if
one had the opportunity. Would it be housing, would it be
health, would it be education? Everything was lacking.
Violence must inevitably breed in conditions of squalor like
those we saw.'

Howard dealt relentlessly with the selfishness and corruption in human nature which he felt created these conditions.
He said it was in men's hearts and wills that the answer lay,
not only in their pockets. Dame Flora found it a difficult
message to accept. Her solutions were political and not moral,
and yet in those days in India she watched Howard deal with
despair and dishonesty in people's lives, taking infinite time
with each individual. Her faith in God which had been entirely
conventional began to grow. Howard included her in his work,
as he did all the delegation, and he invited her advice on his
major speeches. It was a gift he had for making everyone feel
part of his life, and he often adopted her suggestions. Although
Dame Flora did not always share his views, this was an
atmosphere in which she flourished. She never refused a
speaking engagement, whether it was a rally for 2,000 women
in Lucknow, or tea with a Swami. She spoke always without
notes, and if she was specially nervous she would hold a
postcard of the Fairy Flag in her hand.

One afternoon in Calcutta, as she was returning home in a
taxi, a street urchin climbed on to the running-board of the
car to beg. Dame Flora immediately looked in her purse for
money. The driver of the cab urged her to desist, advising her
that it would do no good and cause much trouble. For a
moment she hesitated but at the next red light, the urchin tried
again—this time singing a sad little song through the window.
It touched Dame Flora's heart. She opened the window and
threw a handful of coins out into the street. From every alley

and by-way they ran in their hundreds, naked little boys, marked with the stigma of neglect and poverty, dark-eyed and charming, singing at the tops of their voices, climbing over the taxi like ants, clinging on for grim death between the traffic lights. The cab drivers cursed and hooted their horns to avoid the children as a huge traffic jam developed. Dame Flora sat bewildered, her eyes full of tears, unmoved by the curses of those around her, touched only by the dark, sad eyes of the children. She remained a dedicated sentimentalist. In Madras one evening she astonished Rajmohan Gandhi by taking off her shoes and stockings on the public beach, pacing briskly across the vast sands down to the water's edge and wading in up to her knees because, she said, 'I had to feel I was stepping into the Indian Ocean.'

Gandhi took Dame Flora to meet his family, including his grandfather, Shri Rajagopalachari, the first Indian Governor-General following Independence. Subsequently, he took her to see the Viceroy's Palace in Delhi and fascinated her with stories of its history. 'I was impressed to think, after all these years of liberation, what small changes have been made in these tremendous rooms.' She wrote afterwards, 'I remember the portraits of the Queen and the portraits of the Viceroys still in their places. It was an extraordinary contrast, a shattering relevation, to pass Mahatma Gandhi's ashes which were standing in a humble little place outside a door.'

In Bombay, Dame Flora drove up to Government House, which she had last visited as a girl of twenty when Aunt Alice was in residence. She signed the visitors' book and a few of the oldest servants rushed up to shake her hand.

When Peter Howard found he had to remain behind in India, he asked Dame Flora, Doë and Anne to fulfil his engagements in Iran. Escorted by a British diplomat, Mr. A. R. K. Mackenzie,* and Major Oliver Corderoy, they flew to Teheran. It was an unusual female trio, particularly as the engagements were predominantly for men. There was a reception by the President, and an official luncheon at the Military Academy—an audience entirely composed of high-ranking officers without their wives. Dame Flora rose nervously to speak for the guests at the end of lunch and

---

* Later the British Ambassador to Tunis and Minister for Social and Economic Affairs at the United Nations.

performed so well that one of the officers in his reply suggested making her a general.

Dame Flora's first journey with Peter Howard lasted only six weeks but was so successful that within seven months, in November 1963, she joined him again. This time she travelled to Paris, Rome, Athens, Cyprus and finally India. Following in the footsteps of his famous grandfather, Rajmohan Gandhi had planned a 4,500 mile March-on-Wheels from Cape Comarin in the south to the nation's capital. It was a march to end corruption and build national character. His concepts stirred the hearts of ordinary Indians, and 100,000 people had gathered to see him off on his great journey. Dame Flora was captured by this initiative and, equipped with a stout pair of walking shoes, she joined the march at Lucknow. 'We arrived here from Cyprus at what the Indians think was five in the morning and we thought of as two-thirty,' she wrote from Delhi. 'The dawn was the fiercest fiery red. We leave again at five-thirty tomorrow morning to meet Rajmohan at Lucknow. We have been told to have essential night things packed in an air bag as the luggage does not always catch up in time (by lorry). The march will have been 3,400 miles, for they went all up the east coast to Calcutta and then across India. It seems to have been triumphant in its impressiveness. Scores of thousands of people accompanying it to the different places, and Rajmohan addressing vast meetings of industrial workers.'

Once Dame Flora joined the march, Gandhi provided a car in which she resolutely refused to ride even when the march continued for four miles without stopping, in considerable heat. 'I cannot meet people from a car,' she wrote, and marched on. Of all her experiences with MRA, that was to be the one she most valued. 'Yesterday in Kanpur was tremendously thrilling,' she wrote. 'We marched through the poor quarters of the city and narrow streets crowded with very poor and, I am afraid, hungry people who look upon Rajmohan as their saviour. Miserable rags of paper bunting were tied by string and cotton across the streets, and people had been up all night to fill in the road. Garlands innumerable. I was given pigeons to release. It was deeply moving. Young Gandhi has a colossal enterprise to accomplish. He makes me walk with him for he says the people are thrilled and encouraged to know that an old woman from far away cares.

Peter nobly holds my left arm as we march in step after the flag. There are mayoral receptions and parties of all kinds, and of course very important meetings with chambers of commerce and industrial workers. But the intense reality is the adoration and yearning of these desperately poor people.'

When the march reached Delhi, Dame Flora spoke to a gathering of Indian Parliamentarians. 'Kingdoms have come and gone in India,' she said, 'the Mogul kingdom and the British Raj. Now that has all passed away and India is her own great self. The Indian people today are dreaming dreams and seeing visions of the greatest India there has ever been, an India that is free from corruption, and free from poverty. Years ago Mahatma Gandhi marched to the sea and made such an impression that the British left. We remain good friends still. Today, thank God, another Gandhi marches and India looks to him for leadership. And to him I and many others give all the support within our power.' Gandhi's family were grateful for her loyalty. At a breakfast party, Rajago-palachari asked her how old she was. When he discovered she was a few months older than him, he said merrily, 'Thank goodness. Now I cannot marry you.' Throughout the meal they discussed Scotland and Skye, and to her amazement and delight he quoted long sections from Boswell's *Life of Johnson*. With Gandhi's friends, Russi Lala, the editor of his magazine *Himmat*, and R. D. Mathur, responsible for the MRA centre at Panchgani, and with the young Indians who worked with Gandhi, she made close friends. Although she travelled to many countries with Peter Howard, none could rival India in her loyalty. Howard fought vigorously for her to put loyalty to God before her loyalty to men. She never did. She marched for Gandhi in India and she spoke for Howard in Asia and America.

Dame Flora's relationship with MRA was never a commit-ment. It was always a love-affair with people. Some members of her clan who felt their interests were being usurped criticised her journeys with Peter Howard. They need not have worried. The clan always came first, but what Howard tried to give her, which the clan did not, was a faith. How far he succeeded may be questioned. Although she defended MRA in public, particularly to the mass media in Britain where she felt there was unforgivable prejudice, she could be, and often was,

Caroline and Patrick Wolrige Gordon with their great grandmother on her ninety-third birthday

t a London Ceilidh, 1971

Discussing the book with the author at Dunvegan

highly critical in private. Howard welcomed her criticisms and found them valuable, something which won her heart. Some years later, when asked in a BBC radio interview about the happiest years of her life, she answered that they were when she had first discovered the enthusiasm for the clan overseas, and her journeys with Peter Howard.

Dame Flora's faith was never a certainty. She invariably quoted Rabelais, 'Je cherchais un grand peut-être.' Howard, who regarded faith as the most important ingredient in life, tried to help her overcome the obstacles which stood in its way. He dealt with her pride and control. In foreign countries where speakers found her name difficult to pronounce, mistakes were often made in introducing her. She disliked this intensely. Sometimes she got so cross she would stand up and publicly contradict the speaker. Howard tried to explain that what mattered was the man on the platform and not her self-esteem. It was an argument he only partially won, but he always told her to her face what he thought, and because he cared deeply for her, she accepted it. In turn, she was probably more honest with him than she had been with anyone else. 'You must be sensible as well as a saint,' she wrote after one journey. 'An eighteen-hour day is too long. Fourteen hours is better, but twelve hours is best.' To her sorrow it was an argument she also lost.

Because of the hours he worked, Howard occasionally wrote letters to his travelling-companions. One morning in early December 1963, he sat at his typewriter and wrote:

Dear, dear Flora,

Our Asian journey is nearly over. Rome, Athens, Beirut, Delhi, Lucknow, Kanpur, Agra, Delhi, Tokyo, Nikko, Odawara, Tokyo. It has been an adventurous time and many, many more to come. I wanted to tell you this morning how thankful I am not just for your friendship and comradeship, which are a candle in dark days and a constant cocktail in the hearts of Doë and me, but also for your valour and effectiveness.

Christ's challenge however imperfectly expressed by humans has always been resented and resisted by the faintly pious, the self-righteous and the intellectual blue-bloods all down the ages. Why, God knows, but there it is.

Forgive this typing. It is rather dark in this room and very early. We must put the changing of men first. It means moving each morning out of self into Christ, out to others, so that our viewpoints and angles are not so dear to us as the other person's place in God. 'Nothing in my hand I bring. Simply to Thy Cross I cling.' That is my need and decision. It is one of the greatest gifts in life that I can call you 'friend'.

With a grateful heart,
Peter.

Dame Flora travelled twice to America with Peter Howard, but they were journeys which lacked the novelty of unknown places. However, in January 1964, Peter Howard was invited by the Government of Brazil to visit Latin America, and he asked Dame Flora to accompany him. He took with him a delegation of some thirty people, which included Rajmohan Gandhi and the Shibusawas. Among the hundreds of people who turned out to welcome Howard at Rio de Janeiro was a delegation of port-workers and some of the shanty-town dwellers of Rio, who later entertained him and his friends to a dinner in their *favela*. This was a considerable financial sacrifice for them. 'The astonishing and impressive feature here is the *favelas,*' wrote Dame Flora, 'districts inhabited by sometimes thousands of workers at one or kindred trades. Sometimes housing conditions are relatively good. Often the homes are shacks on the slopes of the strange sudden hills which make Rio such a remarkable city, with a mud, pot-holed track leading up them. Peter says they feel themselves apart from the rest of the community, but they are wonderful people, men and women alike, and it was the famous march of the women organised by themselves which brought the overthrow of Goulart's régime. These people have a mystique for Peter, although very few have ever seen him. The amazing women, whom we know and meet personally, decided to give a tea-party for him, and as they had no money they asked for gifts to help provide it. So great was the response that it has become a dinner for 250.'

Dame Flora, dressed in her best green brocade dress to do them honour, was as moved by this glittering occasion held in the midst of squalor as she had been by the poverty in India. Howard's main concern in Latin America was to deal with the corruption which, he felt, created, and would continue to create, revolution. With that in mind he moved to Uruguay. It did not take long for Dame Flora to share his conviction. 'This lovely country is sunk in lethargy and strangled by corruption,' she wrote. 'A man Peter used to know told him this morning that Uruguay was the richest country in the world, but he only had a few thousand pesetas here because all his fortune goes as fast as he makes it to the Swiss banks. He thought this might last another five years. When the crash comes he will leave Uruguay with his future secure. They boast that their social services are the most liberal in the world; a man retires on full pay at fifty; 3 per cent illiteracy, and kindergarten through university free for all. A Catholic told Peter the professors are Communist and only Communists get degrees. Others told him that the Church is infiltrated and corrupt and there was no hope for Uruguay, because people had lost interest. Starting from nothing, Peter nevertheless sees the President and Ministers, Rotary, Press and television, and has an impressive interview with members of the armed forces. But it seems pretty hopeless and like beating the wind. The Government is really Alice in Wonderland. One super President with no power, nine Presidents co-equal, six-to-three government and opposition who never can agree, and nine cabinet ministers. Everyone is fraudulent. They don't think it is wrong—merely common sense. Peter says there are three alternatives—military revolution, a Communist revolution, or Moral Re-Armament. The easy-going folk say there are no Communists and this is nonsense.'

In the Argentine, Dame Flora was invited to preach a sermon in the largest Scottish church in Buenos Aires. 'I chose the tenth chapter of Acts,' she wrote, 'and the analogy for us today that all people and religions are acceptable before God, which is the message of MRA. It is a marvellous church. The Moderator rightly described it as a cathedral, lofty with fine coloured glass. All the world is supposed to be on holiday. I was warned it would be a tiny congregation but over a hundred people were there.'

Throughout her Latin-American journey, Dame Flora was received at the British Embassies and in some cases the Ambassador sent his car to the airport to meet her. She was infuriated that these attentions never included Howard. 'It is curious and unfortunate, I think,' she wrote, 'from a purely

British point of view that our Foreign Office should deny itself contact with people who know the situation in the world as Peter does.' Howard was accustomed to the British attitude and it did not concern him. The pace of the Latin-American journey was arduous, and speaking engagements fell largely upon his shoulders. It was a difficult climate in which to work. He had not slackened his pace for nearly five years. From the Argentine to Chile and on to Peru the journey proceeded relentlessly. Dame Flora wrote home, 'I am sometimes frightened for him.' In the early morning of February 23rd, 1965, twelve hours after he had landed in Lima, Peter Howard was struck down by an intense fever. He was taken to the Anglo-American Hospital suffering from virus-pneumonia. From the ambulance on his way to hospital he sent Dame Flora a bouquet of pink roses, and it was the last time she was ever to hear from him. On February 25th, at the age of fifty-six, he died and his body was taken to lie in state in the City Hall of Lima. Dame Flora wrote to Joan, 'I am sure you understand that for me the sun has ceased to shine.'

Dame Flora had lived through death before, but perhaps none so sudden and unexpected as this. Her mind may have stretched back to a spring day in Spain and another face that she would never see again. It was when Olive died that she found a remarkable inner strength, and here in the sultry heat of Lima she found it again. In the privacy of her room she read aloud from the Bible, and outside it she gave infinite care to Doë and each of Peter's friends. She wrote, 'I wish I could share with you what the last weeks have meant to me, culminating in the last ten days. I am very grateful that I was able to help Doë a little in her overwhelming loss, and share her pride in the miracles which happened in Latin America. The lying-in-state in the City Hall in Lima was an honour that has never before been accorded to any foreigner. The coffin was covered with the Union Jack, and the flag of Peru stood by the head, together with a great silver crucifix and six huge candlesticks. I have so often heard Peter say the first four lines of the hymn which begins, "When I survey the wondrous Cross", that I liked this very much. Hundreds of people filed past and the flowers were lovely. He had planned to go back to Brazil to confirm and repeat what he had done there, and would have received from the President the highest decoration Brazil can give. Now that is over.'

Although Dame Flora travelled to Asia later in the same year, her journeys without Peter Howard were never the same. Her work for MRA was henceforward out of loyalty to his memory rather than for the love of God, for which Howard had lived and died.

Old Age

DAME FLORA HAD ONCE REMARKED HOW SAD WAS THE difference when people ceased to refer to her father as 'a wonderful man' and called him instead 'a wonderful old man'. It was not strange that old age should at last stretch out its tentacles towards her. It was merely astonishing that it had not done so before. Just as she had developed slowly from a girl into a woman, so old age now came towards her gently and at first imperceptibly. In the autumn of 1965 she travelled with Rajmohan Gandhi, Masa Shibusawa, and her grandson, Patrick, to Japan, returning through Ceylon, India and Kenya. Rajmohan Gandhi had her complete loyalty. She admired his work, most particularly the opening of his new MRA centre at Panchgani, although she abhorred the poverty in which she felt most MRA workers in India lived. Dame Flora entertained sixty of his young Indians at Dunvegan Castle in the summer of 1967.

In the winter of 1967, Dame Flora travelled to Norway with Doë Howard as the guests of MRA. 'I was welcomed as the descendant of the great Viking, Harald Hardrada, and chief of a clan which is proud of its Norse descent,' she wrote. 'The television was excited about this and I was told I had hundreds of cousins. I was taken to a village called Hallingdal, where in 1440 a very distinguished young Hebridean couple established themselves and called their home *Dunvegan*.'

The clan now increasingly took pre-eminence over everything else in Dame Flora's life. With the exception of Gandhi in India, she found the world leadership of MRA uninspiring, and it was never again the same for her after Howard's death. 'I think it is very important that leaders should give people the sustenance they require,' she wrote. 'A leader must inspire others to follow him and with that in view the leadership in MRA is inadequate. A Cabinet

198

without a leader is emasculated.' In the past, Dame Flora had met people of national importance with Howard. Henceforward, however mistakenly, her journeys with MRA seemed to her less important, made among people who were struggling both financially and spiritually after the loss of their two leading figures within five years. Although she was given every care it was impossible to provide her with the stream of political, business and Labour figures who had been so much a part of Howard's life. It may seem strange that Dame Flora, who was satisfied with a greater or less important following in an egalitarian clan family, could not accept the same conditions in MRA. This was perhaps for two reasons. The first was that she was ambitious for MRA to succeed and to obtain the recognition which she felt it deserved. The second was that she was in charge of the clan and, therefore, the most important figure in it.

Dunvegan Castle had been the source of Dame Flora's inspiration before. It was here she returned to the healing hills and waters which she loved, along with her close family which now included four great-grandchildren, and her clansmen from around the world. On May 16th, 1965, Dame Flora officially handed the castle and estate to John and became his life tenant. The tourist business and the management of the crofting estate was put under John's control. This decision, made in the interest of the castle, was perhaps the most difficult of her life. Once again she had questioned whether she could not part with the estate and keep the castle for herself. It was an impractical idea, but the pain of the parting between herself and the castle was one from which she never completely recovered. It was as if the stones and harling had become a part of her bone and blood, like the barnacles on a ship. The full force of her ambition was now focused on John. She said hopefully that she did not want to interfere, but she could hardly resist it. Unloved in childhood, disappointed in marriage, Dame Flora had never learned to love her family in a way which made them love her. She offered a strange mixture of worship on the one hand and crippling control on the other, which inevitably repelled them. She did not see it. The fact that she wanted the men in her life to be great blinded her to the fact that her determination often achieved the opposite result. In turn, the family found it hard to express their gratitude for her unlimited generosity, or to appreciate her very great achievements. Yet it was impossible not to love her, for in old age she displayed amazing charm and courage. Known to the family as 'Baloo', the wise old bear in the 'Mowgli' stories, she possessed much of his wisdom.

The tourists poured into the castle in increasing numbers, making life there in the height of summer almost unendurable. Dame Flora did not complain. She had perhaps done more than any other person in Skye to encourage tourism. On August 24th, 1967, she initiated the first Silver Chanter Piping Competition in honour of the nine generations of MacCrimmons, acknowledged as the greatest composers, performers and instructors, whose piping college at Borreraig gathered students from every part of Scotland. 'It was Fairy work,' wrote Dame Flora, 'because the first MacCrimmon was given by the fairies a silver chanter.' The competition was held in the castle drawing-room and only pipers who had won the Gold Medal of London in open competition in Oban or Inverness, or the Dunvegan Medal at Portree, were eligible to take part. It was, therefore, a competition of champions. Each piper was invited to submit a list of four MacCrimmon pibrochs, and the judges selected one. It was an immediate success, attracting to Skye some of the best pipers in the world, who played in unique surroundings and provided a feast of music which lovers of pibroch flocked to hear. Dame Flora herself spoke and presented the silver chanter at the end of the evening. 'We are feeling proud and elated over the success of the Silver Chanter Competition,' she wrote. 'The pibroch were most beautifully played. People were turned away from the doors. The head of Scottish BBC was there and we feel secure that we are truly on the map. We are happy to see Skye once more in the lead.'

It was important to Dame Flora that Skye should excel, just as it was important to her that her family, her country, her clan and MRA should excel.

During the tourist season it was impossible to get out of the castle without passing through crowds of tourists, but in the afternoons—with a walking-stick and stout shoes, and seldom if ever with a coat—Dame Flora would set off down the drive for her walk. As she passed the groups of visitors she would say, 'Is there anybody here from Canada?' or 'How many from Australia?' As the hands shot up she beamed, 'Welcome, welcome'. The owners of other stately homes might shut themselves in a secluded corner and curse the invasion of their privacy, but Dame Flora never did. 'I feel very strongly,' she wrote, 'that if you have opened your house and you are taking money from people for the privilege of seeing it, it would be horribly ungracious to make them feel what a burden it was and how tiresome it could be. You must make them feel they are welcome. Many of them want to take photographs. If it pleases them, why shouldn't they? It is horrid not to ask if they are enjoying their holiday and you hope it will be better weather tomorrow.'

The castle provided glorious summer holidays for her grandchildren and great-grandchildren, and she lavished affection and care upon them in a manner of which she would have heartily disapproved in her youth. She was an expert at children's games, notably 'Old Maid', 'Racing Demon' and 'Grandmother's Footsteps'. Whenever she could she joined fishing expeditions in the boat. Once on a very rough, windy day she accompanied the family party on a day trip to Loch Coruisk. The boat was small and unsteady and the waves broke ceaselessly over the deck. Other members of the party huddled together for shelter, while Dame Flora stood in the bow like a figurehead, her face to the wind, her eyes alight, as torrents of foam drenched first her hair and then her clothing. She regularly attended the Portree Balls when there was a castle party, sitting in the gallery and staying until two or three in the morning. Gradually the inevitable burdens of failing sight and hearing weighed down upon her. Those who knew her well could hardly believe this apparently superhuman figure could be so affected, and she was excellent at deceiving them. She continued to take a lively interest in politics, reading *The Economist* with a magnifying glass and making penetrating comments about de Gaulle and the Common Market. A strong advocate of the EEC, her dislike for de Gaulle knew no bounds when Britain's application to join was rejected. In the library she picked up a copy of the book on The Salvation Army's General Booth entitled, *The General Next to God,* and commented drily, 'This is de Gaulle's book, I suppose.' Sir Alec Douglas-Home's period as Prime Minister and the ensuing rise and fall of Harold Wilson gave her months of

political interest. She never missed an election campaign in
East Aberdeenshire. On polling day she would travel the
eight-hour journey to cast her vote in Skye and then return
immediately for the count in Aberdeen. She remained a
figure of importance in local Skye politics, pulling strings
behind the scenes with the merriment of a child in a puppet
theatre. When an important division took place in the House
of Commons, she would urge that a long-distance call be made
to Patrick to discover the voting figures, for she could
hardly wait for the evening news or the next day's
newspaper.

Dame Flora possessed the lightning mind and self-
confidence which made her an expert performer on television
and she was in constant demand. When in 1967 the BBC
decided to make a colour film of Johnson and Boswell's tour
of the Hebrides under the title *Highland Jaunt,* they invited
Dame Flora to play the part of her ancestress. She was
eighty-nine. 'I was dressed in a beautiful eighteenth-century
dress with a very becoming bonnet,' she wrote, 'so I don't
think my age mattered very much.' Her performance amazed
technicians and producers alike and a national newspaper
described her as a 'starlet'. In 1972, she was interviewed by
Joan Bakewell for BBC television in a programme entitled
The Lady in the Castle, which was a substantial success and
in 1973 Lord Chalfont interviewed her for Welsh television.
As a result of her television appearances the fan mail which
already loaded her desk became ever more heavy. Some
wrote simply to congratulate her or to obtain an autograph.
Clansmen wrote to ask about their ancestors, or beg for a
piece of tartan. Dame Flora had no secretary. With failing
sight and paying the postage out of her own pocket, she
tried in vain to answer every letter which came. For many
months she doggedly refused to face the condition of her
eyes, ordering new spectacles or buying ever larger magnifying glasses in the hope that her sight would be restored. Only
seldom did she reveal what this deprivation meant to her,
as once when she wrote from Dunvegan, 'Last night the light
was so bright that I watched the stars and planets dancing
for joy. I thought I should never see stars again.' Her clear
round hand-writing remained almost perfect with seldom
a crooked line or a fumbled word. Indeed, her correspondence
gave her an occupation without which she would have

perhaps lost interest in life. During the dock strike of 1970 she wrote personally to her grocer to enquire whether it was in the national interest for her to place her usual order for butter and eggs. He framed her letter and hung it on the wall of his office. If her loyalty to Britain was an outsize loyalty, so was the clan's loyalty to her. During the same strike, a clansman from Alabama telegraphed Dame Flora offering to fly supplies to the beleaguered castle in a chartered jet. She declined the offer with the crisp comment that the landing-strip at Broadford—a project which she had strongly opposed —was too small for a jet.

In 1972, Mrs. Nicolson and Miss Katie Matheson, two of Dame Flora's faithful staff at Dunvegan, retired. It proved impossible to replace them and life at the castle without them became a permanent problem. In the same year, Joan's health broke down. She had lived at Dunvegan with her mother for fourteen years, but was now forced to make her home in a less arduous atmosphere. Suddenly and unexpectedly it was the end of an era at the castle. At the invitation of her grandson, Patrick, and his wife, Dame Flora crossed Scotland for several months of the year and made her home at Ythan Lodge, Aberdeenshire. Her personal possessions were so few that she could bring them in three suitcases. Without rancour or bitterness, at the age of ninety-five she pulled up her roots and virtually made for herself a new life.

At Ythan Lodge she was a perfect guest and great-grandmother. She was invariably dressed for breakfast at eight-thirty to see her great-grandchildren off to school. Each afternoon she walked, often alone, round the policies of her grandson's small farm, commenting on the state of the cattle and crops. She insisted that her greatest treat was to be allowed to do the washing-up, something which had been denied to her throughout her life. It is difficult to know how honest this was, for she was determined not to be a burden upon those she loved. Never once did she raise a voice in complaint, though the trials of being unable to hear a conversation or read a newspaper were heavy indeed upon a person so steeped in public life. While she could, she read to her great-grandchildren and played games with them. In the evening she played Scrabble and watched the political pro-grammes on television.

In March 1972, Dame Flora walked out into a bitterly cold

Aberdeenshire afternoon with no overcoat. Two days later she was suffering from her customary 'irritation of the nostril'. In the night a harsh cough developed and echoed through the walls of her bedroom. In the morning she would not allow the doctor to come to the house, and protested that she was perfectly well. Finally, Anne insisted that even if she had to be carried bodily out to the car, she must be taken to the doctor's surgery. From the scene which ensued it looked as if this threat might have to be implemented. Dame Flora climbed angrily into the car and as it set off down the drive, her shoulders slumped and her face turned to Anne. She said quietly, 'I think you are possibly right. I do not feel like jumping over the moon.' The doctor diagnosed acute bronchitis. She had a temperature of 103°. She was put to bed and given antibiotics, but within a day she was better, grumbling about her medicine and agitating to be up. A month later her sturdy figure could be seen walking again down the same country road, perhaps a little more fragile and slightly more frail, but never more determined. Occasionally her health would trouble her but it was a fact she liked to disguise, for she dreaded losing any of her faculties. 'When I go I want to go out like a light,' she would say. 'If I am too old put me in a home. I never want to be nursed by those I love.' Her old age was to her a condemnation and a sorrow, but she suffered it with unforgettable courage. For those who enjoyed her company, for the great-grandchildren who would otherwise never have known her, it was an infinite blessing. 'I think God did something wonderful for the world when He created the seasons,' she once wrote. 'As it is true of nature, I think it is true of human life, and I welcome what is happening to me now because I am slipping into the long sleep. I rejoice that it should be so, for it is inevitable and so compassionate.'

It was at moments like these that Dame Flora's faith was strongest. She would often quote St. Paul's words from Corinthians, 'For now we see through a glass darkly, but then face to face: now I know in part; but then I shall know even as also I am known.' She was a loyal member of her church, seldom missed a service on Sunday, and generously supported many Christian causes. 'I look upon the church as vital,' she once wrote, 'because no great movement can live or exist without being organised. That is why the organised church service means more to me than disorganised forms of worship. The church is not perfect, but through it we share a common faith expressed in many different ways.'

The little girl, born at 10 Downing Street in 1878, whose life had spanned almost a century, did not like looking back, but she must occasionally have asked herself how the years had passed. Her life had been a series of contradictions. Born in England, a child slow to develop, she became the first female Highland chief, with an unlimited passion for power; a wife and mother who often failed in her intimate relationships, she created a brilliantly succesful world family in her clan; a lover of Scotland, cheered by Scots in every city and village across the globe, her heart was always deeply stirred by the beggars of India and the shanty-town dwellers of Rio; a passionate believer in Great Britain, she favoured the power bloc of Europe; in love with the castle—the only possession she ever truly treasured— she was carelessly generous with her money and indifferent to her personal effects; a believer in euthanasia she clung to life with tenacity; a doubter about the next world she had faith in the magic of the Fairy Flag; an admirer of ambition and success, her devotees were mostly people who had neither. Her life has reflected a thousand changing scenes, as swiftly and suddenly as the deep waters of Loch Dunvegan, and she will be remembered, like the Skye she loves, as part of its magic.

Appendix I

THE FAIRY FLAG

THE MACLEODS HAD MANY CONNECTIONS WITH THE FAIRIES, AS did the MacCrimmons. If the theory is accepted that the 'little people' were the original inhabitants, who were much smaller in stature than the Viking invaders, much is explained.

Of the different versions of the fairy origin of the flag, the one preferred is that the 4th chief, Malcolm, married a fairy wife. After many happy years together, they parted at the Fairy Bridge and she gave him the flag with instructions that it would save the clan three times in the hour of great danger. It is believed that Alasdair Crotach twice used the Fairy Flag (for one of the occasions there is strong local oral tradition) and that when the chest was broken open in 1799 in the Chief's absence, this was *not* the third waving of the flag and that its power remains. Local people say that when the flag was carried to safety during the fire of 1938 the flames bowed before it.

In the 1920s, when it was framed to preserve it by the experts in the Victoria and Albert Museum who had handled the Tutankhamun textiles, they said it was Syrian or Rhodian silk of great antiquity, and they thought it must have been a holy relic, perhaps a saint's shirt, as the darns, still bright scarlet and circular, not criss-cross, were nearly as old as the silk. The expert said, 'We know Harold Hardrada was in Constantinople in 1032'. The 27th Chief interrupted, 'That is extremely interesting, but I know my ancestor married a fairy'. The expert replied, 'Sir Reginald, I bow to your superior knowledge.'

It is, however, historical that Harold Hardrada did bring back a powerful and precious banner from the Middle East called 'Land Öde—the land ravager'. The tradition is that, after his defeat at the battle of Stamford Bridge in 1066, the banner was carried away, first to Orkney and then to the Isle of Man by his great friend Godred Crovan. When a powerful and mysterious banner is found in the possession of the descendant and of Olav the Black, the King of the Isle of Man, it is tempting to believe that Land Öde and the Fairy Flag are one and the same. It is impossible of proof, but an attractive hypothesis.

Appendix II

A SHORT CLAN HISTORY

A clan meant originally a close feudal relationship between the chief and the people who sought his protection and leadership in return for service. When economic and political necessities caused the chiefs to sell much of their land, the ties loosened, and many of the more active and energetic clansmen emigrated, and made their fantastic contribution to the creation of a new world in Australia, New Zealand and Canada. Apart from a direct migration to North Carolina, a great many of the MacLeods to be found in the USA now came there via Canada.

The history of the clan is thus in early times the history of the chiefs.

Dame Flora is the twenty-eighth in the direct line from the 1st Chief Leod, born circa 1200. He was the son of Olav the Black, the King of the Isle of Man. He went to Skye and married the only daughter of MacArailt, Viking overlord of the island and already living on the rock of Dunvegan. They had twin sons, Tormod (Norman), progenitor of the MacLeods of Harris and Dunvegan, and Torquil of the MacLeods of Lewis.

The curtain wall of Dunvegan Castle was built by Leod; the great keep, tower and dungeon were probably built by the 3rd Chief, Malcolm, c. 1330, the Fairy Tower in 1502 by the 8th Chief, Alasdair Crotach; the central block containing the present dining-room and library by Rory Mor, 15th Chief, c. 1612, and the south wing, in which the 1938 fire occurred, by Ian Breac, 18th Chief, in 1684. Later generations added, altered and improved the main structure.

Alasdair Crotach, c. 1455-1547 (the hunchbacked, so named from a sword cut across the muscles of his neck), was engaged in almost incessant fighting with the Macdonalds in a series of episodes which include the massacre of the Macdonalds in a cave on the Island of Eigg, and battles at Glendale and on the Wall (at Trumpan) on both of which occasions the Fairy Flag was waved.

He was also a very great patron of the arts. Under him was founded the piping college of the MacCrimmons at Borreraig. This family maintained their supremacy as composers, players and teachers of the 'Ceol Mor'—The Great Music—and their continuous service to MacLeod for 300 years. The last of them played to Sir Walter Scott when he stayed with John Norman, 24th Chief, in 1814. His pipes are still at the castle, as are the earlier set—the 'speckled pipes', on which the MacCrimmon of the day originally played the pibroch 'I had a Kiss of the King's Hand' about Charles II.

Pupils came to the piping college from far and near, and it was said it took seven years and seven generations to make a piper. A pibroch is an intricate piece of music, with a ground and several variations, and it is remarkable that such a sophisticated composition should have originated so early in that wild country.

There are many MacCrimmons in Canada and it is good that one of them has now bought the old school at Borreraig.

In later life Alasdair retired to Rodel in Harris, where he built the church of St. Clement, in the tower of which he spent the last few years of his life as a recluse. His seven predecessors had been buried in Iona but he built himself at Rodel a most beautiful tomb, said to have the finest Renaissance sculpture in the Highlands.

The next chief of great importance to the clan was Sir Rory Mor 1562-1626, the 15th Chief. 'Mor' means great—'not so much from his size or stature of his body which was not remarkably large, as from the strength of his parts'. He steered the clan through troubled waters, fighting in Ireland with the O'Neils against Queen Elizabeth, yet going to London in 1613, where he was knighted by James I, formerly James VI of Scotland. The Statutes of Iona had been an attempt by the Crown to curb the power and independence of the chiefs—their sons had to be educated in Edinburgh and the chiefs themselves had to go yearly to Edinburgh to renew their titles to their lands. Rory Mor sometimes honoured these laws more by the breach than the observance, and was 'put to the horn' (outlawed) more than once, but he survived and maintained his lands intact. He had a great reputation for overflowing hospitality and his death was mourned in the beautiful 'Lament for Rory Mor'.

Two of his five sons were very remarkable men, both of them 'gilded' knights (i.e. knighted by the king himself)—Sir Roderick of Talisker and Sir Norman of Bernera. They led the clan at the Battle of Worcester 1651 (during the minority of their nephew, the 16th Chief) at which the clan suffered severely, and they were imprisoned in the Tower.

These knighthoods were the only rewards the MacLeods had for their devotion to the Stuarts and when, almost a hundred years later, Charles Edward Stuart landed in 1745, the 22nd Chief, Norman (1705-72) was not prepared to sacrifice his clan a second time. Succeeding to the chieftainship as a baby, he was always seeking a father figure to whom to cling, and President Forbes of Culloden was an important influence in keeping MacLeod 'out' of the '45. Norman was an M.P. from 1737-52 and no doubt viewed the Jacobite adventure from a different angle. He was married twice, and the splendid Allan Ramsay portraits of him and his second wife Anne Martin are important treasures at Dunvegan. He is wearing a red and black check, said to be intended to imply tartan without actually breaking the law which proscribed Highland dress. Henceforward the eldest sons of chiefs and heads of families had to be educated in England (it took the 25th Chief four days to travel by coach from Skye to Harrow).

The 22nd chief's only son died in his lifetime and he was succeeded by his grandson, the General Norman (1754-1801) the 23rd Chief, young host to Boswell and Johnson on their visit in 1773. He had a colourful career, raising the 2nd Battalion of the Black Watch and fighting with great distinction in India. He was captured on his way out there and imprisoned in America, where he met and was greatly impressed by Washington. A treacherous wound in the temple at the hand of Tippoo Sahib greatly changed his disposition. He returned from India at the very end of 1789, and became a Member of Parliament. He and his beautiful second wife, Sarah Stackhouse, were painted both by Zoffany and by Raeburn.

His son John Norman, 24th Chief, attended in full regalia the reception for George IV organised by Sir Walter Scott at Holyrood in 1823, and his grandson Norman 25th was the chief during the potato famine to which reference has been made in the text.

It will be seen from this brief summary of a few of the more outstanding chiefs that a capacity for leadership, in whatever form was appropriate to the circumstances of the hour, was apparent in them. The family motto 'Hold Fast' has been an enduring inspiration.

© Joan Wolrige Gordon

THE MACLEODS OF HARRIS AND DUNVEGAN

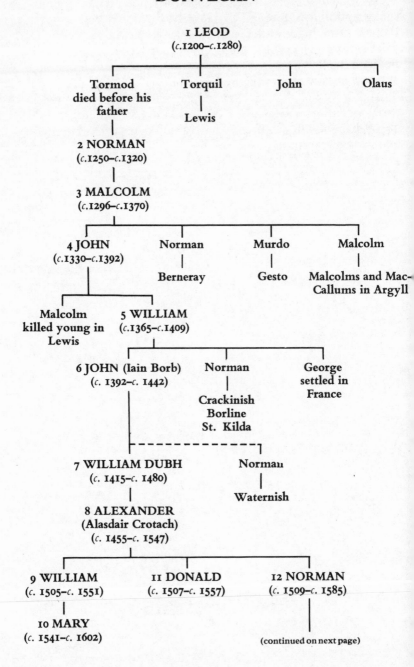

1 LEOD
(c.1200–c.1280)

Tormod
died before his
father

Torquil

Lewis

John

Olaus

2 NORMAN
(c.1250–c.1320)

3 MALCOLM
(c.1296–c.1370)

4 JOHN
(c.1330–c.1392)

Norman

Berneray

Murdo

Gesto

Malcolm

Malcolms and Mac-
Callums in Argyll

Malcolm
killed young in
Lewis

5 WILLIAM
(c.1365–c.1409)

6 JOHN (Iain Borb)
(c. 1392–c. 1442)

Norman

Crackinish
Borline
St. Kilda

George
settled in
France

7 WILLIAM DUBH
(c. 1415–c. 1480)

Norman

Waternish

8 ALEXANDER
(Alasdair Crotach)
(c. 1455–c. 1547)

9 WILLIAM
(c. 1505–c. 1551)

11 DONALD
(c. 1507–c. 1557)

12 NORMAN
(c. 1509–c. 1585)

10 MARY
(c. 1541–c. 1602)

(continued on next page)

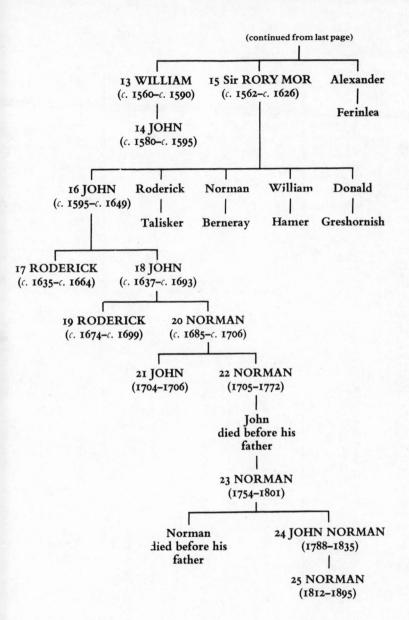

(continued from last page)

13 WILLIAM
(c. 1560–c. 1590)

15 Sir RORY MOR
(c. 1562–c. 1626)

Alexander

Ferinlea

14 JOHN
(c. 1580–c. 1595)

16 JOHN
(c. 1595–c. 1649)

Roderick

Talisker

Norman

Berneray

William

Hamer

Donald

Greshornish

17 RODERICK
(c. 1635–c. 1664)

18 JOHN
(c. 1637–c. 1693)

19 RODERICK
(c. 1674–c. 1699)

20 NORMAN
(c. 1685–c. 1706)

21 JOHN
(1704–1706)

22 NORMAN
(1705–1772)

John
died before his
father

23 NORMAN
(1754–1801)

Norman
died before his
father

24 JOHN NORMAN
(1788–1835)

25 NORMAN
(1812–1895)

DAME FLORA AND HER FAMILY

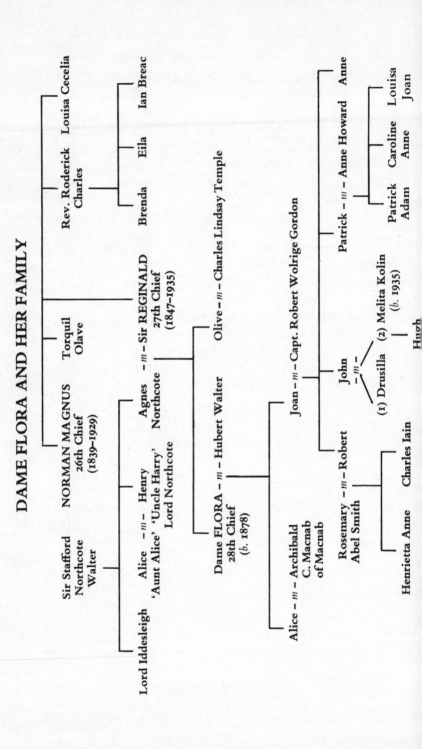

Index

Index

Aberdeen, Marquess of, 76
Aberdeenshire East, 173–4, 179–81, 202
Adelaide, 152–3, 155
Adenauer, Dr. Konrad, 176
Agadir, 79
Agra, 58, 59
Akalkot, Rani of, 50
Albany, Duchess of, 42
Alexander, Boyd, 76–7
Alexandra, Queen (Princess of Wales), 43
Alice, Princess (Countess of Athlone), 42
America, The United States of, 121, 125, 139–50
Argentina, 195
Arnold, Edward, 68
Asquith, Herbert Henry, 62, 66, 78, 82
Asquith, Margot, 62
Asquith, Violet, 61–2, 76–7
Austen, Jane, 66
Australia, 151–7

Bakewell, Joan, 202
Bailey, Mamie, 34
Baldwin, Stanley (Earl Baldwin of Bewdley), 96
Balfour, A. J. (Earl of Balfour), 12, 16
Bayreuth, 36–7
Beaconsfield, Earl of (see Disraeli)
Bearwood, 63–4, 66–7
Beaverbrook, Lord, 178
Belgium, 69, 70–1, 85–6
Bell, Graham, 137
Berlin, 72–6
Bessire School, Edinburgh, 34, 38
Bevin, Ernest, 120
Boer War, 56
Bombay, 47–8; famine fund, 55–6; cricket, 57–8
Bonham-Carter, Maurice, 61
Booth, General, 201

Boothby, Robert (Lord Boothby), 173
Borreraig, 85, 106, 135, 166
Boswell, James, 65, 113–14, 139, 152, 192, 202
Brazil, 194–5, 196
B.B.C., The, 121, 125, 155, 200, 202
British Commonwealth, The, 157
British Travel Association, The, 142
Brussels, 69, 70–1
Buccleuch, Duke of, 32
Buchman, Dr. F. N. D., 177, 179
Buckingham Palace, 43, 126
Burghstaller, Mr., 37

Calcutta, 188–91
Caledonia, P. & O. liner, 46, 47, 59
Cameron, The Hon. Archie, 156
Cameron, Donald of Lochiel, 24th Chief, 26–7
Canada, 79–80, 127–38
Canadian Pacific Railway, 41, 79
Canberra, 156
Cannon, Nanny, 68, 71
Cape Breton, 129–33, 137
Castle Grant, 25, 61
Caux, 176–9
Chad, Lake, 76–7
Chalfont, Lord, 202
Chaucer, 28
Chelsea, Borough Council, 88–91; housing improvement society, 90; Infant Welfare Service, 82–83; war savings movement, 83–4; Conservative Women's branch, 87–8; Barracks, 87; in World War II, 121; Cheyne Place, 78, 81; Christ Church, 98
Chiba, Saburo, 184
Chicago, 144–6, 148
Christchurch, (N.Z.), 157–8
Churchill, Lord Randolph, 27
Churchill, Sir Winston S., 120–1, 186

Clan MacLeod, The, 111–12, 125–6, 133–7, 140–1, 142, 151, 161–8, 208–11
Clan MacLeod Society
of America, 148–50, 168–9
of Australia, 111, 152–3, 157, 170
of Canada, 136–7
of Edinburgh, 36, 111, 170
of London, 170
of New Zealand, 157–60, 170
Clan Parliament, The, 161–7, 183
Conservative Central Office, 91–2
Cook, Captain, 156
Corderoy, Major Oliver, 190
Cranbrook, Earl of, 88
Cricket, at Granton House, 34; in Bombay, 57–8
Croly, Colonel, 52, 53
Crotach, Alasdair (see MacLeod)
Cullen, 25, 61
Cuillins, The, 135
Curzon, Lady, 59
Curzon, Lord, 47, 59
Czechoslovakia, 118

Dallas, 146, 148
de Gaulle, General Charles, 201
Delhi, 58, 192
Disraeli, Benjamin (Lord Beaconsfield), 14, 16, 47
Doubleday, publisher, 140
Douglas-Home, The Rt. Hon. Sir Alec, 121, 171
Downing Street, 10: 16, 28, 205
Downing Street, 11: 14, 171
Drysdale, Mr. 58
Dugdale, Blanche, 61
Dunvegan Castle, additions to, 9–11; holidays at 84; history of, 208; tourists, 127, 200–1; fire at, 116–17; damage to, 149–50, 174–5; repairs, 162, 175; 118–19; preservation of, 165–6; Royal visits to, 105–6, 163–5
Dunvegan, egg depot, 102; school, 171

Economist, The, 133, 156, 201
Edinburgh, Duke of, 164
Edward VII, King, 26
E.E.C., The, 186, 201
Eigg, Island of, 13
Eire, 121
Eisenhower, General Dwight D., 185
Elizabeth II, Queen, 163–165
Elizabeth, Queen Mother, 105
Esslemont House, 98, 116, 119

Etingshausen, Baroness Hanna von (Aunt), 20, 44, 84
Express, The Daily, 178

Faber and Faber, publisher, 139
Fairy Flag, The, 16, 85, 105, 112, 116, 119, 123, 133, 139, 140, 162, 183, 206–7
Famine, in Poona, 55; in Skye, 9
Farrar, Mary (Lady Hobhouse, Aunt), 22
Farrar, Sir William, 65
Fell, Sir Godfrey, 121
Ferguson, Captain, 58
Fettercairn Castle, 114
Fish, Edith Hamilton, 35
Fish, Stuyvesant, 139
France, 120–1
Fraser, family of, 146

Gaelic, 171
Gallagher, Angela (Gally), 98
Gandhi, Mahatma, 178, 183, 190, 192
Gandhi, Rajmohan, 178, 188, 190–2, 194, 198
Ganesh Khind, 54–8
General Strike, The, 96
George VI, King, 95, 113
Gilbert and Sullivan, opera, 31, 185
Girton College, Cambridge, 94
Gladstone, W. E., 14, 19
Glasgow, 101
Glendale, uprising, 18; typhoid, 101
Glengarry (Ontario), 132, 136
Gordon, Archibald (s. of Marquess of Aberdeen), 61, 76
Gordon-Lennox, Lord Walter, 28
Granada (Spain), 97–8, 108
Grant, Dr. I. F., 139–40
Grant, Major and Mrs. of Rothiemurchus, 50
Granton House, 32, 34–40
Gray, Miss, 81
Greenway, Lauder, 140
Greig, Captain, 52, 54
Grenadier Guards, 87, 98
Greville, Captain, 52–4
Grosvenor, Dr. and Mrs. Gilbert, 137

Hardrada, Harold, 105, 183, 198, 207
Harris, Island of, 85, 95; tweed, 102–3, 135, 148
Harrow School, 11
Hatfield House, 42
Haw Haw, Lord, 88
Heron, Charles, 164
Highland clearances, 9

Hill, Lord, 12
Hill, Mr. 52
Hilleary, Major Iain, 134
Hindu religion, 56
Hitler, Adolf, 118
Hoare, Lady Maud, 92
Hoare, Sir Samuel, 87, 91, 92
Hobhouse, Sir Arthur (Lord Hobhouse), 22, 31
Hobhouse, Lady, 31
Holyrood Palace, 39
Home Guard, The, 121
Hong Kong, 152, 188
Hope, Miss Agnes Beresford, 47, 49, 50–4, 58
Hope, Mr., 121
Houlihan, Mr., 92
House of Commons, The, 87, 88, 173, 202
House of Lords, The, 88
Howard, Anne (see Wolrige Gordon)
Howard, Doë, 178, 182, 190, 196, 198
Howard, Peter D., 177–83, 184–97, 199
Hunter, Mary, 34
Hyde, Donald, 139–40
Hyde, Mary, 139–40

India, 47–60, 107–8, 188–92
Indian Civil Service, 56
Indian Mutiny, 58
Inverness-shire, constituency, 26–7; County Council, 122–3; health committee, 99; hospital, 175–6
Iran, 190–1
Isham, Heyward, 188
Isham, Col. Ralph, 114, 120, 139–40

Jain Mosque, 58
James V, King, 164
Japan, 103, 121, 184–8
Johns, Sir Lawrence, 61
Johnson, Dr. Samuel, 65, 113–14, 139, 202
Johnstone, Rt. Hon. Tom, 143

Kabuki Theatre, 186
Kansas City, 146
Kennedy, Robert, 185
Kila Kona Mosque, 58
Kinnaird, Lord, 12
Kipling, Rudyard, 56, 189
Kishi, Nobosuke, 184
Khyber Pass, The, 107
Kneeland, Hopeton, 152–6, 168
Kneeland, Dr. Yale, 139, 143, 152
Knox, John, 78

Lala, Russi, 192
Land Öde (see Fairy Flag)
Latin America, 194–7
Latour, Count Vincent de, 44, 84
League of Nations Union, 92
Leigh, Major, 52
Leod, Eponymous of the MacLeods, 105, 111, 183
Lewis, Island of, 95, 103
Life magazine, 163
Lloyd George, David (Earl Lloyd George), 79, 82
Los Angeles, 146, 148
Luman, Maybelle, 149

McCarthy, Senator, 141
MacCrimmons, The, 85, 106, 125, 135, 200, 209
MacDonald, Lord Alexander of MacDonald, 122
MacDonald, Hon. Angus L., 132
MacDonald, Mayor Earle, 136
MacDonald, Flora, 16, 134, 143–4
MacFadyen, John, 135
MacGibbon, Alison, 157–8
Mackenzie, A. R. K., 190
Mackenzie, Rev. A. W. R., 129
Mackenzie, James, 73–6
Mackenzie, Mrs. Jessie, 158
Mackenzie, Sir Kenneth, 26
Mackie, Maitland, 173
Machlejd, Jerzy, 123–4
Machlejd, Wanda, 124
MacLeod, Agnes of MacLeod, wife of 27th Chief (mother), engagement and marriage, 13–16; as a mother, 23–6; declining health, 29–33, 62–3; death, 94
MacLeod, Alexander (Alasdair Crotach) of MacLeod, 8th Chief, 13, 85, 206, 208–9
MacLeod, Anderson, C. (U.S.A.), 169
MacLeod, Angus and Mary (Dallas), 148
MacLeod, Anthony (New York), 169
MacLeod, Bruce (Sydney), 151–2, 154
MacLeod, Donald (Toronto), 136
MacLeod, Donald B. (New York), 148
MacLeod, Captain Donald D. B. (Sydney, N.S.), 131–2
MacLeod, Gunner D. J., 124
MacLeod, Dame Flora of MacLeod, 28th Chief:
birth, 6–17
early childhood, 18–33

as chief mourner at Lord Iddesleigh's memorial service, 28
at Wiesbaden, 29–30
at Granton House, 34–40
at Dunvegan Castle, 35–6
comes out, 39–46
in India, 1900, 47–60
marries Hubert Walter, 66–8
as mother, 68–9
in Brussels, 70–1
in Berlin, 72–5
in Canada, 79–80, 130–3, 135–7
becomes a nurse, 80–1
public work in Chelsea, 82–93
early years in Skye, 100–3
public work in Inverness-shire, 103–104, 122–3, 134–5
hostess at the Castle, 104–6, 113, 164–5, 183
succeeds father, 107, 111–12
re-visits India, 107–8, 188–92
rebuildings south wing, 116–19
as Chief, 123–6, 156–7
breaks entail, 128–30
Clan tours of America, 139–49, 168–169; of Australia, 151–57, 169–70; of New Zealand, 157–60, 169–70
is made D.B.E., 141
first Clan Parliament, 161–68
campaigns for grandson, 173–4, 180–1
visits Caux, 176–8
meets Peter Howard, 177–82; travels with Howard, 184–97
becomes tenant at Castle, 199
old age, 198–205

MacLeod, Lord George F. of Fuineray, 171
MacLeod, Rt. Hon. Iain, 170–1
MacLeod, James (Gore), 159
MacLeod, John (California), 148
MacLeod, John (Dunvegan), 121, 175
MacLeod, Sir John Lorne, 111
MacLeod, John (Iain Breac) of MacLeod, 18th Chief, 117
MacLeod, John (Iain Breac) s. of Canon R. C. MacLeod (cousin)
birth, 36
death, 84–5
MacLeod, John, Younger of MacLeod (grandson), 107, 116, 128, 130, 135–6, 142–7, 161, 164–5, 176, 199
MacLeod, John H. (Wallingford), 139, 141, 148–50, 163
MacLeod, John Norman of MacLeod, 24th Chief, 36

MacLeod, Kenneth (Coinneach Mor), 170
MacLeod, Lamar (Chicago), 148
MacLeod, Squadron Leader Lewis, 124
MacLeod, Hon. Louisa of MacLeod, wife of 25th Chief (grandmother)
marriage, 9
ill-health, 11
relationship with Reginald, 13
death, 19
MacLeod, Malcolm (Napier), 157–8, 160
MacLeod, Milton (U.S.A.), 169
MacLeod, Col. Norman, 113
MacLeod, Norman of MacLeod, 25th Chief (grandfather)
marriage, 9–10
potato famine, 10–11
wife's death and remarriage, 19–20
death, 35–6, 172
MacLeod, Norman Magnus of MacLeod, 26th Chief (uncle), 13, 36, 95, 100
MacLeod, Rev. Norman (Nova Scotia), 130–3, 137, 158
MacLeod, Norman (Suardal), 170
MacLeod, Olive (Mrs. Charles Lindsay Temple), sister
birth, 19
early childhood, 20–3
at Granton House, 34–40
comes out, 61–2
romance with Boyd Alexander, 76
marriage, 77
death, 97–8, 108–9, 196
MacLeod, Sir Reginald of MacLeod, 27th Chief (father)
birth, 9
education, 11–12
first visits Skye, 12–13
engagement and marriage, 13–16
Conservative Agent, 23–7
stands for Parliament, 27
public life in Scotland, 32–40, 45
at Vinters, 61–2
business career, 79–80
succeeds as 27th Chief, 100
improves Castle, 104–5
death, 107
MacLeod, Canon Roderick Charles of MacLeod (uncle), 13, 36, 106
MacLeod, Sir Roderick (Rory Mor) of MacLeod, 15th Chief
sword of, 16, 111, 123
horn of, 164–5, 208–9
MacLeod, Sayre (New York), 148

MacLeod, of Talisker, 111, 112, 151, 210
MacLeod, Tony, 170
MacLeod, William (Louisiana), 148
MacLure, General Robert B., 147
Macmillan, Rt. Hon. Harold, 186
Macnab, Archibald Corrie of Macnab (son-in-law), 99, 107, 109, 127–30
Macnabb, Flora (see Walter)
MacNeill, Ronald, M. P., 92
MacNeill, Seumas, 135
MacQueen, Mr., 53
Macrae, Mrs. Joanna, 158
Madras, 190
Madrid, 108
Mahableshwar, 48–53
Maidstone, 80
Mail, The Daily, 126
Malabar Point, 48
Malahide, Lady Talbot de, 114–15
Malahide, Lord Talbot de, 114
Manila, 152
Manitoba, 79
Manners, Mr. Henry, 28
Manor Place, Edinburgh, 23–5
Maori welcome, 160
Margaret, H.R.H. Princess, 164
Marseilles, 46
Martin, Major-General J. S. S. (Husabost), 135
Matheson, Katie, 203
Mathur, R. D. 192
Melbourne, William Lamb (2nd Viscount), 41
Menzies, Dame Pattie, 156
Menzies, Sir Robert, 156
Metaxa, Mrs. J., 50
Mitford, Brenda Osbaldeston (cousin), 106
Montgomery of Alamein, Field-Marshal Viscount, 174
Montreal, 79
Moore's Creek, battle of, 144
Moral Re-Armament (MRA), 176–99
Morocco, 79
Mosan, Chief, 160
Mount Stephen, Lady, 41–3
Mount Stephen, Lord, 41–4

Nagasaki, 186–7
National Broadcasting Company (N.B.C. of America), 145–6
National Trust, The, 149
Newfoundland, 131, 142
New South Wales, 152–3

New York, 142–3, 148, 168
New Zealand, 157–60
Niagara Falls, 136
Nicholson, Mrs., 203
Nightingale, Florence, 15
North Carolina, 143–4, 148, 169
Northcote, Agnes Mary Cecilia (see MacLeod)
Northcote, Lady Alice (aunt), 41, 42–5, 47–60, 65–6
Northcote, Sir Henry Stafford (uncle), 41, 45, 49–59
Northcote, Lady (grandmother), 14, 15, 21
Northcote, Margaret, 15
Northcote, Mary (cousin), 98, 109–10, 121,·139, 141, 175
Northcote, Oliver (Uncle Olly), 21, 35, 45, 98, 139
Northcote, Sir Stafford, 1st Earl of Iddesleigh (grandfather), 14, 15, 21, 27–8
Norway, 198; King of (see Olva)
Nova Scotia, 79, 129–33, 136–7, 139

Oban, 101
Olav The Black King, 105, 183, 207
Olav V, King of Norway, 183
Ottawa, 136–7
Oxford University, 95

Pagenstecher, Dr., 29, 73
Paris, 45, 92, 96, 134, 191
Passchendaele, Battle of, 85–6
Perceval, Anne Eliza MacLeod (d. of 23rd Chief), 36
Perceval, Spencer, 36
Perth (W. Australia), 155
Peru, 196–7
Phillimore, Lord and Lady, 66
Phipps, Sir Edmund, 83
Phipps, Lady Margaret, 83
Piping, the Silver Chanter, 200
Poland, 123–4
Poona, 48, 53–8
Portnalong, 102
Portnaskye tweed, 102
Portree, hospital, 101; Games, 134, 163
Potato Famine, 9
Pretoria, Capture of, 56
Prince Edward Island, 136
Purves, Captain, 52
Pynes, 14, 41

Quebec, 79
Queen's Gate School, 94
Queensland, 155

Rabelais, 193
Rajagopalachari, Chakravarty, 190, 192
Reeve, Mrs., 136
Reichstag, The, 72
Reilly, Kate, 43
Reprise du Congo, The, 69, 70–1
Rhode Island, State of, 144
Rhodes, Island of, 105
Rhum, Island of, 13
Richter, Mr., 37
Roberts, Captain, 57
Robertson, MacLeod, 152
Rodel, Harris, 85
Rome, 96, 191
Runciman, Lord, 86
Russell, Bertrand, 91
Russia, 120

St. Giles Cathedral, Edinburgh, 28
St. John of Bletso, 13th Lord, 9
St. John of Bletso, Hon. Louisa (see MacLeod)
St. Laurent, Monsieur, 137
St. Mary Abbots Church, Kensington, 66
St. Mary's Cathedral, Edinburgh, 34
St. Paul's Girls' School, 81, 93
Salisbury, Robert Gasgoyne-Cecil, 3rd Marquess of, 27–8
Samuel, Marcus (Lord Bearsted), 79
San Francisco, 146, 148
Saunders, George, 72
Schönbrunn Palace, 44
Schuman, Robert, 176
Scotland, The Church of, 104, 204
Scotsman, The, 28, 82
Scott, Sir Walter, 14, 17, 35
Scottish Nationalism, 167
Seafield, Caroline, Countess of, 25, 61, 93
Seattle, 80
Shakespeare, 81
Shibusawa, Masahide, 184, 187, 194, 198
Simpson, Dr. Douglas, 116
Sinclair, Dr. Colin, 119
Skye, conditions in, 101–2; people of 116–17; war restrictions in 120–1; Skye Week, 134–5
Sligachan, 106
Smalley, Mr., 64
Sogo, Governor, 184

Sohma, Yasutane, 184
Sohma, Fujiko, 188
Spain, 97, 120
Spectator, The, 171
Stamford Bridge, Battle of, 105, 207
Stanley, Venetia, 61
Strathcona, Lord, 79
Stewart, Charles and Caroline (cousins), 170
Suardal, 106
Suffragette movement, 78
Switzerland, 80, 176–8
Sydney, 152–3
Syria, 105

Taj Mahal, 59
Talbot, Mr. and Mrs., 77
Teck, Duke and Duchess of, 42
Temple, Charles Lindsay (brother-in-law), 77, 97
Times, The, 63–4, 68, 69, 74, 99
Tokyo, 184–6
Toronto, 79, 136
Trade Unions, 96–7
Treptow Park, 74
Trinity College, Cambridge, 12
Tufnell, Miss (2nd Lady Mount Stephen), 43

Uiginish, dower house, 20, 84
Uist, Island of, 135
Unemployment (in Chelsea), 89–90
Uruguay, 195

Vancouver, 80
Vanderveldes, The, 70
Victoria Island, 80
Victoria, Queen, 42–3, 47, 51, 52, 56
Vienna, 44
Vinters Park, 61, 71
Virginia, State of, 144

Wace, Mr. 105
Wagner, Festival, 36–7, music of, 110
Wai, 49, 54
Waipu, 131, 137, 158
Walker, MacLeod, 155
Walter, Alice (daughter), 68–9, 71, 74–8, 80–2, 93–4, 98–9, 103, 116, 119, 130, 135, 141, 151, 174–6
Walter, Flora Macnabb (mother-in-law), 63, 65
Walter, Hubert (husband)
marriage, 63–9
childhood, 63–4

Times correspondent, 70–6, 80, 85–6, 96
declining health, 99
death, 106
Walter, Joan (daughter) see Wolrige Gordon
Walter, John III, 63–4
Walter, Ralph, 64, 75
Waseda University, 185–6
Washington D.C., 147
Westminster Abbey, 16
Whitchurch, Mr. and Mrs., 31
Wiesbaden, 29, 73
Wilson, Rt. Hon. Harold, 201
Winchester, School, 64
Wingate, Lady, 50
Winnipeg, 79
Wolrige Gordon, Anne (wife of Patrick), 179, 190, 204
Wolrige Gordon, Joan (daughter), 68, 71, 74–8, 80–2, 93–4, 98–9, 103, 116, 119, 130, 135, 141, 151, 174–5

Wolrige Gordon, John (see MacLeod Yr. of MacLeod)
Wolrige Gordon, Patrick (grandson), 106, 116, 135–6, 142–7, 173–4, 176–181, 198, 202–3
Wolrige Gordon, Captain Robert (son-in-law), 87, 98–9, 116, 119
Wolrige Gordon, Robert (grandson), 99, 106, 116, 128, 174
Wolseley, Sir Garnet (Lord), 18
Wood, Captain, 49, 52
Woodson, President and Mrs., 144

Yale University, 114
Yamagiwa, Mr., 184
Yellowstone National Park, The, 80
York, Duke and Duchess of, 105, 134
Yorkshire Post, The, 64
Yoshida, Shigeru, 184, 186

Zerwick, Margaret, 149
Zunguru, Nigeria, 77